Learning the bash Shell

Learning the bash Shell
Second Edition

Cameron Newham and Bill Rosenblatt

O'REILLY®

Beijing · Cambridge · Farnham · Köln · Paris · Sebastopol · Taipei · Tokyo

Learning the bash Shell, Second Edition
by Cameron Newham and Bill Rosenblatt

Editor: Mike Loukides
Update Editor: Gigi Estabrook
Production Editor: Nicole Gipson Arigo

Printing History:

October 1995:	First Edition.
January 1998:	Second Edition. Updated to include bash version 2.0.

ISBN: 1-56592-347-2
[M]

Table of Contents

Preface

The first thing users of the UNIX or Linux operating systems come face to face with is the *shell*. "Shell" is the UNIX term for a user interface to the system—something that lets you communicate with the computer via the keyboard and the display. Shells are just separate programs that encapsulate the system, and, as such, there are many to choose from.

Systems are usually set up with a "standard" shell that new users adopt without question. However, some of these standard shells are rather old and lack many features of the newer shells. This is a shame, because shells have a large bearing on one's working environment. Since changing shells is as easy as changing hats, there is no reason not to change to the latest and greatest in shell technology.

Of the many shells to choose from, this book introduces the Bourne Again shell (*bash* for short), a modern general-purpose shell. Other useful modern shells are the Korn shell (*ksh*) and the "Tenex C shell" (*tcsh*); both are also the subjects of O'Reilly handbooks.

bash Versions

This book is relevant to all versions of *bash*, although older versions lack some of the features of the most recent version.* You can easily find out which version you are using by typing **echo $BASH_VERSION**. The earliest public version of *bash* was 1.0, and the most recent is 2.01 (released in May 1997). If you have an older version, you might like to upgrade to the latest one. Chapter 11, *bash for Your System*, shows you how to go about it.

---

* Even though version 2.0 has been out for a while, *bash* version 1.14.*x* is still in widespread use. Throughout this book we have clearly marked with footnotes the features that are not present in the earlier versions.

Summary of bash Features

bash is a backward-compatible evolutionary successor to the Bourne shell that includes most of the C shell's major advantages as well as features from the Korn shell and a few new features of its own. Features appropriated from the C shell include:

- Directory manipulation, with the **pushd**, **popd**, and **dirs** commands.

- Job control, including the **fg** and **bg** commands and the ability to stop jobs with CTRL-Z.

- Brace expansion, for generating arbitrary strings.

- Tilde expansion, a shorthand way to refer to directories.

- Aliases, which allow you to define shorthand names for commands or command lines.

- Command history, which lets you recall previously entered commands.

bash's major new features include:

- Command-line editing, allowing you to use *vi-* or *emacs*-style editing commands on your command lines.

- Key bindings that allow you to set up customized editing key sequences.

- Integrated programming features: the functionality of several external UNIX commands, including *test, expr, getopt,* and *echo,* has been integrated into the shell itself, enabling common programming tasks to be done more cleanly and efficiently.

- Control structures, especially the **select** construct, which enables easy menu generation.

- New options and variables that give you more ways to customize your environment.

- One dimensional arrays that allow easy referencing and manipulation of lists of data.

- Dynamic loading of built-ins, plus the ability to write your own and load them into the running shell.

Intended Audience

This book is designed to address casual UNIX and Linux users who are just above the "raw beginner" level. You should be familiar with the process of logging in, entering commands, and doing simple things with files. Although Chapter 1, *bash Basics*, reviews concepts such as the tree-like file and directory scheme, you may find that it moves too quickly if you're a complete neophyte. In that case, we recommend the O'Reilly & Associates handbook, *Learning the UNIX Operating System*, by Jerry Peek, Grace Todino, and John Strang.

If you're an experienced user, you may wish to skip Chapter 1 altogether. But if your experience is with the C shell, you may find that Chapter 1 reveals a few subtle differences between the *bash* and C shells.

No matter what your level of experience is, you will undoubtedly learn many things in this book that make you a more productive *bash* user—from major features down to details at the "nook-and-cranny" level that you may not have been aware of.

If you are interested in shell programming (writing shell *scripts* and *functions* that automate everyday tasks or serve as system utilities), you should also find this book useful. However, we have deliberately avoided drawing a strong distinction between interactive shell use (entering commands during a login session) and shell programming. We see shell programming as a natural, inevitable outgrowth of increasing experience as a user.

Accordingly, each chapter depends on those previous to it, and although the first three chapters are oriented toward interactive use only, subsequent chapters describe interactive, user-oriented features in addition to programming concepts.

This book aims to show you that writing useful shell programs doesn't require a computing degree. Even if you are completely new to computing, there is no reason why you shouldn't be able to harness the power of *bash* within a short time.

Toward that end, we have decided not to spend too much time on features of interest exclusively to low-level systems programmers. Concepts like file descriptors and special file types can only confuse the casual user, and anyway, we figure that those of you who understand such things are smart enough to extrapolate the necessary information from our cursory discussions.

Code Examples

This book is full of examples of shell commands and programs that are designed to be useful in your everyday life as a user, not just to illustrate the feature being explained. In Chapter 4, *Basic Shell Programming*, and onwards, we include various programming problems, which we call *tasks*, that illustrate particular shell programming concepts. Some tasks have solutions that are refined in subsequent chapters. The later chapters also include programming exercises, many of which build on the tasks in the chapter.

Feel free to use any code you see in this book and to pass it along to friends and colleagues. We especially encourage you to modify and enhance it yourself.

If you want to try examples but you don't use *bash* as your login shell, you must put the following line at the top of each shell script:

```
#!/bin/bash
```

If *bash* isn't installed as the file */bin/bash*, substitute its pathname in the above.

Chapter Summary

If you want to investigate specific topics rather than read the entire book through, here is a chapter-by-chapter summary:

Chapter 1, *bash Basics*, introduces *bash* and tells you how to install it as your login shell. Then it surveys the basics of interactive shell use, including overviews of the UNIX file and directory scheme, standard I/O, and background jobs.

Chapter 2, *Command-Line Editing*, discusses the shell's command history mechanism (including the *emacs-* and *vi*-editing modes), history substitution and the **fc** history command, and key bindings with *readline* and **bind**.

Chapter 3, *Customizing Your Environment*, covers ways to customize your shell environment without programming, by using the startup and environment files. Aliases, options, and shell variables are the customization techniques discussed.

Chapter 4, *Basic Shell Programming*, is an introduction to shell programming. It explains the basics of shell scripts and functions, and discusses several important "nuts-and-bolts" programming features: string manipulation operators, brace expansion, command-line arguments (positional parameters), and command substitution.

Chapter 5, *Flow Control*, continues the discussion of shell programming by describing command exit status, conditional expressions, and the shell's flow-control structures: **if**, **for**, **case**, **select**, **while**, and **until**.

Chapter 6, *Command-Line Options and Typed Variables*, goes into depth about positional parameters and command-line option processing, then discusses special types and properties of variables, integer arithmetic, and arrays.

Chapter 7, *Input/Output and Command-Line Processing*, gives a detailed description of *bash* I/O. All of the shell's I/O redirectors are covered, as are the line-at-a-time I/O commands **read** and **echo**. Then the chapter discusses the shell's command-line processing mechanism and the **eval** command.

Chapter 8, *Process Handling*, covers process-related issues in detail. It starts with a discussion of job control, then gets into various low-level information about processes, including process IDs, signals, and traps. The chapter then moves to a higher level of abstraction to discuss coroutines and subshells.

Chapter 9, *Debugging Shell Programs*, discusses various debugging techniques, like trace and verbose modes, and the "fake" signal traps. We then present in detail a useful shell tool, written using the shell itself: a *bash* debugger.

Chapter 10, *bash Administration*, gives information for system administrators, including techniques for implementing system-wide shell customization and features related to system security.

Chapter 11, *bash for Your System*, shows you how to go about getting *bash* and how to install it on your system. It also outlines what to do in the event of problems along the way.

Appendix A, *Related Shells*, compares *bash* to several similar shells, including the standard Bourne shell, the IEEE 1003.2 POSIX shell standard, the Korn shell (*ksh*) and the public-domain Korn shell (*pdksh*), and the MKS Toolkit shell for MS-DOS and OS/2.

Appendix B, *Reference Lists*, contains lists of shell invocation options, built-in commands, built-in variables, conditional test operators, options, I/O redirection, and *emacs* and *vi* editing mode commands.

Appendix C, *Loadable Built-Ins*, gives information on writing and compiling your own loadable built-ins.

Appendix D, *Syntax*, lists the *bash* reserved words and provides a complete BNF description of the shell.

Appendix E, *Obtaining Sample Programs*, lists the ways that you can obtain the major scripts in this book for free, using anonymous FTP or electronic mail.

Conventions Used in This Handbook

We leave it as understood that, when you enter a shell command, you press RETURN at the end. RETURN is labeled ENTER on some keyboards.

Characters called CTRL-*X*, where *X* is any letter, are entered by holding down the CTRL (or CTL, or CONTROL) key and pressing that letter. Although we give the letter in uppercase, you can press the letter without the SHIFT key.

Other special characters are LINEFEED (which is the same as CTRL-J), BACKSPACE (same as CTRL-H), ESC, TAB, and DEL (sometimes labeled DELETE or RUBOUT).

This book uses the following font conventions:

Italic   is used for UNIX filenames, commands not built into the shell
                   (which are files anyway), and shell functions. *Italic* is also used
                   for dummy parameters that should be replaced with an actual
                   value, to distinguish the *vi* and *emacs* programs from their *bash*
                   modes, and to highlight special terms the first time they are
                   defined.

Bold   is used for *bash* built-in commands, aliases, variables, and
                   options, as well as command lines when they are within regular
                   text. **Bold** is used for all elements typed in by the user within reg-
                   ular text.

Constant   is used in examples to show the contents of files or the output
Width   from commands.

Constant   is used in examples to show interaction between the user and the
Bold   shell; any text the user types in is shown in **Constant Bold**.
                   For example:

```
$ pwd
/home/cam/adventure/carrol
$
```

Constant   is used in displayed command lines for dummy parameters that
Italic   should be replaced with an actual value.

Reverse   is used in Chapter 2, *Command-Line Editing*, to show the posi-
Video   tion of the cursor on the command line being edited. For exam-
                   ple:

```
grep -l Alice < ~cam/book/aiw
```

We use UNIX as a shorthand for "UNIX and Linux." Purists will correctly insist that
Linux is not UNIX—but as far as this book is concerned, they behave identically.

We'd Like to Hear from You

We have tested and verified all of the information in this book to the best of our
ability, but you may find that features have changed (or even that we have made
mistakes!). Please let us know about any errors you find, as well as your suggestions for future editions, by writing:

O'Reilly & Associates, Inc.
101 Morris Street
Sebastopol, CA 95472
1-800-998-9938 (in the US or Canada)
1-707-829-0515 (international/local)
1-707-829-0104 (FAX)

You can also send us messages electronically. To be put on the mailing list or request a catalog, send email to:

info@oreilly.com

To ask technical questions or comment on the book, send email to:

bookquestions@oreilly.com

We have a web site for the book, where we'll list examples, errata, and any plans for future editions. You can access this page at:

http://www.oreilly.com/catalog/bash2/

For more information about this book and others, see the O'Reilly web site:

http://www.oreilly.com

Acknowledgments for the First Edition

This project has been an interesting experience and wouldn't have been possible without the help of a number of people. Firstly, I'd like to thank Brian Fox and Chet Ramey for creating *bash* and making it the polished product it is today. Thanks also to Chet Ramey for promptly answering all of my questions on *bash* and pointing out my errors.

Many thanks to Bill Rosenblatt for *Learning the korn Shell*, on which this book is based; Michael O'Reilly and Michael Malone at iiNet Technologies for their useful comments and suggestions (and my net.connection!); Chris Thorne, Justin Twiss, David Quin-Conroy, and my mum for their comments, suggestions, and corrections; Linus Torvalds for the Linux operating system which introduced me to *bash* and was the platform for all of my work on the book; Brian Fox for providing a short history of *bash*; David Korn for information on the latest Korn shell. Thanks also to Depeche Mode for "101" as a backdrop while I worked, Laurence Durbridge for being a likable pest and never failing to ask "Finished the book yet?" and Adam (for being in my book).

The sharp eyes of our technical reviewers picked up many mistakes. Thanks to Matt Healy, Chet Ramey, Bill Reynolds, Bill Rosenblatt, and Norm Walsh for taking time out to go through the manuscript.

The crew at O'Reilly & Associates were indispensable in getting this book out the door. I'd like to thank Lenny Muellner for providing me with the formatting tools for the job, Chris Reilley for the figures, and Edie Freedman for the cover design. On the production end, I'd like to thank David Sewell for his copyediting, Claire-marie Fisher O'Leary for managing the production process, Michael Deutsch and Jane Ellin for their production assistance, Ellen Siever for tools support, Kismet McDonough for providing quality assurance, and Seth Maislin for the index.

I'm grateful to Frank Willison for taking me up on my first piece of email to ORA: "What about a book on *bash*?"

Last but by no means least, a big thank you to my editor, Mike Loukides, who helped steer me through this project.

Acknowledgments for the Second Edition

Thanks to all the people at O'Reilly & Associates. Gigi Estabrook was the editor for the second edition. Nicole Gipson Arigo was the production editor and project manager. Nancy Wolfe Kotary and Ellie Fountain Maden performed quality control checks. Seth Maislin wrote the index. Edie Freedman designed the cover, and Nancy Priest designed the interior format of the book. Lenny Muellner implemented the format in troff. Robert Romano updated the illustrations for this second edition.

1

bash Basics

Since the early 1970s, when it was first created, the UNIX operating system has become more and more popular. During this time it has branched out into different versions, and taken on such names as Ultrix, AIX, Xenix, SunOS, and Linux. Starting on minicomputers and mainframes, it has moved onto desktop workstations and even personal computers used at work and home. No longer a system used only by academics and computing wizards at universities and research centers, UNIX is used in many businesses, schools, and homes. As time goes on, more people will come into contact with UNIX.

You may have used UNIX at your school, office, or home to run your applications, print documents, and read your electronic mail. But have you ever thought about the process that happens when you type a command and hit RETURN?

Several layers of events take place whenever you enter a command, but we're going to consider only the top layer, known as the *shell*. Generically speaking, a shell is any user interface to the UNIX operating system, i.e., any program that takes input from the user, translates it into instructions that the operating system can understand, and conveys the operating system's output back to the user. Figure 1-1 shows the relationship between user, shell, and operating system.

There are various types of user interfaces. *bash* belongs to the most common category, known as character-based user interfaces. These interfaces accept lines of textual commands that the user types in; they usually produce text-based output. Other types of interfaces include the increasingly common *graphical user interfaces* (GUI), which add the ability to display arbitrary graphics (not just typewriter characters) and to accept input from a mouse or other pointing device, touch-screen interfaces (such as those on some bank teller machines), and so on.

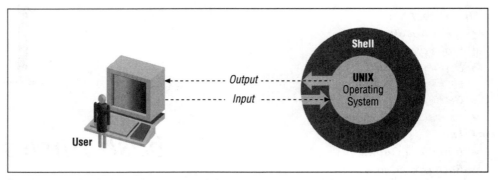

Figure 1-1: The shell is a layer around the UNIX operating system

What Is a Shell?

The shell's job, then, is to translate the user's command lines into operating system instructions. For example, consider this command line:

```
sort -n phonelist > phonelist.sorted
```

This means, "Sort lines in the file *phonelist* in numerical order, and put the result in the file *phonelist.sorted*." Here's what the shell does with this command:

1. Breaks up the line into the pieces *sort*, **−n**, *phonelist*, **>**, and *phonelist.sorted*. These pieces are called words.

2. Determines the purpose of the words: *sort* is a command, **−n** and *phonelist* are arguments, and **>** and *phonelist.sorted*, taken together, are I/O instructions.

3. Sets up the I/O according to **>** *phonelist.sorted* (output to the file *phonelist.sorted*) and some standard, implicit instructions.

4. Finds the command *sort* in a file and runs it with the option **−n** (numerical order) and the argument *phonelist* (input filename).

Of course, each of these steps really involves several substeps, each of which includes a particular instruction to the underlying operating system.

Remember that the shell itself is not UNIX—just the user interface to it. UNIX is one of the first operating systems to make the user interface independent of the operating system.

Scope of This Book

In this book you will learn about *bash*, which is one of the most recent and powerful of the major UNIX shells. There are two ways to use *bash*: as a user interface and as a programming environment.

This chapter and the next cover interactive use. These two chapters should give you enough background to use the shell confidently and productively for most of your everyday tasks.

After you have been using the shell for a while, you will undoubtedly find certain characteristics of your environment (the shell's "look and feel") that you would like to change, and tasks that you would like to automate. Chapter 3 shows several ways of doing this.

Chapter 3, *Customizing Your Environment,* also prepares you for shell programming, the bulk of which is covered in Chapters 4, *Basic Shell Programming,* through 6, *Command-Line Options and Typed Variables.* You need not have any programming experience to understand these chapters and learn shell programming. Chapters 7, *Input/Output and Command-Line Processing,* and 8, *Process Handling,* give more complete descriptions of the shell's I/O and process handling capabilities, while Chapter 9, *Debugging Shell Programs,* discusses various techniques for debugging shell programs.

You'll learn a lot about *bash* in this book; you'll also learn about UNIX utilities and the way the UNIX operating system works in general. It's possible to become a virtuoso shell programmer without any previous programming experience. At the same time, we've carefully avoided going into excessive detail about UNIX internals. We maintain that you shouldn't have to be an internals expert to use and program the shell effectively, and we won't dwell on the few shell features that are intended specifically for low-level systems programmers.

History of UNIX Shells

The independence of the shell from the UNIX operating system *per se* has led to the development of dozens of shells throughout UNIX history—although only a few have achieved widespread use.

The first major shell was the Bourne shell (named after its inventor, Steven Bourne); it was included in the first popular version of UNIX, Version 7, starting in 1979. The Bourne shell is known on the system as *sh.* Although UNIX has gone through many, many changes, the Bourne shell is still popular and essentially unchanged. Several UNIX utilities and administration features depend on it.

The first widely used alternative shell was the C shell, or *csh.* This was written by Bill Joy at the University of California at Berkeley as part of the Berkeley Software Distribution (BSD) version of UNIX that came out a couple of years after Version 7. It's included in most recent UNIX versions.

The C shell gets its name from the resemblance of its commands to statements in the C Programming Language, which makes the shell easier for programmers on

UNIX systems to learn. It supports a number of operating system features (e.g., job control; see Chapter 8) that were unique to BSD UNIX but by now have migrated to most other modern versions. It also has a few important features (e.g., aliases; see Chapter 3) that make it easier to use in general.

In recent years a number of other shells have become popular. The most notable of these is the Korn shell. This shell is a commercial product that incorporates the best features of the Bourne and C shells, plus many features of its own. The Korn shell is similar to *bash* in most respects; both have an abundance of features that make them easy to work with. The advantage of *bash* is that it is free. For further information on the Korn shell see Appendix A, *Related Shells*.

The Bourne Again Shell

The Bourne Again shell (named in punning tribute to Steve Bourne's shell) was created for use in the GNU project.* The GNU project was started by Richard Stallman of the Free Software Foundation (FSF) for the purpose of creating a UNIX-compatible operating system and replacing all of the commercial UNIX utilities with freely distributable ones. GNU embodies not only new software utilities, but a new distribution concept: the *copyleft*. Copylefted software may be freely distributed so long as no restrictions are placed on further distribution (for example, the source code must be made freely available).

bash, intended to be the standard shell for the GNU system, was officially "born" on Sunday, January 10, 1988. Brian Fox wrote the original versions of *bash* and *readline* and continued to improve the shell up until 1993. Early in 1989 he was joined by Chet Ramey, who was responsible for numerous bug fixes and the inclusion of many useful features. Chet Ramey is now the official maintainer of *bash* and continues to make further enhancements.

In keeping with the GNU principles, all versions of *bash* since 0.99 have been freely available from the FSF. *bash* has found its way onto every major version of UNIX and is rapidly becoming the most popular Bourne shell derivative. It is the standard shell included with Linux, a widely used free UNIX operating system.

In 1995 Chet Ramey began working on a major new release, 2.0, which was released to the public for the first time on December 23, 1996. *bash* 2.0 adds a range of new features to the old release (the last being 1.14.7) and brings the shell into better compliance with various standards.

This book describes the latest release of *bash* 2.0 (version 2.01, dated June 1997). It is applicable to all previous releases of *bash*. Any features of the current release that are different in, or missing from, previous releases will be noted in the text.

---

* GNU is a recursive acronym, standing for "GNU's Not UNIX".

Features of bash

Although the Bourne shell is still known as the "standard" shell, *bash* is becoming increasingly popular. In addition to its Bourne shell compatibility, it includes the best features of the C and Korn shells as well as several advantages of its own.

bash's command-line editing modes are the features that tend to attract people to it first. With command-line editing, it's much easier to go back and fix mistakes or modify previous commands than it is with the C shell's history mechanism—and the Bourne shell doesn't let you do this at all.

The other major *bash* feature that is intended mostly for interactive users is job control. As Chapter 8 explains, job control gives you the ability to stop, start, and pause any number of commands at the same time. This feature was borrowed almost verbatim from the C shell.

The rest of *bash*'s important advantages are meant mainly for shell customizers and programmers. It has many new options and variables for customization, and its programming features have been significantly expanded to include function definition, more control structures, integer arithmetic, advanced I/O control, and more.

Getting bash

You may or may not be using *bash* right now. Your system administrator probably set your account up with whatever shell he or she uses as the "standard" on the system. You may not even have been aware that there is more than one shell available.

Yet it's easy for you to determine which shell you are using. Log in to your system and type **echo $SHELL** at the prompt. You will see a response containing **sh**, **csh**, **ksh**, or **bash**; these denote the Bourne, C, Korn, and *bash* shells, respectively. (There's also a chance that you're using another shell such as *tcsh*.)

If you aren't using *bash* and you want to, then you first need to find out if it exists on your system. Just type **bash**. If you get a new prompt consisting of some information followed by a dollar-sign (e.g: **bash2-2.01$**), then all is well; type **exit** to go back to your normal shell.

If you get a "not found" message, your system may not have it. Ask your system administrator or another knowledgeable user; there's a chance that you might have some version of *bash* installed on the system in a place (directory) that is not normally accessible to you. If not, read Chapter 11, *bash for Your System*, to find out how you can obtain a version of *bash*.

Once you know you have *bash* on your system, you can invoke it from whatever other shell you use by typing **bash** as above. However, it's much better to install it as your *login shell*, i.e., the shell that you get automatically whenever you log in. You may be able to do the installation by yourself. Here are instructions that are designed to work on the widest variety of UNIX systems. If something doesn't work (e.g., you type in a command and get a "not found" error message or a blank line as the response), you'll have to abort the process and see your system administrator or, alternatively, turn to Chapter 11 where we demonstrate a less straightforward way of replacing your current shell.

You need to find out where *bash* is on your system, i.e., in which directory it's installed. You might be able to find the location by typing **whereis bash** (especially if you are using the C shell); if that doesn't work, try **whence bash**, **which bash**, or this complex command:*

```
grep bash /etc/passwd | awk -F: '{print $7}' | sort -u
```

You should see a response that looks like */bin/bash* or */usr/local/bin/bash*.

To install *bash* as your login shell, type **chsh** *bash-name*, where *bash-name* is the response you got to your **whereis** command (or whatever worked). For example:

```
% chsh /usr/local/bin/bash
```

You'll either get an error message saying that the shell is invalid, or you'll be prompted for your password.† Type in your password, then log out and log back in again to start using *bash*.

Interactive Shell Use

When you use the shell interactively, you engage in a login session that begins when you log in and ends when you type **exit** or **logout** or press CTRL-D.‡ During a login session, you type in *command lines* to the shell; these are lines of text ending in RETURN that you type in to your terminal or workstation.

By default, the shell prompts you for each command with an information string followed by a dollar sign, though as you will see in Chapter 3, the entire prompt can be changed.

---

* Make sure you use the correct quotation mark in this command: ´ rather than `.

† For system security reasons, only certain programs are allowed to be installed as login shells.

‡ The shell can be set up so that it ignores a single CTRL-D to end the session. We recommend doing this, because CTRL-D is too easy to type by accident. See the section on options in Chapter 3 for further details.

Commands, Arguments, and Options

Shell command lines consist of one or more words, which are separated on a command line by blanks or TABs. The first word on the line is the *command*. The rest (if any) are *arguments* (also called *parameters*) to the command, which are names of things on which the command will act.

For example, the command line **lp myfile** consists of the command *lp* (print a file) and the single argument **myfile**. *lp* treats **myfile** as the name of a file to print. Arguments are often names of files, but not necessarily: in the command line **mail cam**, the *mail* program treats **cam** as the username to which a message will be sent.

An *option* is a special type of argument that gives the command specific information on what it is supposed to do. Options usually consist of a dash followed by a letter; we say "usually" because this is a convention rather than a hard-and-fast rule. The command **lp −h myfile** contains the option **−h**, which tells *lp* not to print the "banner page" before it prints the file.

Sometimes options take their own arguments. For example, **lp −d lp1 −h myfile** has two options and one argument. The first option is **−d lp1**, which means "Send the output to the printer (destination) called **lp1**." The second option and argument are the same as in the previous example.

Files

Although arguments to commands aren't always files, files are the most important types of "things" on any UNIX system. A file can contain any kind of information, and indeed there are different types of files. Three types are by far the most important:

Regular files

Also called text files; these contain readable characters. For example, this book was created from several regular files that contain the text of the book plus human-readable formatting instructions to the *troff* word processor.

Executable files

Also called programs; these are invoked as commands. Some can't be read by humans; others—the shell scripts that we'll examine in this book—are just special text files. The shell itself is a (non-human-readable) executable file called *bash*.

Directories

These are like folders that contain other files—possibly other directories (called *subdirectories*).

Directories

Let's review the most important concepts about directories. The fact that directories can contain other directories leads to a hierarchical structure, more popularly known as a *tree*, for all files on a UNIX system.

Figure 1-2 shows part of a typical directory tree; rectangles are directories and ovals are regular files.

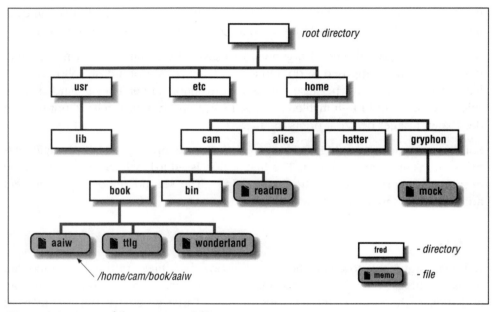

Figure 1-2: A tree of directories and files

The top of the tree is a directory called *root* that has no name on the system.* All files can be named by expressing their location on the system relative to *root*; such names are built by listing all of the directory names (in order from *root*), separated by slashes (/), followed by the file's name. This way of naming files is called a *full* (or *absolute*) *pathname*.

For example, say there is a file called *aaiw* that is in the directory *book*, which is in the directory *cam*, which is in the directory *home*, which is in the root directory. This file's full pathname is */home/cam/book/aaiw*.

---

* Most UNIX tutorials say that *root* has the name /. We stand by this alternative explanation because it is more logically consistent with the rest of the UNIX filename conventions.

The working directory

Of course, it's annoying to have to use full pathnames whenever you need to specify a file. So there is also the concept of the working directory (sometimes called the current directory), which is the directory you are "in" at any given time. If you give a pathname with no leading slash, then the location of the file is worked out relative to the working directory. Such pathnames are called *relative* pathnames; you'll use them much more often than full pathnames.

When you log in to the system, your working directory is initially set to a special directory called your *home* (or *login*) directory. System administrators often set up the system so that everyone's home directory name is the same as their login name, and all home directories are contained in a common directory under *root*.

For example, */home/cam* is a typical home directory. If this is your working directory and you give the command **lp memo**, then the system looks for the file *memo* in */home/cam*. If you have a directory called *hatter* in your home directory, and it contains the file *teatime*, then you can print it with the command **lp hatter/teatime**.

Tilde notation

As you can well imagine, home directories occur often in pathnames. Although many systems are organized so that all home directories have a common parent (such as */home* or */users*), you should not rely on that being the case, nor should you even have to know the absolute pathname of someone's home directory.

Therefore, *bash* has a way of abbreviating home directories: just precede the name of the user with a tilde (˜). For example, you could refer to the file *story* in user **alice**'s home directory as ˜*alice/story*. This is an absolute pathname, so it doesn't matter what your working directory is when you use it. If **alice**'s home directory has a subdirectory called *adventure* and the file is in there instead, you can use ˜*alice/adventure/story* as its name.

Even more convenient, a tilde by itself refers to your own home directory. You can refer to a file called *notes* in your home directory as ˜*/notes* (note the difference between that and ˜*notes*, which the shell would try to interpret as user *notes*'s home directory). If *notes* is in your *adventure* subdirectory, then you can call it ˜*/adventure/notes*. This notation is handiest when your working directory is not in your home directory tree, e.g., when it's some system directory like */tmp*.

Changing working directories

If you want to change your working directory, use the command **cd**. If you don't remember your working directory, the command **pwd** tells the shell to print it.

cd takes as an argument the name of the directory you want to become your working directory. It can be relative to your current directory, it can contain a tilde, or it can be absolute (starting with a slash). If you omit the argument, **cd** changes to your home directory (i.e., it's the same as **cd ˜**).

Table 1-1 gives some sample **cd** commands. Each command assumes that your working directory is */home/cam* just before the command is executed, and that your directory structure looks like Figure 1-2.

Table 1-1: Sample cd Commands

Command	New Working Directory
cd book	*/home/cam/book*
cd book/wonderland	*/home/cam/book/wonderland*
cd ˜/book/wonderland	*/home/cam/book/wonderland*
cd /usr/lib	*/usr/lib*
cd ..	*/home*
cd ../gryphon	*/home/gryphon*
cd ˜gryphon	*/home/gryphon*

The first four are straightforward. The next two use a special directory called **..** (two dots), which means "parent of this directory." Every directory has one of these; it's a universal way to get to the directory above the current one in the hierarchy—which is called the parent directory.*

Another feature of *bash*'s **cd** command is the form **cd −**, which changes to whatever directory you were in before the current one. For example, if you start out in */usr/lib*, type **cd** without an argument to go to your home directory, and then type **cd −**, you will be back in */usr/lib*.

Filenames, Wildcards, and Pathname Expansion

Sometimes you need to run a command on more than one file at a time. The most common example of such a command is *ls*, which lists information about files. In its simplest form, without options or arguments, it lists the names of all files in the working directory except special hidden files, whose names begin with a dot (.).

If you give *ls* filename arguments, it will list those files—which is sort of silly: if your current directory has the files *duchess* and *queen* in it and you type **ls duchess queen**, the system will simply print those filenames.

---

* Each directory also has the special directory **.** (single dot), which just means "this directory." Thus, **cd .** effectively does nothing. Both **.** and **..** are actually special hidden files in each directory that point to the directory itself and to its parent directory, respectively. *root* is its own parent.

Actually, *ls* is more often used with options that tell it to list information about the files, like the **−l** (long) option, which tells *ls* to list the file's owner, size, time of last modification, and other information, or **−a** (all), which also lists the hidden files described above. But sometimes you want to verify the existence of a certain group of files without having to know all of their names; for example, if you use a text editor, you might want to see which files in your current directory have names that end in *.txt*.

Filenames are so important in UNIX that the shell provides a built-in way to specify the pattern of a set of filenames without having to know all of the names themselves. You can use special characters, called *wildcards*, in filenames to turn them into patterns. Table 1-2 lists the basic wildcards.

Table 1-2: Basic Wildcards

Wildcard	Matches
?	Any single character
*	Any string of characters
[*set*]	Any character in *set*
[!*set*]	Any character *not* in *set*

The **?** wildcard matches any single character, so that if your directory contains the files *program.c*, *program.log*, and *program.o*, then the expression **program.?** matches *program.c* and *program.o* but not *program.log*.

The asterisk (*****) is more powerful and far more widely used; it matches any string of characters. The expression **program.*** will match all three files in the previous paragraph; text editor users can use the expression ***.txt** to match their input files.*

Table 1-3 should help demonstrate how the asterisk works. Assume that you have the files *bob*, *darlene*, *dave*, *ed*, *frank*, and *fred* in your working directory.

Table 1-3: Using the * Wildcard

Expression	Yields
fr*	frank fred
*ed	ed fred
b*	bob
e	darlene dave ed fred
r	darlene frank fred

---

* MS-DOS and VAX/VMS users should note that there is *nothing special* about the dot (.) in UNIX filenames (aside from the leading dot, which "hides" the file); it's just another character. For example, **ls *** lists all files in the current directory; you don't need ***.*** as you do on other systems. Indeed, **ls *.*** won't list all the files—only those that have at least one dot in the middle of the name.

*Table 1-3: Using the * Wildcard* (continued)

Expression	Yields
*	bob darlene dave ed frank fred
d*e	darlene dave
g*	g*

Notice that * can stand for nothing: both *ed and *e* match *ed*. Also notice that the last example shows what the shell does if it can't match anything: it just leaves the string with the wildcard untouched.

The remaining wildcard is the *set* construct. A set is a list of characters (e.g., abc), an inclusive range (e.g., a–z), or some combination of the two. If you want the dash character to be part of a list, just list it first or last. Table 1-4 should explain things more clearly.

Table 1-4: Using the Set Construct Wildcards

Expression	Matches
[abc]	a, b, or c
[., ;]	Period, comma, or semicolon
[-_]	Dash or underscore
[a-c]	a, b, or c
[a-z]	All lowercase letters
[!0-9]	All non-digits
[0-9!]	All digits and exclamation point
[a-zA-Z]	All lower- and uppercase letters
[a-zA-Z0-9_-]	All letters, all digits, underscore, and dash

In the original wildcard example, **program.[co]** and **program.[a-z]** both match *program.c* and *program.o*, but not *program.log*.

An exclamation point after the left bracket lets you "negate" a set. For example, [!. ;] matches any character except period and semicolon; [!a-zA-Z] matches any character that isn't a letter. To match ! itself, place it after the first character in the set, or precede it with a backslash, as in [\!].

The range notation is handy, but you shouldn't make too many assumptions about what characters are included in a range. It's safe to use a range for uppercase letters, lowercase letters, digits, or any subranges thereof (e.g., [f-q], [2-6]). Don't use ranges on punctuation characters or mixed-case letters: e.g., [a-Z] and [A-z] should not be trusted to include all of the letters and nothing more. The problem is that such ranges are not entirely portable between different types of computers.*

The process of matching expressions containing wildcards to filenames is called *wildcard expansion* or *globbing*. This is just one of several steps the shell takes when reading and processing a command line; another that we have already seen is tilde expansion, where tildes are replaced with home directories where applicable. We'll see others in later chapters, and the full details of the process are enumerated in Chapter 7.

However, it's important to be aware that the commands that you run only see the results of wildcard expansion. That is, they just see a list of arguments, and they have no knowledge of how those arguments came into being. For example, if you type **ls fr*** and your files are as on the previous page, then the shell expands the command line to **ls fred frank** and invokes the command *ls* with arguments **fred** and **frank**. If you type **ls g***, then (because there is no match) *ls* will be given the literal string **g*** and will complain with the error message, **g*: No such file or directory**.†

Here is an example that should help make things clearer. Suppose you are a C programmer. This means that you deal with files whose names end in *.c* (programs, also known as source files), *.h* (header files for programs), and *.o* (object code files that aren't human-readable) as well as other files. Let's say you want to list all source, object, and header files in your working directory. The command **ls *.[cho]** does the trick. The shell expands ***.[cho]** to all files whose names end in a period followed by a **c**, **h**, or **o** and passes the resulting list to *ls* as arguments. In other words, *ls* will see the filenames just as if they were all typed in individually—but notice that we required no knowledge of the actual filenames whatsoever! We let the wildcards do the work.

The wildcard examples that we have seen so far are actually part of a more general concept called *pathname expansion*. Just as it is possible to use wildcards in the current directory, they can also be used as part of a pathname. For example, if you wanted to list all of the files in the directories */usr* and */usr2*, you could type **ls /usr***. If you were only interested in the files beginning with the letters *b* and *e* in these directories, you could type **ls /usr*/[be]*** to list them.

---

* Specifically, ranges depend on the character encoding scheme your computer uses. The vast majority use ASCII, but IBM mainframes use EBCDIC.

† This is different from the C shell's wildcard mechanism, which prints an error message and doesn't execute the command at all.

Brace Expansion

A concept closely related to pathname expansion is brace expansion. Whereas pathname expansion wildcards will expand to files and directories that exist, brace expansion expands to an arbitrary string of a given form: an optional *preamble*, followed by comma-separated strings between braces, and followed by an optional *postscript*. If you type **echo b{ed,olt,ar}s**, you'll see the words *beds*, *bolts*, and *bars* printed. Each instance of a string inside the braces is combined with the preamble *b* and the postscript *s*. Notice that these are not filenames—the strings produced are independent of filenames. It is also possible to nest the braces, as in **b{ar{d,n,k},ed}s**. This will result in the expansion *bards*, *barns*, *barks*, and *beds*.

Brace expansion can also be used with wildcard expansions. In the example from the previous section where we listed the source, object, and header files in the working directory, we could have used **ls *.{c,h,o}.***

Input and Output

The software field—really, any scientific field—tends to advance most quickly and impressively on those few occasions when someone (i.e., not a committee) comes up with an idea that is small in concept yet enormous in its implications. The standard input and output scheme of UNIX has to be on the short list of such ideas, along with such classic innovations as the LISP language, the relational data model, and object-oriented programming.

The UNIX I/O scheme is based on two dazzlingly simple ideas. First, UNIX file I/O takes the form of arbitrarily long sequences of characters (bytes). In contrast, file systems of older vintage have more complicated I/O schemes (e.g., "block," "record," "card image," etc.). Second, everything on the system that produces or accepts data is treated as a file; this includes hardware devices like disk drives and terminals. Older systems treated every device differently. Both of these ideas have made systems programmers' lives much more pleasant.

Standard I/O

By convention, each UNIX program has a single way of accepting input called *standard input*, a single way of producing output called *standard output*, and a single way of producing error messages called *standard error output*, usually shortened to *standard error*. Of course, a program can have other input and output sources as well, as we will see in Chapter 7.

---

* This differs slightly from C shell brace expansion. *bash* requires at least one unquoted comma to perform an expansion, otherwise the word is left unchanged, e.g., b{o}lt remains as b{o}lt.

Standard I/O was the first scheme of its kind that was designed specifically for interactive users at terminals, rather than the older batch style of use that usually involved decks of punch-cards. Since the UNIX shell provides the user interface, it should come as no surprise that standard I/O was designed to fit in very neatly with the shell.

All shells handle standard I/O in basically the same way. Each program that you invoke has all three standard I/O channels set to your terminal or workstation, so that standard input is your keyboard, and standard output and error are your screen or window. For example, the *mail* utility prints messages to you on the standard output, and when you use it to send messages to other users, it accepts your input on the standard input. This means that you view messages on your screen and type new ones in on your keyboard.

When necessary, you can redirect input and output to come from or go to a file instead. If you want to send the contents of a pre-existing file to someone as mail, you redirect *mail*'s standard input so that it reads from that file instead of your keyboard.

You can also hook programs together in a *pipeline*, in which the standard output of one program feeds directly into the standard input of another; for example, you could feed *mail* output directly to the *lp* program so that messages are printed instead of shown on the screen.

This makes it possible to use UNIX utilities as building blocks for bigger programs. Many UNIX utility programs are meant to be used in this way: they each perform a specific type of filtering operation on input text. Although this isn't a textbook on UNIX utilities, they are essential to productive shell use. The more popular filtering utilities are listed in Table 1-5.

Table 1-5: Popular UNIX Data Filtering Utilities

Utility	Purpose
cat	Copy input to output
grep	Search for strings in the input
sort	Sort lines in the input
cut	Extract columns from input
sed	Perform editing operations on input
tr	Translate characters in the input to other characters

You may have used some of these before and noticed that they take names of input files as arguments and produce output on standard output. You may not know, however, that all of them (and most other UNIX utilities) accept input from standard input if you omit the argument.*

For example, the most basic utility is *cat*, which simply copies its input to its output. If you type **cat** with a filename argument, it will print out the contents of that file on your screen. But if you invoke it with no arguments, it will expect standard input and copy it to standard output. Try it: *cat* will wait for you to type a line of text; when you type RETURN, *cat* will repeat the text back to you. To stop the process, hit CTRL-D at the beginning of a line. You will see ^**D** when you type CTRL-D. Here's what this should look like:

```
$ cat
Here is a line of text.
Here is a line of text.
This is another line of text.
This is another line of text.
^D
$
```

I/O Redirection

cat is short for "catenate," i.e., link together. It accepts multiple filename arguments and copies them to the standard output. But let's pretend, for now, that *cat* and other utilities don't accept filename arguments and accept only standard input. As we said above, the shell lets you redirect standard input so that it comes from a file. The notation *command < filename* does this; it sets things up so that *command* takes standard input from a file instead of from a terminal.

For example, if you have a file called *cheshire* that contains some text, then **cat < cheshire** will print *cheshire*'s contents out onto your terminal. **sort < cheshire** will sort the lines in the *cheshire* file and print the result on your terminal (remember: we're pretending that these utilities don't take filename arguments).

Similarly, *command > filename* causes the *command*'s standard output to be redirected to the named file. The classic "canonical" example of this is **date > now**: the *date* command prints the current date and time on the standard output; the previous command saves it in a file called *now*.

Input and output redirectors can be combined. For example: the *cp* command is normally used to copy files; if for some reason it didn't exist or was broken, you could use *cat* in this way:

```
$ cat < file1 > file2
```

This would be similar to **cp file1 file2**.

---

* If a particular UNIX utility doesn't accept standard input when you leave out the filename argument, try using a dash (–) as the argument.

Pipelines

It is also possible to redirect the output of a command into the standard input of another command instead of a file. The construct that does this is called the pipe, notated as |. A command line that includes two or more commands connected with pipes is called a pipeline.

Pipes are very often used with the *more* command, which works just like *cat* except that it prints its output screen by screen, pausing for the user to type SPACE (next screen), RETURN (next line), or other commands. If you're in a directory with a large number of files and you want to see details about them, **ls –l | more** will give you a detailed listing a screen at a time.

Pipelines can get very complex, and they can also be combined with other I/O directors. To see a sorted listing of the file *cheshire* a screen at a time, type **sort < cheshire | more**. To print it instead of viewing it on your terminal, type **sort < cheshire | lp**.

Here's a more complicated example. The file */etc/passwd* stores information about users' accounts on a UNIX system. Each line in the file contains a user's login name, user ID number, encrypted password, home directory, login shell, and other information. The first field of each line is the login name; fields are separated by colons (:). A sample line might look like this:

```
cam:LM1c7GhNesD4GhF3iEHrH4FeCKB/:501:100:Cameron Newham:/home/cam:/bin/bash
```

To get a sorted listing of all users on the system, type:

```
$ cut -d: -f1 < /etc/passwd | sort
```

(Actually, you can omit the <, since *cut* accepts input filename arguments.) The *cut* command extracts the first field (–f1), where fields are separated by colons (–d:), from the input. The entire pipeline will print a list that looks like this:

```
adm
bin
cam
daemon
davidqc
ftp
games
gonzo
...
```

If you want to send the list directly to the printer (instead of your screen), you can extend the pipeline like this:

```
$ cut -d: -f1 < /etc/passwd | sort | lp
```

Now you should see how I/O directors and pipelines support the UNIX building block philosophy. The notation is extremely terse and powerful. Just as important, the pipe concept eliminates the need for messy temporary files to store command output before it is fed into other commands.

For example, to do the same sort of thing as the above command line on other operating systems (assuming that equivalent utilities are available ...), you need three commands. On DEC's VAX/VMS system, they might look like this:

```
$ cut [etc]passwd /d=":" /f=1 /out=temp1
$ sort temp1 /out=temp2
$ print temp2
$ delete temp1 temp2
```

After sufficient practice, you will find yourself routinely typing in powerful command pipelines that do in one line what it would take several commands (and temporary files) in other operating systems to accomplish.

Background Jobs

Pipes are actually a special case of a more general feature: doing more than one thing at a time. This is a capability that many other commercial operating systems don't have, because of the rigid limits that they tend to impose upon users. UNIX, on the other hand, was developed in a research lab and meant for internal use, so it does relatively little to impose limits on the resources available to users on a computer—as usual, leaning towards uncluttered simplicity rather than overcomplexity.

"Doing more than one thing at a time" means running more than one program at the same time. You do this when you invoke a pipeline; you can also do it by logging on to a UNIX system as many times simultaneously as you wish. (If you try that on an IBM's VM/CMS system, for example, you will get an obnoxious "already logged in" message.)

The shell also lets you run more than one command at a time during a single login session. Normally, when you type a command and hit RETURN, the shell will let the command have control of your terminal until it is done; you can't type in further commands until the first one is done. But if you want to run a command that does not require user input and you want to do other things while the command is running, put an ampersand (&) after the command.

This is called running the command in the background, and a command that runs in this way is called a background job; by contrast, a job run the normal way is called a foreground job. When you start a background job, you get your shell prompt back immediately, enabling you to enter other commands.

The most obvious use for background jobs is programs that take a long time to run, such as *sort* or *uncompress* on large files. For example, assume you just got an enormous compressed file loaded into your directory from magnetic tape.* Let's say the file is *gcc.tar.Z*, which is a compressed archive file that contains well over 10 MB of source code files.

Type **uncompress gcc.tar &** (you can omit the .Z), and the system will start a job in the background that uncompresses the data "in place" and ends up with the file *gcc.tar*. Right after you type the command, you will see a line like this:

    [1] 175

followed by your shell prompt, meaning that you can enter other commands. Those numbers give you ways of referring to your background job; Chapter 8, explains them in detail.

You can check on background jobs with the command **jobs**. For each background job, **jobs** prints a line similar to the above but with an indication of the job's status:

    [1]+ Running   uncompress gcc.tar &

When the job finishes, you will see a message like this right before your shell prompt:

    [1]+ Done   uncompress gcc.tar

The message changes if your background job terminated with an error; again, see Chapter 8 for details.

Background I/O

Jobs you put in the background should not do I/O to your terminal. Just think about it for a moment and you'll understand why.

By definition, a background job doesn't have control over your terminal. Among other things, this means that only the foreground process (or, if none, the shell itself) is "listening" for input from your keyboard. If a background job needs keyboard input, it will often just sit there doing nothing until you do something about it (as described in Chapter 8).

If a background job produces screen output, the output will just appear on your screen. If you are running a job in the foreground that produces output too, then the output from the two jobs will be randomly (and often annoyingly) interspersed.

---

* Compressed files are created by the *compress* utility, which packs files into smaller amounts of space; they have names of the form *filename.Z*, where *filename* is the name of the original uncompressed file.

If you want to run a job in the background that expects standard input or produces standard output, you usually want to redirect the I/O so that it comes from
or goes to a file. Programs that produce small, one-line messages (warnings,
"done" messages, etc.) are an exception to this general rule; you may not mind if
these are interspersed with whatever other output you are seeing at a given time.

For example, the *diff* utility examines two files, whose names are given as arguments, and prints a summary of their differences on the standard output. If the
files are exactly the same, *diff* is silent. Usually, you invoke *diff* expecting to see a
few lines that are different.

diff, like *sort* and *compress*, can take a long time to run if the input files are very
large. Suppose that you have two large files that are called *warandpeace.txt* and
warandpeace.txt.old. The command **diff warandpeace.txt warandpeace.txt.old***
reveals that the author decided to change the name "Ivan" to "Aleksandr" throughout the entire file—i.e., hundreds of differences, resulting in very large amounts of
output.

If you type **diff warandpeace.txt warandpeace.txt.old &**, then the system will spew
lots and lots of output at you, which will be difficult to stop—even with the techniques explained in Chapter 7. However, if you type:

```
$ diff warandpeace.txt warandpeace.txt.old > txtdiff &
```

then the differences will be saved in the file *txtdiff* for you to examine later.

Background Jobs and Priorities

Background jobs can save you a lot of thumb-twiddling time. Just remember that
such jobs eat up lots of system resources like memory and the processor (CPU).
Just because you're running several jobs at once doesn't mean that they will run
faster than they would if run sequentially—in fact, performance is usually slightly
worse.

Every job on the system is assigned a *priority*, a number that tells the operating
system how much priority to give the job when it doles out resources (the higher
the number, the lower the priority). Commands that you enter from the shell,
whether foreground or background jobs, usually have the same priority. The system administrator is able to run commands at a higher priority than normal users.

Note that if you're on a multiuser system, running lots of background jobs may eat
up more than your fair share of resources, and you should consider whether

---

* You could use **diff warandpeace*** as a shorthand to save typing—as long as there are no other files
with names of that form. Remember that *diff* doesn't see the arguments until after the shell has
expanded the wildcards. Many people overlook this use of wildcards.

having your job run as fast as possible is really more important than being a good citizen.

Speaking of good citizenship, there is also a UNIX command that lets you lower the priority of any job: the aptly named *nice*. If you type **nice** *command*, where *command* can be a complex shell command line with pipes, redirectors, etc., then the command will run at a lower priority.* You can control just how much lower by giving *nice* a numerical argument; consult the *nice* manpage for details.†

Special Characters and Quoting

The characters <, >, |, and & are four examples of *special characters* that have particular meanings to the shell. The wildcards we saw earlier in this chapter (*, ?, and [. . .]) are also special characters.

Table 1-6 gives the meanings of all special characters within shell command lines only. Other characters have special meanings in specific situations, such as the regular expressions and string-handling operators that we'll see in Chapter 3 and Chapter 4.

Table 1-6: Special Characters

Character	Meaning	See Chapter
~	Home directory	1
`	Command substitution (archaic)	4
#	Comment	4
$	Variable expression	3
&	Background job	1
*	String wildcard	1
(	Start subshell	8
)	End subshell	8
\	Quote next character	1
		Pipe	1
[	Start character-set wildcard	1
]	End character-set wildcard	1
{	Start command block	7
}	End command block	7
;	Shell command separator	3
'	Strong quote	1
"	Weak quote	1

---

* Complex commands following *nice* should be quoted.

† If you are a system administrator logged in as **root**, then you can also use *nice* to raise a job's priority.

Table 1-6: Special Characters (continued)

Character	Meaning	See Chapter
<	Input redirect	1
>	Output redirect	1
/	Pathname directory separator	1
?	Single-character wildcard	1
!	Pipeline logical NOT	5

Quoting

Sometimes you will want to use special characters literally, i.e., without their special meanings. This is called *quoting*. If you surround a string of characters with single quotation marks (or *quotes*), you strip all characters within the quotes of any special meaning they might have.

The most obvious situation where you might need to quote a string is with the **echo** command, which just takes its arguments and prints them to the standard output. What is the point of this? As you will see in later chapters, the shell does quite a bit of processing on command lines—most of which involves some of the special characters listed in Table 1-6. **echo** is a way of making the result of that processing available on the standard output.

But what if we wanted to print the string **2 * 3 > 5 is a valid inequality**? Suppose you typed this:

```
$ echo 2 * 3 > 5 is a valid inequality.
```

You would get your shell prompt back, as if nothing happened! But then there would be a new file, with the name *5*, containing "2", the names of all files in your current directory, and then the string **3 is a valid inequality**. Make sure you understand why.*

However, if you type:

```
$ echo '2 * 3 > 5 is a valid inequality.'
```

the result is the string, taken literally. You needn't quote the entire line, just the portion containing special characters (or characters you think *might* be special, if you just want to be sure):

```
$ echo '2 * 3 > 5' is a valid inequality.
```

This has exactly the same result.

---

* This should also teach you something about the flexibility of placing I/O redirectors anywhere on the command line—even in places where they don't seem to make sense.

Notice that Table 1-6 lists double quotes (") as weak quotes. A string in double quotes is subjected to *some* of the steps the shell takes to process command lines, but not all. (In other words, it treats only some special characters as special.) You'll see in later chapters why double quotes are sometimes preferable; Chapter 7 contains the most comprehensive explanation of the shell's rules for quoting and other aspects of command-line processing. For now, though, you should stick to single quotes.

Backslash-Escaping

Another way to change the meaning of a character is to precede it with a back-slash (\). This is called *backslash-escaping* the character. In most cases, when you backslash-escape a character, you quote it. For example:

```
$ echo 2 \* 3 \> 5 is a valid inequality.
```

will produce the same results as if you surrounded the string with single quotes. To use a literal backslash, just surround it with quotes (' \ ') or, even better, back-slash-escape it (\\).

Here is a more practical example of quoting special characters. A few UNIX commands take arguments that often include wildcard characters, which need to be escaped so the shell doesn't process them first. The most common such command is *find*, which searches for files throughout entire directory trees.

To use *find*, you supply the root of the tree you want to search and arguments that describe the characteristics of the file(s) you want to find. For example, the command **find** . −*name string* searches the directory tree whose root is your current directory for files whose names match the string. (Other arguments allow you to search by the file's size, owner, permissions, date of last access, etc.)

You can use wildcards in the string, but you must quote them, so that the *find* command itself can match them against names of files in each directory it searches. The command **find** . −**name** '*.c' will match all files whose names end in *.c* anywhere in your current directory, subdirectories, sub-subdirectories, etc.

Quoting Quotation Marks

You can also use a backslash to include double quotes within a quoted string. For example:

```
$ echo \"2 \* 3 \> 5\" is a valid inequality.
```

produces the following output:

```
"2 * 3 > 5" is a valid inequality.
```

However, this won't work with single quotes inside quoted expressions. For example, **echo 'Hatter\'s tea party'** will not give you **Hatter's tea party**. You can get around this limitation in various ways. First, try eliminating the quotes:

```
$ echo Hatter\'s tea party
```

If no other characters are special (as is the case here), this works. Otherwise, you can use the following command:

```
$ echo 'Hatter'\''s tea party'
```

That is, `'\''` (i.e., single quote, backslash, single quote, single quote) acts like a single quote within a quoted string. Why? The first `'` in `'\''` ends the quoted string we started with (`'Hatter`), the `\'` inserts a literal single quote, and the next `'` starts another quoted string that ends with the word "party". If you understand this, then you will have no trouble resolving the other bewildering issues that arise from the shell's often cryptic syntax.

Continuing Lines

A related issue is how to continue the text of a command beyond a single line on your terminal or workstation window. The answer is conceptually simple: just quote the RETURN key. After all, RETURN is really just another character.

You can do this in two ways: by ending a line with a backslash, or by not closing a quote mark (i.e., by including RETURN in a quoted string). If you use the backslash, there must be nothing between it and the end of the line—not even spaces or TABs.

Whether you use a backslash or a single quote, you are telling the shell to ignore the special meaning of the RETURN character. After you press RETURN, the shell understands that you haven't finished your command line (i.e., since you haven't typed a "real" RETURN), so it responds with a secondary prompt, which is > by default, and waits for you to finish the line. You can continue a line as many times as you wish.

For example, if you want the shell to print the first sentence of Chapter 5 of Lewis Carroll's *Alice's Adventures in Wonderland*, you can type this:

```
$ echo The Caterpillar and Alice looked at each other for some \
> time in silence: at last Caterpillar took the hookah out of its \
> mouth, and addressed her in a languid, sleepy voice.
```

Or you can do it this way:

```
$ echo 'The Caterpillar and Alice looked at each other for some
> time in silence: at last Caterpillar took the hookah out of its
> mouth, and addressed her in a languid, sleepy voice.'
```

Control Keys

Control keys—those that you type by holding down the CONTROL (or CTRL) key and hitting another key—are another type of special character. These normally don't print anything on your screen, but the operating system interprets a few of them as special commands. You already know one of them: RETURN is actually the same as CTRL-M (try it and see). You have probably also used the BACKSPACE or DEL key to erase typos on your command line.

Actually, many control keys have functions that don't really concern you—yet you should know about them for future reference and in case you type them by accident.

Perhaps the most difficult thing about control keys is that they can differ from system to system. The usual arrangement is shown in Table 1-7, which lists the control keys that all major modern versions of UNIX support. Note that DEL and CTRL-? are the same character.

You can use the **stty** command to find out what your settings are and change them if you wish; see Chapter 8 for details. If the version of UNIX on your system is one of those that derive from BSD (such as SunOS and Ultrix), type **stty all** to see your control-key settings; you will see something like this:

```
erase  kill   werase rprnt  flush  lnext  susp   intr   quit   stop   eof
^?     ^U     ^W     ^R     ^O     ^V     ^Z/^Y  ^C     ^\     ^S/^Q  ^D
```

Table 1-7: Control Keys

Control Key	stty Name	Function Description
CTRL-C	**intr**	Stop current command
CTRL-D	**eof**	End of input
CTRL-\	**quit**	Stop current command, if CTRL-C doesn't work
CTRL-S	**stop**	Halt output to screen
CTRL-Q		Restart output to screen
DEL or CTRL-?	**erase**	Erase last character
CTRL-U	**kill**	Erase entire command line
CTRL-Z	**susp**	Suspend current command (see Chapter 8)

The *^X* notation stands for CTRL-*X*. If your UNIX version derives from System III or System V (this includes AIX, HP/UX, SCO, Linux, and Xenix), type **stty −a**.

The resulting output will include this information:

```
intr = ^c; quit = ^|; erase = DEL; kill = ^u; eof = ^d; eol = ^`;
swtch = ^`; susp = ^z; dsusp <undef>;
```

The control key you will probably use most often is CTRL-C, sometimes called the *interrupt* key. This stops—or tries to stop—the command that is currently running. You will want to use this when you enter a command and find that it's taking too long, you gave it the wrong arguments, you change your mind about wanting to run it, or whatever.

Sometimes CTRL-C doesn't work; in that case, if you really want to stop a job, try CTRL-\. But don't just type CTRL-\; always try CTRL-C first! Chapter 8 explains why in detail. For now, suffice it to say that CTRL-C gives the running job more of a chance to clean up before exiting, so that files and other resources are not left in funny states.

We've already seen an example of CTRL-D. When you are running a command that accepts standard input from your keyboard, CTRL-D tells the process that your input is finished—as if the process were reading a file and it reached the end of the file. *mail* is a utility in which this happens often. When you are typing in a message, you end by typing CTRL-D. This tells *mail* that your message is complete and ready to be sent. Most utilities that accept standard input understand CTRL-D as the end-of-input character, though many such programs accept commands like **q**, **quit**, **exit**, etc.

CTRL-S and CTRL-Q are called flow-control characters. They represent an antiquated way of stopping and restarting the flow of output from one device to another (e.g., from the computer to your terminal) that was useful when the speed of such output was low. They are rather obsolete in these days of high-speed local networks and dialup lines. In fact, under the latter conditions, CTRL-S and CTRL-Q are basically a nuisance. The only thing you really need to know about them is that if your screen output becomes "stuck," then you may have hit CTRL-S by accident. Type CTRL-Q to restart the output; any keys you may have hit in between will then take effect.

The final group of control characters gives you rudimentary ways to edit your command line. DEL acts as a backspace key (in fact, some systems use the actual BACKSPACE or CTRL-H key as "erase" instead of DEL); CTRL-U erases the entire line and lets you start over. Again, these have been superseded.* The next chapter will look at *bash*'s editing modes, which are among its most useful features and far more powerful than the limited editing capabilities described here.

---

* Why are so many outmoded control keys still in use? They have nothing to do with the shell *per se*; instead, they are recognized by the *tty driver*, an old and hoary part of the operating system's lower depths that controls input and output to/from your terminal.

Help

A feature in *bash* that no other shell has is an online help system. The **help** command gives information on commands in *bash*. If you type **help** by itself, you'll get a list of the built-in shell commands along with their options.

If you provide **help** with a shell command name it will give you a detailed description of the command:

```
$ help cd
cd: cd [-PL] [dir]
    Change the current directory to DIR.  The variable $HOME is the
    default DIR.  The variable $CDPATH defines the search path for
    the directory containing DIR.  Alternative directory names in
    CDPATH are separated by a colon (:).  A null directory name is
    the same as the current directory, i.e. '.'.  If DIR begins with
    a slash (/), then $CDPATH is not used.  If the directory is not
    found, and the shell option 'cdable_vars' is set, then try the
    word as a variable name.  If that variable has a value, then cd
    to the value of that variable.  The -P option says to use the
    physical directory structure instead of following symbolic links;
    the -L option forces symbolic links to be followed.
```

You can also provide **help** with a partial name, in which case it will return details on all commands matching the partial name. For example, **help re** will provide details on **read**, **readonly**, and **return**. The partial name can also include wildcards. You'll need to quote the name to ensure that the wildcard is not expanded to a filename. So the last example is equivalent to **help 're*'**, and **help 're??'** will only return details on **read**.

Sometimes **help** will show more than a screenful of information and it will scroll the screen. You can use the *more* command to show one screenful at a time by typing **help** *command* **| more**.

2

Command-Line Editing

It's always possible to make mistakes when you type at a computer keyboard, but perhaps even more so when you are using a UNIX shell. UNIX shell syntax is powerful, yet terse, full of odd characters, and not particularly mnemonic, making it possible to construct command lines that are as cryptic as they are complex. The Bourne and C shells exacerbate this situation by giving you extremely limited ways of editing your command lines.

In particular, there is no way to recall a previous command line so that you can fix a mistake. If you are an experienced Bourne shell user, undoubtedly you know the frustration of having to retype long command lines. You can use the BACKSPACE key to edit, but once you hit RETURN, it's gone forever!

The C shell provided a small improvement via its *history* mechanism, which provides a few very awkward ways of editing previous commands. But there are more than a few people who have wondered, "Why can't I edit my UNIX command lines in the same way I can edit text with an editor?"

This is exactly what *bash* allows you to do. It has editing modes that allow you to edit command lines with editing commands similar to those of the two most popular UNIX editors, *vi* and *emacs*. It also provides a much-extended analog to the C shell history mechanism called **fc** (for fix command) that, among other things, allows you to use your favorite editor directly for editing your command lines. To round things out, *bash* also provides the original C shell history mechanism.

In this chapter, we will discuss the features that are common to all of *bash*'s command-history facilities; after that, we will deal with each facility in detail. If you use either *vi* or *emacs*, you may wish to read the section on the emulation mode for only the one you use.* If you use neither *vi* or *emacs*, but are interested in learning one of the editing modes anyway, we suggest emacs-mode, because it is more of a natural extension of the minimal editing capability you get with the bare shell.

We should mention up front that both emacs- and vi-modes introduce the potential for clashes with control keys set up by the UNIX terminal interface. Recall the control keys shown in Chapter 1, *bash Basics*, in Table 1-7 and the sample *stty* command output. The control keys shown there override their functions in the editing modes.

During the rest of this chapter, we'll warn you when an editing command clashes with the *default setting* of a terminal-interface control key.

Enabling Command-Line Editing

bash initially starts interactively with emacs-mode as the default (unless you have started *bash* with the **−noediting** option;† see Chapter 10, *bash Administration*). There are two ways to enter either editing mode while in the shell. First, you can use the **set** command:

```
$ set -o emacs
```

or:

```
$ set -o vi
```

The second way of selecting the editing mode is to set a *readline* variable in the file *.inputrc*. We will look at this method later in this chapter.

You will find that the vi- and emacs-editing modes are good at emulating the basic commands of these editors, but not their advanced features; their main purpose is to let you transfer "keyboard habits" from your favorite editor to the shell. **fc** is quite a powerful facility; it is mainly meant to supplant C shell history and as an "escape hatch" for users of editors other than *vi* or *emacs*. Therefore the section on **fc** is mainly recommended to C shell users and those who don't use either standard editor.

---

* You will get the most out of these sections if you are already familiar with the editor(s) in question. Good sources for more complete information on the editors are the O'Reilly & Associates books *Learning the vi Editor*, by Linda Lamb, and *Learning GNU Emacs*, by Debra Cameron and Bill Rosenblatt.

† **−nolineediting** in versions of *bash* prior to 2.0.

The History File

All of *bash*'s command history facilities depend on a list that records commands as you type them into the shell. Whenever you log in or start another interactive shell, *bash* reads an initial history list from the file *.bash_history* in your home directory. From that point on, every *bash* interactive session maintains its own list of commands. When you exit from a shell, it saves the list in *.bash_history*. You can call this file whatever you like by setting the environment variable **HISTFILE**. We'll look more closely at **HISTFILE** and some other related command history variables in the next chapter.

emacs Editing Mode

If you are an *emacs* user, you will find it most useful to think of *emacs* editing mode as a simplified *emacs* with a single, one-line window. All of the basic commands are available for cursor motion, cut-and-paste, and search.

Basic Commands

emacs-mode uses control keys for the most basic editing functions. If you aren't familiar with *emacs*, you can think of these as extensions of the rudimentary "erase" character (usually BACKSPACE or DEL) that UNIX provides through its interface to users' terminals. For the sake of consistency, we'll assume your erase character is DEL from now on; if it is CTRL-H or something else, you will need to make a mental substitution. The most basic control-key commands are shown in Table 2-1. (*Important:* remember that typing CTRL-D when your command line is empty may log you off!) The basic keyboard habits of emacs-mode are easy to learn, but they do require that you assimilate a couple of concepts that are peculiar to the *emacs* editor.

Table 2-1: Basic emacs-Mode Commands

Command	Description
CTRL-B	Move backward one character (without deleting)
CTRL-F	Move forward one character
DEL	Delete one character backward
CTRL-D	Delete one character forward

The first of these is the use of CTRL-B and CTRL-F for backward and forward cursor motion. These keys have the advantage of being obvious mnemonics. You can also use the left and right cursor motion keys ("arrow" keys), but for the rest of this discussion we will use the control keys, as they work on all keyboards. In emacs-mode, the *point* (sometimes also called *dot*) is an imaginary place just to the left of the character the cursor is on. In the command descriptions in Table 2-1, some say "forward" while others say "backward." Think of forward as "to the right of point" and backward as "to the left of point."

For example, let's say you type in a line and, instead of typing RETURN, you type CTRL-B and hold it down so that it repeats. The cursor will move to the left until it is over the first character on the line, like this:

```
$ █grep -l Duchess < ~cam/book/alice_in_wonderland
```

Now the cursor is on the **f**, and point is at the beginning of the line, just before the **f**. If you type DEL, nothing will happen because there are no characters to the left of point. However, if you press CTRL-D (the "delete character forward" command) you will delete the first letter:

```
$ █rep -l Duchess < ~cam/book/alice_in_wonderland
```

Point is still at the beginning of the line. If this were the desired command, you could hit RETURN now and run it; you don't need to move the cursor back to the end of the line. However, you could type CTRL-F repeatedly to get there:

```
$ grep -l Duchess < ~cam/book/alice_in_wonderland█
```

At this point, typing CTRL-D wouldn't do anything, but hitting DEL would erase the final **d**.

Word Commands

The basic commands are really all you need to get around a command line, but a set of more advanced commands lets you do it with fewer keystrokes. These commands operate on *words* rather than single characters; emacs-mode defines a word as a sequence of one or more alphanumeric characters.

The word commands are shown in Table 2-2. The basic commands are all single characters, whereas these consist of two keystrokes, ESC followed by a letter. You will notice that the command ESC *X*, where *X* is any letter, often does for a word what CTRL-*X* does for a single character. "Kill" is another word for "delete"; it is the standard term used in the *readline* library documentation for an "undoable" deletion.

Table 2-2: emacs-Mode Word Commands

Command	Description
ESC-B	Move one word backward
ESC-F	Move one word forward
ESC-DEL	Kill one word backward
ESC-CTRL-H	Kill one word backward

Table 2-2: emacs-Mode Word Commands (continued)

Command	Description
ESC-D	Kill one word forward
CTRL-Y	Retrieve ("yank") last item killed

To return to our example: if we type ESC-B, point will move back a word. Since the underscore (_) is not an alphanumeric character, emacs-mode will stop there:

    $ grep -1 Duchess < ~cam/book/alice_in_wonderland

The cursor is on the **w** in *wonderland,* and point is between the _ and the **w**. Now let's say we want to change the **–1** option of this command from *Duchess* to *Cheshire.* We need to move back on the command line, so we type ESC-B four more times. This gets us here:

    $ grep -1 Duchess < ~cam/book/alice_in_wonderland

If we type ESC-B again, we end up at the beginning of *Duchess*:

    $ grep -1 Duchess < ~cam/book/alice_in_wonderland

Why? Remember that a word is defined as a sequence of alphanumeric characters only. Therefore < is not a word; the next word in the backward direction is *Duchess.* We are now in position to delete *Duchess,* so we type ESC-D and get:

    $ grep -1 < ~cam/book/alice_in_wonderland

Now we can type in the desired argument:

    $ grep -1 Cheshire < ~cam/book/alice_in_wonderland

If you want *Duchess* back again you can use the CTRL-Y command. The CTRL-Y "yank" command will undelete a word if the word was the last thing deleted. In this case, CTRL-Y would insert *Duchess* at the point.

Line Commands

There are still more efficient ways of moving around a command line in emacs-mode. A few commands deal with the entire line; they are shown in Table 2-3.

Table 2-3: emacs-Mode Line Commands

Command	Description
CTRL-A	Move to beginning of line
CTRL-E	Move to end of line
CTRL-K	Kill forward to end of line

Using CTRL-A, CTRL-E, and CTRL-K should be straightforward. Remember that CTRL-Y will always undelete the last thing deleted; if you use CTRL-K, that could be quite a few characters.

Moving Around in the History File

Now we know how to get around the command line efficiently and make changes. But that doesn't address the original issue of recalling previous commands by accessing the history file. emacs-mode has several commands for doing this, summarized in Table 2-4.

Table 2-4: emacs-Mode Commands for Moving Through the History File

Command	Description
CTRL-P	Move to previous line
CTRL-N	Move to next line
CTRL-R	Search backward
ESC-<	Move to first line of history file
ESC->	Move to last line of history file

CTRL-P and CTRL-N move you through the command history. If you have cursor motion keys (arrow keys) you can use them instead. The up-arrow is the same as CTRL-P and the down-arrow is the same as CTRL-N. For the rest of this discussion, we'll stick to using the control keys because they can be used on all keyboards.

CTRL-P is by far the one you will use most often—it's the "I made a mistake, let me go back and fix it" key. You can use it as many times as you wish to scroll back through the history file. If you want to get back to the last command you entered, you can hold down CTRL-N until *bash* beeps at you, or just type ESC->. As an example, you hit RETURN to run the command above, but you get an error message telling you that your option letter was incorrect. You want to change it without retyping the whole thing.

First, you would type CTRL-P to recall the bad command. You get it back with point at the end:

```
$ grep -l Duchess < ~cam/book/alice_in_wonderland█
```

After CTRL-A, ESC-F, two CTRL-Fs, and CTRL-D, you have:

```
$ grep -█Duchess < ~cam/book/alice_in_wonderland
```

You decide to try −s instead of −l, so you type **s** and hit RETURN. You get the same error message, so you give up and look it up in the manual. You find out that the command you want is *fgrep*—not *grep*—after all.

You sigh heavily and go back and find the *fgrep* command you typed in an hour ago. To do this, you type CTRL-R; whatever was on the line will disappear and be replaced by **(reverse-i-search)**` `` `:. Then type **fgrep**, and you will see this:

```
$ (reverse-i-search)`fgrep': fgrep -l Duchess <~cam/book/ \
  alice_in_wonderland
```

The shell dynamically searches back through the command history each time you type a letter, looking for the current substring in the previous commands. In this example, when you typed **f** the shell would have printed the most recent command in the history with that letter in it. As you typed more letters, the shell narrowed the search until you ended up with the line displayed above. Of course, this may not have been the particular line you wanted. Typing CTRL-R again makes the shell search further back in the history list for a line with "fgrep" in it. If the shell doesn't find the substring again, it will beep.

If you try the *fgrep* command by hitting RETURN, two things will happen. First, of course, the command will run. Second, this line will be entered into the history file at the end, and your "current line" will be at the end as well. You will no longer be somewhere else in the command history.

CTRL-P, CTRL-N, and CTRL-R are clearly the most important emacs-mode commands that deal with the command history. The others are less useful but are included for compatibility with the full *emacs* editor.

Textual Completion

One of the most powerful (and typically underused) features of emacs-mode is its *textual completion* facility, inspired by similar features in the full *emacs* editor, the C shell, and (originally) the old DEC TOPS-20 operating system.

The premise behind textual completion is simple: you should have to type only as much of a filename, user name, function, etc., to identify it unambiguously. This is an excellent feature; there is an analogous one in vi-mode. We recommend that you take the time to learn it, since it will save you quite a bit of typing.

There are three commands in emacs-mode that relate to textual completion. The most important is TAB.* When you type in a word of text followed by TAB, *bash* will attempt to complete the name. Then one of four things can happen:

1. If there is nothing whose name begins with the word, the shell will beep and nothing further will happen.

---

* *emacs* users will recognize this as minibuffer completion.

2. If there is a command name in the search path, a function name, or a filename that the string uniquely matches, the shell will type the rest of it, followed by a space in case you want to type in more command arguments. Command name completion is only attempted when the word is in a command position (e.g., at the start of a line).

3. If there is a directory that the string uniquely matches, the shell will complete the filename, followed by a slash.

4. If there is more than one way to complete the name, the shell will complete out to the longest common prefix among the available choices. Commands in the search path and functions take precedence over filenames.

For example, assume you have a directory with the files *tweedledee.c* and *tweedledum.c*. You want to compile the first of these by typing **cc tweedledee.c**. You type **cc twee** followed by TAB. This is not an unambiguous prefix, since the prefix "twee" is common to both filenames, so the shell only completes out to **cc tweedled**. You need to type more letters to distinguish between them, so you type **e** and hit TAB again. Then the shell completes out to "**cc tweedledee.c** ", leaving the extra space for you to type in other filenames or options.

If you didn't know what options were available after trying to complete **cc twee**, you could press TAB again. *bash* prints out the possible completions for you and presents your input line again:

```
$ cc tweedled
tweedledee.c   tweedledum.c
$ cc tweedled
```

A related command is ESC-?, which expands the prefix to all possible choices, listing them to standard output. Be aware that the completion mechanism doesn't necessarily expand to a filename. If there are functions and commands that satisfy the string you provide, the shell expands those first and ignores any files in the current directory. As we'll see, you can force completion to a particular type.

It is also possible to complete other environment entities. If the text being completed is preceded by a dollar sign ($), the shell attempts to expand the name to that of a shell variable (see Chapter 3, *Customizing Your Environment*, for a discussion of shell variables). If the text is preceded by a tilde (~), completion to a username is attempted; if preceded by an at sign (@), a hostname is attempted.

For example, suppose there was a username **cameron** on the system. If you wanted to change to this user's home directory, you could just use tilde notation and type the first few letters of the name, followed by a TAB:

```
$ cd ~ca
```

which would expand to:

```
$ cd ~cameron/
```

You can force the shell to complete to specific things. Table 2-5 lists the standard keys for these.

Table 2-5: Completion Commands

Command	Description
TAB	Attempt to perform general completion of the text
ESC-?	List the possible completions
ESC-/	Attempt filename completion
CTRL-X /	List the possible filename completions
ESC-~	Attempt username completion
CTRL-X ~	List the possible username completions
ESC-$	Attempt variable completion
CTRL-X $	List the possible variable completions
ESC-@	Attempt hostname completion
CTRL-X @	List the possible hostname completions
ESC-!	Attempt command completion
CTRL-X !	List the possible command completions
ESC-TAB	Attempt completion from previous commands in the history list

If you find that you are interested only in completing long filenames, you are probably better off using ESC-/ rather than TAB. This ensures that the result will be a filename and not a function or command name.

Miscellaneous Commands

Several miscellaneous commands complete *emacs* editing mode; they are shown in Table 2-6.

Table 2-6: emacs-Mode Miscellaneous Commands

Command	Description
CTRL-J	Same as RETURN
CTRL-L	Clears the screen, placing the current line at the top of the screen
CTRL-M	Same as RETURN
CTRL-O	Same as RETURN, then display next line in command history
CTRL-T	Transpose two characters on either side of point and move point forward by one
CTRL-U	Kills the line from the beginning to point
CTRL-V	Quoted insert
CTRL-[	Same as ESC (most keyboards)

Table 2-6: emacs-Mode Miscellaneous Commands (continued)

Command	Description
ESC-C	Capitalize word after point
ESC-U	Change word after point to all capital letters
ESC-L	Change word after point to all lowercase letters
ESC-.	Insert last word in previous command line after point
ESC-_	Same as ESC-.

BSD-derived systems use CTRL-V and CTRL-W as default settings for the "quote next character" and "word erase" terminal interface functions, respectively.

A few of these miscellaneous commands are worth discussing, even though they may not be among the most useful emacs-mode commands.

CTRL-O is useful for repeating a sequence of commands you have already entered. Just go back to the first command in the sequence and press CTRL-O instead of RETURN. This will execute the command and bring up the next command in the history file. Press CTRL-O again to enter this command and bring up the next one. Repeat this until you see the last command in the sequence; then just hit RETURN.

Of the case-changing commands, ESC-L is useful when you hit the CAPS LOCK key by accident and don't notice it immediately. Since all-caps words aren't used too often in the UNIX world, you probably won't use ESC-U very often.

CTRL-V will cause the next character you type to appear in the command line as is; i.e., if it is an editing command (or an otherwise special character like CTRL-D), it will be stripped of its special meaning.

If it seems like there are too many synonyms for RETURN, bear in mind that CTRL-M is actually the same (ASCII) character as RETURN, and that CTRL-J is actually the same as LINEFEED, which UNIX usually accepts in lieu of RETURN anyway.

ESC-. and ESC-_ are useful if you want to run several commands on a given file. The usual UNIX convention is that a filename is the last argument to a command. Therefore you can save typing by just entering each command followed by SPACE and then typing ESC-. or ESC-_. For example, say you want to examine a file using *more*, so you type:

```
$ more myfilewithaverylongname
```

Then you decide you want to print it, so you type the print command *lp*. You can avoid typing the very long name by typing **lp** followed by a space and then ESC-. or ESC-_; *bash* will insert *myfilewithaverylongname* for you.

vi Editing Mode

Like emacs-mode, vi-mode essentially creates a one-line editing window into the history file. vi-mode is popular because *vi* is the most standard UNIX editor. But the function for which *vi* was designed, writing C programs, has different editing requirements from those of command interpreters. As a result, although it is possible to do complex things in *vi* with relatively few keystrokes, the relatively simple things you need to do in *bash* sometimes take too many keystrokes.

Like *vi*, vi-mode has two modes of its own: *input* and *control* mode. The former is for typing commands (as in normal *bash* use); the latter is for moving around the command line and the history file. When you are in input mode, you can type commands in and hit RETURN to run them. In addition, you have minimal editing capabilities via control characters, which are summarized in Table 2-7.

Table 2-7: Editing Commands in vi Input Mode

Command	Description
DEL	Delete previous character
CTRL-W	Erase previous word (i.e., erase until a blank)
CTRL-V	Quote the next character
ESC	Enter control mode (see below)

Note that at least some of these—depending on which version of UNIX you have—are the same as the editing commands provided by UNIX through its terminal interface.* vi-mode will use your "erase" character as the "delete previous character" key; usually it is set to DEL or CTRL-H (BACKSPACE). CTRL-V works the same way as in emacs-mode; it causes the next character to appear in the command line as is and lose its special meaning.

Under normal circumstances, you just stay in input mode. But if you want to go back and make changes to your command line, or if you want to recall previous commands, you need to go into control mode. To do this, hit ESC.

Simple Control Mode Commands

A full range of *vi* editing commands are available to you in control mode. The simplest of these move you around the command line and are summarized in Table 2-8. vi-mode contains two "word" concepts. The simplest is any sequence of non-blank characters; we'll call this a *non-blank word*. The other is any sequence of

---

* In particular, versions of UNIX derived from 4.x BSD have all of these commands built in.

only alphanumeric characters (letters and digits) plus the underscore (_), or any sequence of only non-alphanumeric characters; we'll just call this a *word.**

Table 2-8: Basic vi Control Mode Commands

Command	Description
h	Move left one character
l	Move right one character
w	Move right one word
b	Move left one word
W	Move to beginning of next non-blank word
B	Move to beginning of preceding non-blank word
e	Move to end of current word
E	Move to end of current non-blank word
0	Move to beginning of line
^	Move to first non-blank character in line
$	Move to end of line

All of these commands except the last three can be preceded by a number that acts as a repeat count. Whenever you type a number for the repeat count, the number replaces the command prompt for the duration of the repeat command. If your keyboard has cursor motion keys ("arrow" keys), you can use the left and right arrows to move between characters instead of the h and l keys. Repeat counts will work with the cursor keys as well.

The last two will be familiar to users of UNIX utilities (such as *grep*) that use regular expressions, as well as to *vi* users.

Time for a few examples. Let's say you type in this line and, before you hit RETURN, decide you want to change it:

```
$ fgrep -l Duchess < ~cam/book/alice_in_wonderland
```

As shown, your cursor is beyond the last character of the line. First, type **ESC** to enter control mode; your cursor will move back one space so that it is on the **d**. Then if you type **h**, your cursor will move back to the **n**. If you type **3h** from the **n**, you will end up at the **r**.

Now we will see the difference between the two "word" concepts. Go back to the end of the line by typing **$**. If you type **b**, the word in question is *alice_in_wonderland*, and the cursor will end up on the **a**:

```
$ fgrep -l Duchess < ~cam/book/alice_in_wonderland
```

---

* Neither of these definitions is the same as the definition of a word in emacs-mode.

If you type **b** again, the next word is the slash (it's a "sequence" of non-alphanumeric characters), so the cursor ends up over it:

```
$ fgrep -l Duchess < ~cam/book/alice_in_wonderland
```

However, if you typed **B** instead of **b**, the non-blank word would be the entire pathname, and the cursor would end up at the beginning of it—over the tilde:

```
$ fgrep -l Duchess < ~cam/book/alice_in_wonderland
```

You would have had to type **b** four times—or just **4b**—to get the same effect, since there are four "words" in the part of the pathname to the left of */alice_in_wonderland*: *book*, slash, *cam*, and the leading tilde.

At this point, **w** and **W** do the opposite: typing **w** gets you over the **c**, since the tilde is a "word," while typing **W** brings you to the end of the line. But whereas **w** and **W** take you to the beginning of the next word, **e** and **E** take you to the end of the current word. Thus, if you type **w** with the cursor on the tilde, you get to:

```
$ fgrep -l Duchess < ~cam/book/alice_in_wonderland
```

Then typing **e** gets you to:

```
$ fgrep -l Duchess < ~cam/book/alice_in_wonderland
```

And typing an additional **w** gets you to:

```
$ fgrep -l Duchess < ~cam/book/alice_in_wonderland
```

On the other hand, **E** gets you to the end of the current non-blank word—in this case, the end of the line. (If you find these commands non-mnemonic, you're right. The only way to assimilate them is through lots of practice.)

Entering and Changing Text

Now that you know how to enter control mode and move around on the command line, you need to know how to get back into input mode so you can make changes and type in additional commands. A number of commands take you from control mode into input mode; they are listed in Table 2-9. All of them enter input mode a bit differently.

Table 2-9: Commands for Entering vi Input Mode

Command	Description
i	Text inserted before current character (insert)
a	Text inserted after current character (append)
I	Text inserted at beginning of line

Table 2-9: Commands for Entering vi Input Mode (continued)

Command	Description
A	Text inserted at end of line
R	Text overwrites existing text

Most likely, you will use either **i** or **a** consistently, and you may use **R** occasionally. **I** and **A** are abbreviations for **0i** and **$a** respectively. To illustrate the difference between **i**, **a**, and **R**, say we start out with our example line:

```
$ fgrep -l Duchess < ~cam/book/alice_in_wonderland
```

If you type **i** followed by **end**, you will get:

```
$ fgrep -l Duchess < ~cam/bookend/alice_in_wonderland
```

That is, the cursor will always appear to be under the / before *alice_in_wonderland*. But if you type **a** instead of **i**, you will notice the cursor move one space to the right. Then if you type **miss_**, you will get:

```
$ fgrep -l Duchess < ~cam/book/miss_alice_in_wonderland
```

That is, the cursor will always be just after the last character you typed, until you type ESC to end your input. Finally, if you go back to the first **a** in *alice_in_wonderland*, type **R** instead, and then type **through_the_looking_glass**, you will see:

```
$ fgrep -l Duchess < ~cam/book/through_the_looking_glass
```

In other words, you will be *replacing* (hence *R*) instead of inserting text.

Why capital **R** instead of lowercase **r**? The latter is a slightly different command, which replaces only one character and does not enter input mode. With **r**, the next single character overwrites the character under the cursor. So if we start with the original command line and type **r** followed by a semicolon, we get:

```
$ fgrep -l Duchess < ~cam/book;alice_in_wonderland
```

If you precede **r** with a number *N*, it will allow you to replace the next *N* existing characters on the line—but still not enter input mode. Lowercase **r** is effective for fixing erroneous option letters, I/O redirection characters, punctuation, and so on.

Deletion Commands

Now that you know how to enter commands and move around the line, you need to know how to delete. The basic deletion command in vi-mode is **d** followed by one other letter. This letter determines what the unit and direction of deletion is, and it corresponds to a motion command, as listed previously in Table 2-8.

Table 2-10 shows some commonly used examples.

Table 2-10: Some vi-Mode Deletion Commands

Command	Description
dh	Delete one character backwards
dl	Delete one character forwards
db	Delete one word backwards
dw	Delete one word forwards
dB	Delete one non-blank word backwards
dW	Delete one non-blank word forwards
d$	Delete to end of line
d0	Delete to beginning of line

These commands have a few variations and abbreviations. If you use a **c** instead of **d**, you will enter input mode after it does the deletion. You can supply a numeric repeat count either before or after the **d** (or **c**). Table 2-11 lists the available abbreviations.

Table 2-11: Abbreviations for vi-Mode Delete Commands

Command	Description
D	Equivalent to **d$** (delete to end of line)
dd	Equivalent to **0d$** (delete entire line)
C	Equivalent to **c$** (delete to end of line, enter input mode)
cc	Equivalent to **0c$** (delete entire line, enter input mode)
X	Equivalent to **dl** (delete character backwards)
x	Equivalent to **dh** (delete character forwards)

Most people tend to use **D** to delete to end of line, **dd** to delete an entire line, and **x** (as "backspace") to delete single characters. If you aren't a hardcore *vi* user, you may find it difficult to get some of the more esoteric deletion commands under your fingers.

Every good editor provides "un-delete" commands as well as delete commands, and vi-mode is no exception. vi-mode maintains a *delete buffer* that stores all of the modifications to text on the current line only (note that this is different from the full *vi* editor). The command **u** undoes previous text modifications. If you type **u**, it will undo the last change. Typing it again will undo the change before that. When there are no more undo's, *bash* will beep. A related command is **.** (dot), which repeats the last text modification command.

There is also a way to save text in the delete buffer without having to delete it in the first place: just type in a delete command but use **y** ("yank") instead of **d**. This does not modify anything, but it allows you to retrieve the yanked text as many times as you like later on. The commands to retrieve yanked text are **p**, which inserts the text on the current line to the right of the cursor, and **P**, which inserts it to the left of the cursor. The **y**, **p**, and **P** commands are powerful but far better suited to "real *vi*" tasks like making global changes to documents or programs than to shell commands, so we doubt you'll use them very often.

Moving Around in the History File

The next group of *vi* control mode commands we cover allows you to move around in and search your command history. This is the all-important functionality that lets you go back and fix an erroneous command without retyping the entire line. These commands are summarized in Table 2-12.

Table 2-12: vi Control Mode Commands for Searching the Command History

Command	Description
k or −	Move backward one line
j or +	Move forward one line
G	Move to line given by repeat count
/*string*	Search backward for string
?*string*	Search forward for string
n	Repeat search in same direction as previous
N	Repeat search in opposite direction of previous

The first two can also be accomplished with the up and down cursor movement keys if your keyboard has them. The first three can be preceded by repeat counts (e.g., **3k** or **3−** moves back three lines in the command history).

If you aren't familiar with *vi* and its cultural history, you may be wondering at the wisdom of choosing such seemingly poor mnemonics as **h**, **j**, **k**, and **l** for backward character, forward line, backward line, and forward character, respectively. Well, there actually is a rationale for the choices—other than that they are all together on the standard keyboard. Bill Joy originally developed *vi* to run on Lear-Siegler ADM-3a terminals, which were the first popular models with addressable cursors (meaning that a program could send an ADM-3a command to move the cursor to a specified location on the screen). The ADM-3a's **h**, **j**, **k**, and **l** keys had little arrows on them, so Joy decided to use those keys for appropriate commands in *vi*. Another (partial) rationale for the command choices is that CTRL-H is the traditional backspace key, and CTRL-J denotes linefeed.

Perhaps + and − are better mnemonics than **j** and **k**, but the latter have the advantage of being more easily accessible to touch typists. In either case, these are the most basic commands for moving around the history file. To see how they work, let's use the same examples from the emacs-mode section earlier.

You enter the example command (RETURN works in both input and control modes, as does LINEFEED or CTRL-J):

```
$ fgrep -l Duchess < ~cam/book/alice_in_wonderland
```

but you get an error message saying that your option letter was wrong. You want to change it to −s without having to retype the entire command. Assuming you are in control mode (you may have to type ESC to put yourself in control mode), you type **k** or − to get the command back. Your cursor will be at the beginning of the line:

```
$ fgrep -l Duchess < ~cam/book/alice_in_wonderland
```

Type **w** to get to the −, then **l** to get to the **l**. Now you can replace it by typing **rs**; press RETURN to run the command.

Now let's say you get another error message, and you finally decide to look at the manual page for the *fgrep* command. You remember having done this a while ago today, so rather than typing in the entire *man* command, you search for the last one you used. To do this, type ESC to enter control mode (if you are already in control mode, this will have no effect), then type / followed by **man** or **ma**. To be on the safe side, you can also type **^ma**; the **^** means match only lines that begin with **ma**.*

But typing /**^ma** doesn't give you what you want: instead, the shell gives you:

```
$ make myprogram
```

To search for "man" again, you can type **n**, which does another backward search using the last search string. Typing / again without an argument and hitting **RETURN** will accomplish the same thing.

The **G** command retrieves the command whose number is the same as the numeric prefix argument you supply. **G** depends on the command numbering scheme described in Chapter 3, in the section "Prompting Variables." Without a prefix argument, it goes to command number 1. This may be useful to former C shell users who still want to use command numbers.

Character-Finding Commands

There are some additional motion commands in vi-mode, although they are less useful than the ones we saw earlier in the chapter. These commands allow you to move to the position of a particular character in the line. They are summarized in Table 2-13, in which *x* denotes any character.

---

* Fans of *vi* and search utilities like *grep* should note that caret (^) for beginning-of-line is the only context operator vi-mode provides for search strings.

All of these commands can be preceded by a repeat count.

Table 2-13: vi-Mode Character-Finding Commands

Command	Description
f*x*	Move right to next occurrence of *x*
F*x*	Move left to previous occurrence of *x*
t*x*	Move right to next occurrence of *x*, then back one space
T*x*	Move left to previous occurrence of *x*, then forward one space
;	Redo last character-finding command
,	Redo last character-finding command in opposite direction

Starting with the previous example: let's say you want to change *Duchess* to *Duckess*. Make sure that you're at the end of the line (or, in any case, to the left of the *h* in *Duchess*); then, if you type **Fh**, your cursor will move to the **h**:

```
$ fgrep -l Duchess < ~cam/book/alice_in_wonderland
```

At this point, you could type **r** to replace the **h** with **k**. But let's say you wanted to change *Duchess* to *Dutchess*. You would need to move one space to the right of the **u**. Of course, you could just type l. But, given that you're somewhere to the right of *Duchess*, the fastest way to move to the **c** would be to type **Tu** instead of **Fu** followed by l.

As an example of how the repeat count can be used with character-finding commands, let's say you want to change the filename from *alice_in_wonderland* to *alice*. In this case, assuming your cursor is still on the **D**, you need to get to one character beyond the second slash. To do this, you can type **2fa**. Your cursor will then be on the **a** in *alice_in_wonderland*.

The character-finding commands also have associated delete commands. Read the command definitions in the previous table and mentally substitute "delete" for move. You'll get what happens when you precede the given character-finding command with a **d**. The deletion includes the character given as argument. For example, assume that your cursor is under the **a** in *alice_in_wonderland*:

```
$ fgrep -l Duchess < ~cam/book/alice_in_wonderland
```

If you want to change *alice_in_wonderland* to *natalie_in_wonderland*, one possibility is to type **dfc**. This means "delete right to next occurrence of c," i.e., delete "alic". Then you can type **i** (to enter input mode) and then "natali" to complete the change.

One final command rounds out the *vi* control mode commands for getting around on the current line: you can use the pipe character (|) to move to a specific column, whose number is given by a numeric prefix argument. Column counts start at 1; count only your input, not the space taken up by the prompt string. The default repeat count is 1, of course, which means that typing | by itself is equivalent to 0 (see Table 2-8).

Textual Completion

Although the character-finding commands and | are not particularly useful, vi-mode provides one additional feature that we think you will use quite often: textual completion. This feature is not part of the real *vi* editor, and it was undoubtedly inspired by similar features in *emacs* and, originally, in the TOPS-20 operating system for DEC mainframes.

The rationale behind textual completion is simple: you should have to type only as much of a filename, user name, function, etc, as is necessary. Backslash (\) is the command that tells *bash* to do completion in vi-mode. If you type in a word, hit ESC to enter control mode, and then type \, one of four things will happen; they are the same as for TAB in emacs-mode:

1. If there is nothing whose name begins with the word, the shell will beep and nothing further will happen.

2. If there is a command name in the search path, a function name, or a filename that the string uniquely matches, the shell will type the rest of it, followed by a space in case you want to type in more command arguments. Command name completion is only attempted when the word is in a command position (e.g: at the start of a line).

3. If there is a directory that the string uniquely matches, the shell will complete the filename, followed by a slash.

4. If there is more than one way to complete the name, the shell will complete out to the longest common prefix among the available choices. Commands in the search path and functions take precedence over filenames.

A related command is *. It behaves similarly to ESC-\, but if there is more than one completion possibility (number four in the previous list), it lists all of them and allows you to type further. Thus, it resembles the * shell wildcard character.

Less useful is the command =, which does the same kind of expansion as *, but in a different way. Instead of expanding the names onto the command line, it prints them, then gives you your shell prompt back and retypes whatever was on your command line before you typed =. For example, if the files in your directory include *tweedledee.c* and *tweedledum.c*, and you type **tweedl** followed by ESC and then =, you will see this:

```
$ cc tweedl
tweedledee.c tweedledum.c
```

It is also possible to expand other environment entities, as we saw in emacs-mode. If the text being expanded is preceded by a dollar sign ($), the shell will attempt to expand the name to that of a shell variable. If the text is preceded by a tilde (~), expansion to a username is attempted; if preceded by an at sign (@), a hostname.

Miscellaneous Commands

Several miscellaneous commands round out vi-mode; some of them are quite esoteric. They are listed in Table 2-14.

Table 2-14: Miscellaneous vi-Mode Commands

Command	Description
~	Invert (twiddle) case of current character(s)
_	Append last word of previous command, enter input mode
CTRL-L	Clear the screen and redraw the current line on it; good for when your screen becomes garbled
#	Prepend # (comment character) to the line and send it to the history file; useful for saving a command to be executed later without having to retype it[a]

a. The line is also "executed" by the shell. However, # is the shell's comment character, so the shell ignores it.

The first of these can be preceded by a repeat count. A repeat count of *n* preceding the ~ changes the case of the next *n* characters. The cursor will advance accordingly.

A repeat count preceding _ causes the *n*th word in the previous command to be inserted in the current line; without the count, the last word is used. Omitting the repeat count is useful because a filename is usually the last thing on a UNIX command line, and because users often run several commands in a row on the same file. With this feature, you can type all of the commands (except the first) followed by ESC-_, and the shell will insert the filename.

The fc Command

fc is a built-in shell command that provides a superset of the C shell history mechanism. You can use it to examine the most recent commands you entered, to edit one or more commands with your favorite "real" editor, and to run old commands with changes without having to type the entire command in again. We'll look at each of these uses in turn.

The −l option to **fc** lists previous commands. It takes arguments that refer to commands in the history file. Arguments can be numbers or alphanumeric strings; numbers refer to the commands in the history file, while strings refer to the most recent command beginning with the string. **fc** treats arguments in a rather complex way:

- If you give two arguments, they serve as the first and last commands to be shown.

- If you specify one number argument, only the command with that number is shown.

- With a single string argument, it searches for the most recent command start-ing with that string and shows you everything from that command to the most recent command.

- If you specify no arguments, you will see the last 16 commands you entered. *bash* also has a built-in command for displaying the history: **history**.

A few examples should make these options clearer. Let's say you logged in and entered these commands:

```
ls -l
more myfile
vi myfile
wc -l myfile
pr myfile | lp -h
```

If you type **fc −l** with no arguments, you will see the above list with command numbers, as in:

```
1       ls -l
2       more myfile
3       vi myfile
4       wc -l myfile
5       pr myfile | lp -h
```

Adding another option, **−n**, suppresses the line numbers. If you want to see only commands 2 through 4, type **fc −l 2 4**. If you want to see only the *vi* command, type **fc −l 3**. To see everything from the *vi* command up to the present, type **fc −l v**. Finally, if you want to see commands between *more* and *wc*, you can type **fc −l m w**, **fc −l m 4**, **fc −l 2 4**, etc.

The other important option to **fc** is **−e** for "edit." This is useful as an "escape hatch" from vi- and emacs-modes if you aren't used to either of those editors. You can specify the pathname of your favorite editor and edit commands from your history file; then when you have made the changes, the shell will actually execute the new lines.

Let's say your favorite editor is a little home-brew gem called *zed*. You could edit your commands by typing:

```
$ fc -e /usr/local/bin/zed
```

This seems like a lot of work just to fix a typo in your previous command; fortunately, there is a better way. You can set the environment variable FCEDIT to the pathname of the editor you want **fc** to use. If you put a line in your *.bash_profile* or environment file saying:*

```
FCEDIT=/usr/local/bin/zed
```

you will get *zed* when you invoke **fc**. If **FCEDIT** isn't set, then *bash* uses whatever the variable **EDITOR** is set to. If that's also not set, then *bash* defaults to *vi*.

fc is usually used to fix a recent command. When used without options, it handles arguments a bit differently than it does for the **fc −l** variation discussed earlier:

- With no arguments, **fc** loads the editor with the most recent command.

- With a numeric argument, **fc** loads the editor with the command with that number.

- With a string argument, **fc** loads the most recent command starting with that string.

- With two arguments to **fc**, the arguments specify the beginning and end of a range of commands, as above.

Remember that **fc** actually runs the command(s) after you edit them. Therefore, the last-named choice can be dangerous. *bash* will attempt to execute all commands in the range you specify when you exit your editor. If you have typed in any multiline constructs (like those we will cover in Chapter 5, *Flow Control*), the results could be even more dangerous. Although these might seem like valid ways of generating "instant shell programs," a far better strategy would be to direct the output of **fc −ln** with the same arguments to a file; then edit that file and execute the commands when you're satisfied with them:

```
$ fc -l cp > lastcommands
$ vi lastcommands
$ source lastcommands
```

In this case, the shell will not try to execute the file when you leave the editor!

There is one final option with **fc**. **fc −s** allows you to rerun a command. With an argument, **fc** will rerun the last command starting with the given string. Without an argument, it will rerun the previous command. The **−s** option also allows you to provide a pattern and replacement. For example, if you typed:

```
$ cs prog.c
```

You could correct it with **fc −s cs=cc**. This can be combined with the string search: **fc −s cs=cc cs**. The last occurence of *cs* will be found and replaced with *cc*.

---

* See Chapter 3 for information on the *bash* startup file *.bash_profile*.

History Expansion

If you are a C shell user, you may be familiar with the history expansion mechanism that it provides. *bash* provides a similar set of features. History expansion is a primitive way to recall and edit commands in the history list. The way to recall commands is by the use of *event designators*. Table 2-15 gives a complete list.

Table 2-15: Event Designators

Command	Description
!	Start a history substitution
!!	Refers to the last command
!*n*	Refers to command line *n*
!-*n*	Refers to the current command line minus *n*
!*string*	Refers to the most recent command starting with *string*
!?*string*?	Refers to the most recent command containing *string*. The ending ? is optional
^*string1*^*string2*	Repeat the last command, replacing *string1* with *string2*

By far the most useful command is !!. Typing !! on the command line re-executes the last command. If you know the command number of a specific command, you can use the !*n* form, where *n* is the command number. Command numbers can be determined from the **history** command. Alternatively, you can re-execute the most recent command beginning with the specified string by using !*string*.

You might also find the last expansion in the table to be of some use if you've made a typing mistake. For example, you might have typed

```
$ cat through_the_loking_glass | grep Tweedledee > dee.list
```

Instead of moving back to the line and changing *loking* to *looking*, you could just type ^lok^look. This will change the string *lok* to *look* and then execute the resulting command.

It's also possible to refer to certain words in a previous command by the use of a *word designator*. Table 2-16 lists available designators. Note that when counting words, *bash* (like most UNIX programs) starts counting with zero, not with one.

Table 2-16: Word Designators

Designator	Description
0	The zeroth (first) word in a line
n	The *n*th word in a line
^	The first argument (the second word)
$	The last argument in a line
%	The word matched by the most recent ?*string* search

Table 2-16: Word Designators (continued)

Designator	Description
x–y	A range of words from *x* to *y*. –*y* is synonymous with 0–*y*.
*	All words but the zeroth (first). Synonymous with 1–$. If there is only one word on the line, an empty string is returned.
*x**	Synonymous with *x*–$
x–	The words from *x* to the second last word

The word designator follows the event designator, separated by a colon. You could, for example, repeat the previous command with different arguments by typing !!:0 followed by the new arguments.

Event designators may also be followed by *modifiers*. The modifiers follow the word designator, if there is one. Table 2-17 lists the available modifiers.

Table 2-17: Modifiers

Modifier	Description
h	Removes a trailing pathname component, leaving the head
r	Removes a trailing suffix of the form *.xxx*
e	Removes all but the trailing suffix
t	Removes all leading pathname components, leaving the tail
p	Prints the resulting command but doesn't execute it
q	Quote the substituted words, escaping further substitutions
x	Quote the substituted words, breaking them into words at blanks and newlines
s/*old*/*new*/	Substitutes *new* for *old*

More than one modifier may be used with an event designator; each one is separated by a colon.

History expansion is fine for re-executing a command quickly, but it has been superseded by the command-line editing facilities that we looked at earlier in this chapter. Its inclusion is really only for completeness, and we feel you are better off mastering the techniques offered in the *vi* or *emacs* editing modes.

readline

bash's command-line editing interface is *readline*. It is actually a library of software developed for the GNU project that can be used by applications requiring a text-based interface. It provides editing and text-manipulation features to make it easier for the user to enter and edit text. Just as importantly, it allows standardization, in terms of both key strokes and customization methods, across all applications that use it.

readline provides default editing in either of two modes: *vi* or *emacs*. Both modes provide a subset of the editing commands found in the full editors. We've already looked at the command sets of these modes in the previous sections of this chapter. We'll now look at how you can make your own command sets.

readline gives *bash* added flexibility compared to other shells because it can be customized through the use of key bindings, either from the command line or in a special startup file. You can also set *readline* variables. We'll see how you can set up *readline* using your own startup file now, and then go on to examine how the binding capability can be used from the command line.

The readline Startup File

The default startup file is called *.inputrc* and must exist in your home directory if you wish to customize *readline*. You can change the default filename by setting the environment variable **INPUTRC** (see Chapter 3 for further information on environment variables).

When *bash* starts up, it reads the startup file (if there is one) and any settings there come into effect. The startup file is just a sequence of lines that bind a *keyname* to a *macro* or *readline* function name. You can also place comments in the file by preceding any line with a #.

You can use either an English name or a key escape sequence for the keyname. For example, to bind CTRL-T to the movement command for moving to the end of the current line, you could place **Control-t: end-of-line** in your *.inputrc*. If you wanted to use a key escape sequence you could have put "**\C-t**": **end-of-line**. The \C- is the escape sequence prefix for Control. The advantage of the key sequence is that you can specify a sequence of keys for an action. In our example, once *readline* has read this line, typing a CTRL-T will cause the cursor to move to the end of the line.

The **end-of-line** in the previous example is a *readline* function. There are over 60 functions that allow you to control everything from cursor motions to changing text and command completion (for a complete list, see the *bash* manual page). All of the *emacs* and *vi* editing mode commands that we looked at in this chapter have associated functions. This allows you to customize the default modes or make up completely new ones using your own key sequences.

Besides the *readline* functions, you can also bind a macro to a key sequence. A macro is simply a sequence of keystrokes inside single or double quotes. Typing the key sequence causes the keys in the macro to be entered as though you had typed them. For example, we could bind some text to CTRL-T; "**\C-t**": "**Curiouser and curiouser!**". Hitting CTRL-T would cause the phrase **Curiouser and curiouser!** to appear on the command line.

If you want to use single or double quotes in your macros or key sequence, you can escape them by using a backslash (\). Table 2-18 lists the common escape sequences.

Table 2-18: Escape Sequences

Sequence	Description
\C-	Control key prefix
\M-	Meta (Escape) key prefix
\e	The escape character
\\	The backslash character (\)
\"	The double quote character (")
\'	The single quote character (')

readline also allows simple conditionals in the *.inputrc*. There are three directives: **$if**, **$else**, and **$endif**. The conditional of the **$if** can be an editing mode, a terminal type, or an application-specific condition.

To test for an editing mode, you can use the form **mode=** and test for either *vi* or *emacs*. For instance, to set up *readline* so that setting CTRL-T will take place only in *emacs* mode, you could put the following in your *.inputrc*:

```
$if mode=emacs
"\C-t": "Curiouser and curiouser!"
$endif
```

Likewise, to test for a terminal type, you can use the form **term=**. You must provide the full terminal name on the right-hand side of the test. This is useful when you need a terminal-specific key binding. You may, for instance, want to bind the function keys of a particular terminal type to key sequences.

If you have other applications that use *readline*, you might like to keep your *bash*-specific bindings separate. You can do this with the last of the conditionals. Each application that uses *readline* sets its own variable which you can test for. To test for *bash* specifics, you could put **$if bash** into your *.inputrc*.

readline variables

readline has its own set of variables that you can set from within your *.inputrc*. Table 2-19 lists them.*

---

* The variables **disable-completion**, **enable-keypad**, **input-meta**, **mark-directories**, and **visible-stats** are not available in versions of *bash* prior to 2.0.

Table 2-19: readline Variables

Variable	Description
bell-style	If set to *none*, *readline* never rings the bell (beeps). If set to *visible*, *readline* will attempt to use a visible bell. If set to *audible*, it will attempt to ring the bell. The default is *audible*.
comment-begin	The string to insert when the *readline* **insert-comment** command is executed. The default is a #.
completion-query-items	Determines when the user is asked to see further completions if the number of completions is greater than that given. The default is 100.
convert-meta	If set to *On*, converts characters with the eighth bit set to an ASCII key sequence by stripping the eighth bit and prepending an escape character. The default is *On*.
disable-completion	If set to *On*, inhibits word completion. Completion characters will be inserted into the line as if they had been mapped to **self-insert**. The default is *Off*.
editing-mode	Sets the editing mode to *vi* or *emacs*.
enable-keypad	If set to *On*, *readline* tries to enable the keyboard's application keypad when it is called. Some systems need this to enable the arrow keys. The default is *Off*.
expand-tilde	If set to *On*, tilde expansion is attempted when *readline* attempts word completion. The default is *Off*.
horizontal-scroll-mode	Set to *On* means that lines will scroll horizontally if you type beyond the right-hand side of the screen. The default is *Off*, which wraps the line onto a new screen line.
input-meta	If set to *On*, eight-bit input will be accepted. The default is *Off*. This is synonymous with **meta-flag**.
keymap	Sets *readline*'s current keymap for bindings. Acceptable names are *emacs, emacs-standard, emacs-meta, emacs-ctlx, vi, vi-move, vi-command* and *vi-insert*. The default is *emacs*. Note that the value of **editing-mode** also affects the keymap.
mark-directories	If set to *On*, completed directory names have a slash appended.
mark-modified-lines	If set to *On*, displays an asterisk at the start of history lines that have been modified. The default is *Off*.
meta-flag	If set to *On*, eight-bit input will be accepted. The default is *Off*.
output-meta	If set to *On*, displays characters with the eighth bit set directly. The default is *Off*.
show-all-if-ambiguous	If set to *On*, words with more than one possible completion are listed instead of ringing the bell. The default is *Off*.
visible-stats	If set to *On*, a character denoting a file's type as reported by the **stat** system call is appended to the filename when listing possible completions. The default is *Off*.

To set any of the variables, you can use the **set** command in your *.inputrc*. For example, to set vi-mode when you start up, you could place the line **set editing-mode vi** in your *.inputrc*. Every time *bash* starts it would change to vi-mode.

Key Bindings Using bind

If you want to try out key bindings or you want to see what the current settings are, you can do it from the *bash* command line by using the **bind** command. The binding syntax is the same as that of the *.inputrc* file, but you have to surround each binding in quotes so that it is taken as one argument.

To bind a string to CTRL-T, we could type **bind ' "\C-t": "Curiouser and curiouser!" '**. This would bind the given string to CTRL-T just as in the *.inputrc*, except that the binding will apply only to the current shell and will cease once you log out.

bind also allows you to print out the bindings currently in effect by typing **bind −P.*** If you do so, you'll see things like:

```
abort can be found on "\C-g", "\C-x\C-g", "\e\C-g".
accept-line can be found on "\C-j", "\C-m".
alias-expand-line is not bound to any keys
arrow-key-prefix is not bound to any keys
backward-char can be found on "\C-b", "\eOD", "\e[D".
...
```

If you just want to see the names of the *readline* functions, you can use **bind −l**.

Another option you might find useful is **−p**. This prints out the bindings to standard output in a format that can be re-read by **bind**, or used as a *.inputrc* file. So, to create a complete *.inputrc* file that you can then edit, you could type **bind −p >** .inputrc.

To read the file back in again you can use another option, **−f**. This option takes a filename as its argument and reads the key bindings from that file. You can also use it to update the key bindings if you've just modified your *.inputrc*.

Keyboard Habits

In this chapter we have seen that *bash* provides command-line editing with two modes: *vi* and *emacs*. You may be wondering why these two editors were chosen. The primary reason is because *vi* and *emacs* are the most widely used editors for UNIX. People who have used either editor will find familiar editing facilities.

---

* Versions of *bash* prior to 2.0 use **−d** instead of **−p**, and **−v** instead of **−P**. Also, the **−r**, **−V**, **−S**, **−s** and the new **−v** options are not available in these older versions.

If you are not familiar with either of these editors, you should seriously consider adopting emacs-mode keyboard habits. Because it is based on control keys and doesn't require you to think in terms of a "command mode" and "insert mode," you will find emacs-mode easier to assimilate. Although the full *emacs* is an extremely powerful editor, its command structure lends itself very well to small subsetting: there are several "mini-emacs" editors floating around for UNIX, MS-DOS, and other systems.

The same cannot be said for *vi*, because its command structure is really meant for use in a full-screen editor. *vi* is quite powerful too, in its way, but its power becomes evident only when it is used for purposes similar to that for which it was designed: editing source code in C and LISP. As mentioned earlier, a *vi* user has the power to move mountains in few keystrokes—but at the cost of being unable to do anything meaningful in very few keystrokes. Unfortunately, the latter is most desired in a command interpreter, especially nowadays when users are spending more time within applications and less time working with the shell. In short, if you don't already know *vi*, you will probably find its commands obscure and confusing.

Both *bash* editing modes have quite a few commands; you will undoubtedly develop keyboard habits that include just a few of them. If you use emacs-mode and you aren't familiar with the full *emacs*, here is a subset that is easy to learn yet enables you to do just about anything:

- For cursor motion around a command line, stick to CTRL-A and CTRL-E for beginning and end of line, and CTRL-F and CTRL-B for moving around.

- Delete using DEL (or whatever your "erase" key is) and CTRL-D; as with CTRL-F and CTRL-B, hold down to repeat if necessary. Use CTRL-K to erase the entire line.

- Use CTRL-P and CTRL-N (or the up and down arrow keys) to move through the command history.

- Use CTRL-R to search for a command you need to run again.

- Use TAB for filename completion.

After a few hours spent learning these keystrokes, you will wonder how you ever got along without command-line editing.

3

*Customizing Your
Environment*

An *environment* is a collection of concepts that express the things a computer system or other set of tools does in terms designed to be understandable and coherent, and a look and feel that is comfortable. For example, your desk at work is an environment. Concepts involved in desk work usually include memos, phone calls, letters, forms, etc. The tools on or in your desk that you use to deal with these things include paper, staples, envelopes, pens, a telephone, a calculator, etc. Every one of these has a set of characteristics that express how you use it; such characteristics range from location on your desk or in a drawer (for simple tools) to more sophisticated things like which numbers the memory buttons on your phone are set to. Taken together, these characteristics make up your desk's look and feel.

You customize the look and feel of your desk environment by putting pens where you can most easily reach them, programming your phone buttons, etc. In general, the more customization you have done, the more tailored to your personal needs—and therefore the more productive—your environment is.

Similarly, UNIX shells present you with such concepts as files, directories, and standard input and output, while UNIX itself gives you tools to work with these, such as file manipulation commands, text editors, and print queues. Your UNIX environment's look and feel is determined by your keyboard and display, of course, but also by how you set up your directories, where you put each kind of file, and what names you give to files, directories, and commands. There are also more sophisticated ways of customizing your shell environment.

This chapter will look at the four most important features that *bash* provides for customizing your environment.

Special files

> The files *.bash_profile*, *.bash_logout*, and *.bashrc* that are read by *bash* when you log in and out or start a new shell.

Aliases

> Synonyms for commands or command strings that you can define for convenience.

Options

> Controls for various aspects of your environment, which you can turn on and off.

Variables

> Changeable values that are referred to by a name. The shell and other programs can modify their behavior according to the values stored in the variables.

Although these features are not the only ones available, they form the basis for doing more advanced customization. They are also the features that are common to the various shells available on UNIX. Later chapters will cover more advanced shell features, such as the ability to program the shell.

The *.bash_profile*, *.bash_logout*, and *.bashrc* Files

Three files in your home directory have a special meaning to *bash*, providing a way for you to set up your account environment automatically when you log in and when you invoke another *bash* shell, and allowing you to perform commands when you log out. These files may already exist in your home directory, depending on how your system administrator has set up your account. If they don't exist, your account is using only the default system file */etc/profile*. You can easily create your own *bash* files using your favorite text editor. If you are unfamiliar with text editors available under UNIX, we suggest that you familiarize yourself with one of the better-known ones such as *vi* or *emacs* before proceeding further with the techniques described in this chapter.

The most important *bash* file, *.bash_profile*, is read and the commands in it executed by *bash* every time you log in to the system. If you examine your *.bash_profile* you will probably see lines similar to:

```
PATH=/sbin:/usr/sbin:/bin:/usr/bin:/usr/local/bin
SHELL=/bin/bash
MANPATH=/usr/man:/usr/X11/man
EDITOR=/usr/bin/vi
```

```
PS1='\h:\w\$ '
PS2='> '
export EDITOR
```

These lines define the basic environment for your login account. For the moment, it is probably best to leave these lines alone until you understand what they do. When editing your *.bash_profile*, just add your new lines after the existing ones.

Note that whatever you add to your *.bash_profile* won't take effect until the file is re-read by logging out and then logging in again. Alternatively, you can also use the *source* command.* For example:

```
source .bash_profile
```

source executes the commands in the specified file, in this case *.bash_profile*, including any commands that you have added.

bash allows two synonyms for *.bash_profile*: *.bash_login*, derived from the C shell's file named *.login*, and *.profile*, derived from the Bourne shell and Korn shell files named *.profile*. Only one of these three is read when you log in. If *.bash_profile* doesn't exist in your home directory, then *bash* will look for *.bash_login*. If that doesn't exist it will look for *.profile*.

One advantage of *bash*'s ability to look for either synonym is that you can retain your *.profile* if you have been using the Bourne shell. If you need to add *bash*-specific commands, you can put them in *.bash_profile* followed by the command **source .profile**. When you log in, all the *bash*-specific commands will be executed, and *bash* will source *.profile*, executing the remaining commands. If you decide to switch to using the Bourne shell you don't have to modify your existing files. A similar approach was intended for *.bash_login* and the C shell *.login*, but due to differences in the basic syntax of the shells, this is not a good idea.

.bash_profile is read and executed only by the login shell. If you start up a new shell (a *subshell*) by typing **bash** on the command line, it will attempt to read commands from the file *.bashrc*. This scheme allows you the flexibility to separate startup commands needed at login time from those you might need when you run a subshell. If you need to have the same commands run regardless of whether it is a login shell or a subshell, you can just use the *source* command from within *.bash_profile* to execute *.bashrc*. If *.bashrc* doesn't exist then no commands are executed when you start up a subshell.

The file *.bash_logout* is read and executed every time a login shell exits. It is provided to round out the capabilities for customizing your environment. If you wanted to execute some commands that remove temporary files from your account or record how much time you have spent logged in to the system then

---

* You can also use the synonymous command dot (.).

you would place the commands in *.bash_logout*. This file doesn't have to exist in your account—if it isn't there when you log out, then no extra commands are executed.

Aliases

If you have used UNIX for any length of time you will have noticed that there are many commands available and that some of them have cryptic names. Sometimes the commands you use the most have a string of options and arguments that need to be specified. Wouldn't it be nice if there was a feature that let you rename the commands or allowed you to type in something simple instead of half a dozen options? Fortunately, *bash* provides such a feature: the *alias.**

Aliases can be defined on the command line, in your *.bash_profile*, or in your *.bashrc*, using this form:

```
alias name=command
```

This syntax specifies that *name* is an alias for *command*. Whenever you type **name** as a command, *bash* will substitute *command* in its place when it executes the line. Notice that there are no spaces on either side of the equal sign (=); this is the required syntax.

There are a few basic ways to use an alias. The first, and simplest, is as a more mnemonic name for an existing command. Many commonly used UNIX commands have names that are poor mnemonics and are therefore excellent candidates for aliasing, the classic example being:

```
alias search=grep
```

grep, the UNIX file-searching utility, was named as an acronym for something like "Generalized Regular Expression Parser."† This acronym may mean something to a computer scientist, but not to the office administrator who has to find **Fred** in a list of phone numbers. If you have to find **Fred** and you have the word *search* defined as an alias for *grep*, you can type:

```
$ search Fred phonelist
```

Some people who aren't particularly good typists like to use aliases for typographical errors they make often. For example:

---

* C shell users should note that the *bash* alias feature does not support arguments in alias expansions, as C shell aliases do. This functionality is provided by *functions*, which we'll look at in Chapter 4, *Basic Shell Programming*.

† Another theory has it that *grep* stands for the command "g/re/p", in the old *ed* text editor, which does essentially the same thing as *grep*.

```
alias emcas=emacs
alias mali=mail
alias gerp=grep
```

This can be handy, but we feel you're probably better off suffering with the error message and getting the correct spelling under your fingers. Another common way to use an alias is as a shorthand for a longer command string. For example, you may have a directory to which you need to go often. It's buried deep in your directory hierarchy, so you want to set up an alias that will allow you to **cd** there without typing (or even remembering) the entire pathname:

```
alias cdvoy='cd sipp/demo/animation/voyager'
```

Notice the quotes around the full **cd** command; these are necessary if the string being aliased consists of more than one word.*

As another example, a useful option to the *ls* command is **−F**: it puts a slash (/) after directory files and an asterisk (*) after executable files. Since typing a dash followed by a capital letter is inconvenient, many people define an alias like this:

```
alias lf='ls -F'
```

A few things about aliases are important to remember. First, *bash* makes a textual substitution of the alias for that which it is aliasing; it may help to imagine *bash* passing your command through a text editor or word processor and issuing a "change" or "substitute" command before interpreting and executing it. Any special characters (such as wildcards like * and ?) that result when the alias is expanded are interpreted properly by the shell.† For example, to make it easier to print all of the files in your directory, you could define the alias:

```
alias printall='pr * | lpr'
```

Second, keep in mind that aliases are recursive, which means that it is possible to alias an alias. A legitimate objection to the previous example is that the alias, while mnemonic, is too long and doesn't save enough typing. If we want to keep this alias but add a shorter abbreviation, we could define:

```
alias pa=printall
```

With recursive aliasing available it would seem possible to create an infinite loop:

```
alias ls='ls -l'
```

bash ensures that this loop cannot happen, because only the first word of the replacement text is checked for further aliasing; if that word is identical to the alias

---

* This contrasts with C shell aliases, in which the quotes aren't required.

† An important corollary: wildcards and other special characters cannot be used in the names of aliases, i.e., on the left side of the equal sign.

being expanded, it is not expanded a second time. The above command will work as expected (typing **ls** produces a long list with permissions, sizes, owners, etc.), while in more meaningless situations such as:

```
alias listfile=ls
alias ls=listfile
```

the alias *listfile* is ignored.

Aliases can be used only for the beginning of a command string—albeit with certain exceptions. In the **cd** example above, you might want to define an alias for the directory name alone, not for the entire command. But if you define:

```
alias anim=sipp/demo/animation/voyager
```

and then type **cd anim**, *bash* will probably print a message like **anim: No such file or directory**.

An obscure feature of *bash*'s alias facility—one not present in the analogous C shell feature—provides a way around this problem. If the value of an alias (the right side of the equal sign) ends in a blank, then *bash* tries to do alias substitution on the next word on the command line. To make the value of an alias end in a blank, you need to surround it with quotes.

Here is how you would use this capability to allow aliases for directory names, at least for use with the **cd** command. Just define:

```
alias cd='cd '
```

This causes *bash* to search for an alias for the directory name argument to **cd**, which in the previous example would enable it to expand the alias *anim* correctly.

Another way to define a directory variable for use with the **cd** command is to use the environment variable **cdable_vars**, discussed later in this chapter.

Finally, there are a few useful adjuncts to the basic **alias** command. If you type **alias** *name* without an equal sign (=) and value, the shell will print the alias's value or **alias** *name* **not found** if it is undefined. If you type **alias** without any arguments, you get a list of all the aliases you have defined. The command **unalias** *name* removes any alias definition for its argument.

Aliases are very handy for creating a comfortable environment, but they have essentially been superseded by shell scripts and functions, which we will look at in the next chapter. These give you everything aliases do plus much more, so if you become proficient at them, you may find that you don't need aliases anymore. However, aliases are ideal for novices who find UNIX to be a rather forbidding place, full of terseness and devoid of good mnemonics. Chapter 4 shows the order of precedence when, for example, an alias and a function have the same name.

Options

While aliases let you create convenient names for commands, they don't really let you change the shell's behavior. *Options* are one way of doing this. A shell option is a setting that is either "on" or "off." While several options relate to arcane shell features that are of interest only to programmers, those that we will cover here are of interest to all users.

The basic commands that relate to options are **set −o** *optionname* and **set +o** *optionname*. You can change more than one option with the one **set** command by preceding each *optionname* with a **−o** or **+o**. The use of plus (+) and minus (−) signs is counterintuitive: the − turns the named option on, while the + turns it off. The reason for this incongruity is that the dash (−) is the conventional UNIX way of specifying options to a command, while the use of + is an afterthought.

Most options also have one-letter abbreviations that can be used in lieu of the **set −o** command; for example, **set −o noglob** can be abbreviated **set −f**. These abbreviations are carryovers from the Bourne shell. Like several other "extra" *bash* features, they exist to ensure upward compatibility; otherwise, their use is not encouraged.

Table 3-1 lists the options that are useful to general UNIX users. All of them are off by default except as noted.

Table 3-1: Basic Shell Options

Option	Description
emacs	Enter *emacs* editing mode (on by default)
ignoreeof	Don't allow use of a single CTRL-D to log off; use the **exit** command to log off immediately. This has the same effect as setting the shell variable IGNOREEOF=10.
noclobber	Don't allow output redirection (>) to overwrite an existing file
noglob	Don't expand filename wildcards like * and ? (wildcard expansion is sometimes called *globbing*)
nounset	Indicate an error when trying to use a variable that is undefined
vi	Enter *vi* editing mode

There are several other options (21 in all; Appendix B, *Reference Lists*, lists them). To check the status of an option, just type **set −o**. *bash* will print a list of all options along with their settings.

shopt

bash 2.0 introduces a new built-in for configuring shell behaviour, **shopt**. This built-in is meant as a replacement for option configuration originally done through environment variables and the **set** command.*

The **shopt -o** functionality is a duplication of parts of the **set** command and is provided for completeness on the part of **shopt**, while retaining backward compatibility by its continued inclusion in **set**.

The format for this command is **shopt** *options option-names*. Table 3-2 lists **shopt**'s options.

Table 3-2: Options to shopt

Option	Meaning
-p	Display a list of the settable options and their current values
-s	Sets each option name
-u	Unset each option name
-q	Suppress normal output; the return status indicates if a variable is set or unset
-o	Allows the values of the option names to be those defined for the -o option of the **set** command

The default action is to unset (turn off) the named options. If no options and arguments are given, or the **-p** option is used, **shopt** displays a list of the settable options and the values that they currently have. If **-s** or **-u** is also given, the list is confined to only those options that are set or unset, respectively.

A list of the most useful option names is given in Table 3-3. A complete list is given in Appendix B.

Table 3-3: shopt Option Names

Option	Meaning
cdable_vars	If set, an argument to the **cd** built-in command that is not a directory is assumed to be the name of a variable whose value is the directory to change to.
checkhash	If set, *bash* checks that a command found in the hash table exists before trying to execute it. If a hashed command no longer exists, a normal path search is performed.
cmdhist	If set, *bash* attempts to save all lines of a multiple-line command in the same history entry.

---

* Appendix B provides a complete list of **shopt** shell options and the corresponding environment variables in earlier versions of the shell.

Table 3-3: shopt Option Names (continued)

Option	Meaning
dotglob	If set, *bash* includes filenames beginning with a . (dot) in the results of pathname expansion.
execfail	If set, a non-interactive shell will not exit if it cannot execute the file specified as an argument to the **exec** command. An interactive shell does not exit if **exec** fails.
histappend	If set, the history list is appended to the file named by the value of the **HISTFILE** variable when the shell exits, rather than overwriting the file.
lithist	If set, and the **cmdhist** option is enabled, multiline commands are saved to the history with embedded newlines, rather than using semicolon separators where possible.
mailwarn	If set, and a file that *bash* is checking for mail has been accessed since the last time it was checked, the message "The mail in *mailfile* has been read" is displayed.

We'll look at the use of the various options later in this chapter.

Shell Variables

There are several characteristics of your environment that you may want to customize but that cannot be expressed as an on/off choice. Characteristics of this type are specified in shell variables. Shell variables can specify everything from your prompt string to how often the shell checks for new mail.

Like an alias, a shell variable is a name that has a value associated with it. *bash* keeps track of several built-in shell variables; shell programmers can add their own. By convention, built-in variables should have names in all capital letters. *bash* does, however, have two exceptions.* The syntax for defining variables is somewhat similar to the syntax for aliases:

```
varname=value
```

There must be no space on either side of the equal sign, and if the value is more than one word, it must be surrounded by quotes. To use the value of a variable in a command, precede its name by a dollar sign ($).

You can delete a variable with the command **unset** *varname*. Normally this isn't useful, since all variables that don't exist are assumed to be null, i.e., equal to the empty string "". But if you use the option **nounset**, which causes the shell to indi-

---

* Versions prior to 2.0 have many more lowercase built-in variables. Most of these are now obsolete, the functionality having been moved to the **shopt** command.

cate an error when it encounters an undefined variable, then you may be interested in **unset**.

The easiest way to check a variable's value is to use the **echo** built-in command. All **echo** does is print its arguments, but not until the shell has evaluated them. This includes—among other things that will be discussed later—taking the values of variables and expanding filename wildcards. So, if the variable **wonderland** has the value **alice**, typing:

```
$ echo "$wonderland"
```

will cause the shell to simply print **alice**. If the variable is undefined, the shell will print a blank line. A more verbose way to do this is:

```
$ echo "The value of \$varname is \"$varname\"."
```

The first dollar sign and the inner double quotes are backslash-escaped (i.e., preceded with \ so the shell doesn't try to interpret them; see Chapter 1, *bash Basics*), so that they appear literally in the output, which for the above example would be:

```
The value of $wonderland is "alice".
```

Variables and Quoting

Notice that we used double quotes around variables (and strings containing them) in these **echo** examples. In Chapter 1, we said that some special characters inside double quotes are still interpreted, while none are interpreted inside single quotes.

A special character that "survives" double quotes is the dollar sign—meaning that variables are evaluated. It's possible to do without the double quotes in some cases; for example, we could have written the above **echo** command this way:

```
$ echo The value of \$varname is \"$varname\".
```

But double quotes are more generally correct. Here's why. Suppose we did this:

```
$ fred='Four spaces between these    words.'
```

Then if we entered the command **echo $fred**, the result would be:

```
Four spaces between these words.
```

What happened to the extra spaces? Without the double quotes, the shell splits the string into words after substituting the variable's value, as it normally does when it processes command lines. The double quotes circumvent this part of the process (by making the shell think that the whole quoted string is a single word).

Therefore the command **echo "$fred"** prints this:

```
Four spaces between these    words.
```

The distinction between single and double quotes becomes particularly important when we start dealing with variables that contain user or file input later on.

Double quotes also allow other special characters to work, as we'll see in Chapters 4, *Basic Shell Programming*, 6, *Command-Line Options and Typed Variables*, and 7, *Input/Output and Command-Line Processing*. But for now, we'll revise the "When in doubt, use single quotes" rule in Chapter 1 by adding, "...unless a string contains a variable, in which case you should use double quotes."

Built-In Variables

As with options, some built-in shell variables are meaningful to general UNIX users, while others are arcana for hackers. We'll look at the more generally useful ones here, and we'll save some of the more obscure ones for later chapters. Again, Appendix B contains a complete list.

Editing mode variables

Several shell variables relate to the command-line editing modes that we saw in the previous chapter. These are listed in Table 3-4.

Table 3-4: Editing Mode Variables

Variable	Meaning
HISTCMD	The history number of the current command
HISTCONTROL	If set to the value of *ignorespace*, lines beginning with a space are not entered into the history list. If set to *ignoredups*, lines matching the last history line are not entered. Setting it to *ignoreboth* enables both options.[a]
HISTIGNORE	A list of patterns, separated by colons (:), used to decide which command lines to save in the history list. Patterns are considered to start at the beginning of the command line and must fully specify the line, i.e., no wildcard (*) is implicitly appended. The patterns are checked against the line after **HISTCONTROL** is applied. An ampersand (**&**) matches the previous line. An explicit **&** may be generated by escaping it with a backslash.[b]
HISTFILE	Name of history file in which the command history is saved. The default is ~/.bash_history.
HISTFILESIZE	The maximum number of lines to store in the history file. The default is 500. When this variable is assigned a value, the history file is truncated, if necessary, to the given number of lines.

Table 3-4: Editing Mode Variables (continued)

Variable	Meaning
HISTSIZE	The maximum number of commands to remember in the command history. The default is 500.
FCEDIT	Pathname of the editor to use with the **fc** command.

a. history_control is synonymous with HISTCONTROL in versions of *bash* prior to 2.0. Versions prior to 1.14 only define history_control. *ignoreboth* is not available in *bash* versions prior to 1.14. HISTCONTROL is now considered to be obsolete, having been superseded by HISTIGNORE.
b. This variable is not available in versions of *bash* prior to 2.0.

In the previous chapter, we saw how *bash* numbers commands. To find out the current command number in an interactive shell, you can use the HISTCMD. Note that if you unset HISTCMD, it will lose its special meaning, even if you subsequently set it again.

We also saw in the last chapter how *bash* keeps the history list in memory and saves it to a file when you exit a shell session. The variables HISTFILESIZE and HISTSIZE allow you to set the maximum number of lines that the shell saves in the history file, and the maximum number of lines to "remember" in the history list, i.e., the lines that it displays with the **history** command.

Suppose you wanted to maintain a small history file in your home directory. By setting HISTFILESIZE to 100, you immediately cause the history file to allow a maximum of 100 lines. If it is already larger than the size you specify, it will be truncated.

HISTSIZE works in the same way, but only on the history that the current shell has in memory. When you exit an interactive shell, HISTSIZE will be the maximum number of lines saved in your history file. If you have already set HISTFILESIZE to be less than HISTSIZE, the saved list will be truncated.

You can also cut down on the size of your history file and history list by use of the HISTCONTROL variable. If set to **ignorespace**, any commands that you type that start with a space won't appear in the history. Even more useful is the **ignoredups** option. This discards consecutive entries from the history list that are duplicated. Suppose you want to monitor the size of a file with *ls* as it is being created. Normally, every time you type *ls* it will appear in your history. By setting HISTCONTROL to **ignoredups**, only the first *ls* will appear in the history.

bash 2.0 introduced a new and more flexible type of history control variable. HISTIGNORE allows you to specify a list of patterns which the command line is checked against. If the command line matches one of the patterns, it is not entered into the history list. You can also request that it ignore duplicates by using the pattern **&**.

For example, suppose you didn't want any command starting with *l*, nor any duplicates, to appear in the history. Setting **HISTIGNORE** to *l*:& will do just that. Just as with other pattern matching we have seen, the wildcard after the *l* will match any command line starting with that letter.

Mail variables

Since the *mail* program is not running all the time, there is no way for it to inform you when you get new mail; therefore the shell does this instead.* The shell can't actually check for incoming mail, but it can look at your mail file periodically and determine whether the file has been modified since the last check. The variables listed in Table 3-5 let you control how this works.

Table 3-5: Mail Variables

Variable	Meaning
MAIL	Name of file to check for incoming mail
MAILCHECK	How often, in seconds, to check for new mail (default 60 seconds)
MAILPATH	List of filenames, separated by colons (:), to check for incoming mail

Under the simplest scenario, you use the standard UNIX mail program, and your mail file is */usr/mail/yourname* or something similar. In this case, you would just set the variable **MAIL** to this filename if you want your mail checked:

```
MAIL=/usr/mail/yourname
```

If your system administrator hasn't already done it for you, put a line like this in your *.bash_profile*.

However, some people use nonstandard mailers that use multiple mail files; **MAIL-PATH** was designed to accommodate this. *bash* will use the value of **MAIL** as the name of the file to check, unless **MAILPATH** is set, in which case the shell will check each file in the **MAILPATH** list for new mail. You can use this mechanism to have the shell print a different message for each mail file: for each mail filename in **MAILPATH**, append a question mark followed by the message you want printed.

For example, let's say you have a mail system that automatically sorts your mail into files according to the username of the sender. You have mail files called */usr/mail/you/martin*, */usr/mail/you/geoffm*, */usr/mail/you/paulr*, etc. You define your **MAILPATH** as follows:

---

* BSD UNIX users should note that the *biff* command on those systems does a better job of informing you about new mail; while *bash* only prints "you have new mail" messages right before it prints command prompts, *biff* can do so at any time.

```
MAILPATH=/usr/mail/you/martin:/usr/mail/you/geoffm:\
/usr/mail/you/paulr
```

If you get mail from Martin Lee, the file */usr/mail/you/martin* will change. *bash* will notice the change within one minute and print the message:

```
You have new mail in /usr/mail/you/martin
```

If you are in the middle of running a command, the shell will wait until the command finishes (or is suspended) to print the message. To customize this further, you could define **MAILPATH** to be:

```
MAILPATH="\
/usr/mail/you/martin?You have mail from Martin.:\
/usr/mail/you/geoffm?Mail from Geoff has arrived.:\
/usr/mail/you/paulr?There is new mail from Paul."
```

The backslashes at the end of each line allow you to continue your command on the next line. But be careful: you can't indent subsequent lines. Now, if you get mail from Martin, the shell will print:

```
You have mail from Martin.
```

You can also use the variable **$_** in the message to print the name of the current mail file. For example:

```
MAILPATH='/usr/mail/you?You have some new mail in $_'
```

When new mail arrives, this will print the line:

```
You have some new mail in /usr/mail/you
```

The ability to receive notification of mail can be switched on and off by using the **mailwarn** option to the **shopt** command.

Prompting variables

If you have seen enough experienced UNIX users at work, you may already have realized that the shell's prompt is not engraved in stone. Many of these users have all kinds of things encoded in their prompts. It is possible to put useful information into the prompt, including the date and the current directory. We'll give you some of the information you need to modify your own here; the rest will come in the next chapter.

Actually, *bash* uses four prompt strings. They are stored in the variables **PS1**, **PS2**, **PS3**, and **PS4**.[*] The first of these is called the primary prompt string; it is your

---

[*] PS3 was not defined in *bash* versions prior to 1.14.

usual shell prompt, and its default value is "\s-\v\$ ".* Many people like to set their primary prompt string to something containing their login name. Here is one way to do this:

```
PS1="\u--> "
```

The \u tells *bash* to insert the name of the current user into the prompt string. If your user name is **alice**, your prompt string will be "**alice- ->**". If you are a C shell user and, like many such people, are used to having a history number in your prompt string, *bash* can do this similarly to the C shell: if the sequence \! is used in the prompt string, it will substitute the history number. Thus, if you define your prompt string to be:

```
PS1="\u \!--> "
```

then your prompts will be like **alice 1- ->**, **alice 2- ->**, and so on.

But perhaps the most useful way to set up your prompt string is so that it always contains your current directory. This way, you needn't type **pwd** to remember where you are. Here's how:

```
PS1="\w--> "
```

Table 3-6 lists the prompt customizations that are available.†

Table 3-6: Prompt String Customizations

Command	Meaning
\a	The ASCII bell character (007)
\d	The date in "Weekday Month Day" format
\e	The ASCII escape character (033)
\H	The hostname
\h	The hostname up to the first "."
\n	A carriage return and line feed
\s	The name of the shell
\T	The current time in 12-hour HH:MM:SS format
\t	The current time in HH:MM:SS format
\@	The current time in 12-hour am/pm format
\u	The username of the current user
\v	The version of *bash* (e.g., 2.00)
\V	The release of *bash*; the version and patchlevel (e.g., 2.00.0)
\w	The current working directory
\W	The basename of the current working directory

---

* In versions of *bash* prior to 2.0, the default was "**bash\$** ".

† \[and \] are not available in *bash* versions prior to 1.14. \a, \e, \H, \T, \@, \v, and \V are not available in versions prior to 2.0.

Table 3-6: Prompt String Customizations (continued)

Command	Meaning
\#	The command number of the current command
\!	The history number of the current command
\$	If the effective UID is 0 print a #, otherwise print a $
\nnn	Character code in octal
\\	Print a backslash
\[	Begin a sequence of non-printing characters, such as terminal control sequences
\]	End a sequence of non-printing characters

PS2 is called the secondary prompt string; its default value is >. It is used when you type an incomplete line and hit RETURN, as an indication that you must finish your command. For example, assume that you start a quoted string but don't close the quote. Then if you hit RETURN, the shell will print > and wait for you to finish the string:

```
$ echo "This is a long line,        # PS1 for the command
> which is terminated down here"     # PS2 for the continuation
$                                    # PS1 for the next command
```

PS3 and **PS4** relate to shell programming and debugging. They will be explained in Chapter 5, *Flow Control*, and Chapter 9, *Debugging Shell Programs*.

Command search path

Another important variable is **PATH**, which helps the shell find the commands you enter.

As you probably know, every command you use is actually a file that contains code for your machine to run.* These files are called executable files or just executables for short. They are stored in various directories. Some directories, like */bin* or */usr/bin*, are standard on all UNIX systems; some depend on the particular version of UNIX you are using; some are unique to your machine; if you are a programmer, some may even be your own. In any case, there is no reason why you should have to know where a command's executable file is in order to run it.

That is where **PATH** comes in. Its value is a list of directories that the shell searches every time you enter a command;† the directory names are separated by colons (:), just like the files in **MAILPATH**.

---

* Unless it's a built-in command (one of those shown in **boldface**, like **cd** and **echo**), in which case the code is simply part of the executable file for the entire shell.

† Unless the command name contains a slash (/), in which case the search does not take place.

For example, if you type **echo $PATH**, you will see something like this:

```
/bin:/usr/bin:/usr/local/bin:/usr/X386/bin
```

Why should you care about your path? There are two main reasons. First, once you have read the later chapters of this book and you try writing your own shell programs, you will want to test them and eventually set aside a directory for them. Second, your system may be set up so that certain restricted commands' executable files are kept in directories that are not listed in **PATH**. For example, there may be a directory */usr/games* in which there are executables that are verboten during regular working hours.

Therefore you may want to add directories to your **PATH**. Let's say you have created a *bin* directory under your login directory, which is */home/you*, for your own shell scripts and programs. To add this directory to your **PATH** so that it is there every time you log in, put this line in your *.bash_profile*:

```
PATH=$PATH":/home/you/bin"
```

This sets **PATH** to whatever it was before, followed immediately by a colon and */home/you/bin*.

This is the safe way of doing it. When you enter a command, the shell searches directories in the order they appear in **PATH** until it finds an executable file. Therefore, if you have a shell script or program whose name is the same as an existing command, the shell will use the existing command—unless you type in the command's full pathname to make it clear. For example, if you have created your own version of the *more* command in the above directory and your **PATH** is set up as in the last example, you will need to type **/home/you/bin/more** (or just **~/bin/more**) to get your version.

The more reckless way of resetting your path is to put your own directory before the other directories:

```
PATH="/home/you/bin:"$PATH
```

This is unsafe because you are trusting that your own version of the *more* command works properly. But it is also risky for a more important reason: system security. If your **PATH** is set up in this way, you leave open a "hole" that is well known to computer crackers and mischief makers: they can install "Trojan horses" and do other things to steal files or do damage. (See Chapter 10, *bash Administration*, for more details.) Therefore, unless you have complete control of (and confidence in) everyone who uses your system, use the first of the two methods of adding your own command directory.

If you need to know which directory a command comes from, you need not look at directories in your **PATH** until you find it. The shell built-in command **type** prints the full pathname of the command you give it as argument, or just the command's name and its type if it's a built-in command itself (like **cd**), an alias, or a function (as we'll see in Chapter 4).

Command hashing

You may be thinking that having to go and find a command in a large list of possible places would take a long time, and you'd be right. To speed things up, *bash* uses what is known as a *hash* table.

Every time the shell goes and finds a command in the search path, it enters it in the hash table. If you then use the command again, *bash* first checks the hash table to see if the command is listed. If it is, it uses the path given in the table and executes the command; otherwise, it just has to go and look for the command in the search path.

You can see what is currently in the hash table with the command **hash**:

```
$ hash
hits    command
   2    /bin/cat
   1    /usr/bin/stat
   2    /usr/bin/less
   1    /usr/bin/man
   2    /usr/bin/apropos
   2    /bin/more
   1    /bin/ln
   3    /bin/ls
   1    /bin/ps
   2    /bin/vi
```

This not only shows the hashed commands, but how many times they have been executed (the *hits*) during the current login session.

Supplying a command name to **hash** forces the shell to look up the command in the search path and enter it in the hash table. You can also make *bash* "forget" what is in the hash table by using the –r option to **hash**. Another option, –p, allows you to enter a command into the hash table, even if the command doesn't exist.*

Command hashing can be turned on and off with the **hashall** option to **set**. In general use, there shouldn't be any need to turn it off.

Don't be too concerned about the details of hashing. The command hashing and lookup is all done by *bash* without you knowing it's taking place.

---

* The –p option is not available in versions of *bash* prior to 2.0.

Directory search path and variables

CDPATH is a variable whose value, like that of **PATH**, is a list of directories separated by colons. Its purpose is to augment the functionality of the **cd** built-in command.

By default, **CDPATH** isn't set (meaning that it is null), and when you type **cd** *dirname*, the shell will look in the current directory for a subdirectory that is called *dirname*.* If you set **CDPATH**, you give the shell a list of places to look for *dirname*; the list may or may not include the current directory.

Here is an example. Consider the alias for the long **cd** command from earlier in this chapter:

```
alias cdvoy='cd sipp/demo/animation/voyager'
```

Now suppose there were a few directories under this directory to which you need to go often; they are called *src, bin,* and *doc*. You define your **CDPATH** like this:

```
CDPATH=:~/sipp/demo/animation/voyager
```

In other words, you define your **CDPATH** to be the empty string (meaning the current directory) followed by *~/sipp/demo/animation/voyager*.

With this setup, if you type **cd doc**, then the shell will look in the current directory for a (sub)directory called *doc*. Assuming that it doesn't find one, it looks in the directory *~/sipp/demo/animation/voyager*. The shell finds the *doc* directory there, so you go *directly* there.

If you often find yourself going to a specific group of directories as you work on a particular project, you can use **CDPATH** to get there quickly. Note that this feature will only be useful if you update it whenever your work habits change.

bash provides another shorthand mechanism for referring to directories; if you set the shell option **cdable_vars** using **shopt**,† any argument supplied to the **cd** command that is not a directory is assumed to be a variable.

We might define the variable **anim** to be *~/sipp/demo/animation/voyager*. If we set **cdable_vars** and then type:

```
cd anim
```

the current directory will become *~/sipp/demo/animation/voyager*.

---

* This search is disabled when *dirname* starts with a slash. It is also disabled when *dirname* starts with `./` or `../`.

† In versions of *bash* prior to 2.0, **cdable_vars** is a shell variable that you can set and unset.

Miscellaneous variables

We have covered the shell variables that are important from the standpoint of customization. There are also several that serve as status indicators and for various other miscellaneous purposes. Their meanings are relatively straightforward; the more basic ones are summarized in Table 3-7.

Table 3-7: Status Variables

Variable	Meaning
HOME	Name of your home (login) directory
SECONDS	Number of seconds since the shell was invoked
BASH	Pathname of this instance of the shell you are running
BASH_VERSION	The version number of the shell you are running
BASH_VERSINFO	An array of version information for the shell you are running
PWD	Current directory
OLDPWD	Previous directory before the last **cd** command

The shell sets the values of these variables, except **HOME** (which is set by the login process: *login, rshd,* etc.). The first five are set at login time, the last two whenever you change directories. Although you can also set their values, just like any other variables, it is difficult to imagine any situation where you would want to. In the case of **SECONDS**, if you set it to a new value it will start counting from the value you give it, but if you unset **SECONDS** it will lose its special meaning, even if you subsequently set it again.

Customization and Subprocesses

Some of the variables discussed above are used by commands you may run—as opposed to the shell itself—so that they can determine certain aspects of your environment. The majority, however, are not even known outside the shell.

This dichotomy begs an important question: which shell "things" are known outside the shell, and which are only internal? This question is at the heart of many misunderstandings about the shell and shell programming. Before we answer, we'll ask it again in a more precise way: which shell "things" are known to subprocesses? Remember that whenever you enter a command, you are telling the shell to run that command in a subprocess; furthermore, some complex programs may start their own subprocesses.

Now for the answer, which (like many UNIX concepts) is unfortunately not as simple as you might like. A few things are known to subprocesses, but the reverse is not true: subprocesses can never make these things known to the processes that created them.

Which things are known depends on whether the subprocess in question is a *bash* program (see Chapter 4) or an interactive shell. If the subprocess is a *bash* program, then it's possible to propagate nearly every type of thing we've seen in this chapter—options and variables—plus a few we'll see later.

Environment Variables

By default, only one kind of thing is known to all kinds of subprocesses: a special class of shell variables called *environment variables.* Some of the built-in variables we have seen are actually environment variables: **HOME, MAIL, PATH,** and **PWD.**

It should be clear why these and other variables need to be known by subprocesses. For example, text editors like *vi* and *emacs* need to know what kind of terminal you are using; the environment variable **TERM** is their way of determining this. As another example, most UNIX mail programs allow you to edit a message with your favorite text editor. How does *mail* know which editor to use? The value of **EDITOR** (or sometimes **VISUAL**).

Any variable can become an environment variable. First it must be defined as usual; then it must be *exported* with the command:*

```
export varnames
```

(*varnames* can be a list of variable names separated by blanks). You can combine variable assignment and the export into one statement:

```
export wonderland=alice
```

It is also possible to define variables to be in the environment of a particular subprocess (command) only, by preceding the command with the variable assignment, like this:

```
varname=value command
```

You can put as many assignments before the command as you want.† For example, assume that you're using the *emacs* editor. You are having problems getting it to work with your terminal, so you're experimenting with different values of **TERM**. You can do this most easily by entering commands that look like:

```
TERM=trythisone emacs filename
```

emacs will have *trythisone* defined as its value of **TERM**, yet the environment variable in your shell will keep whatever value (if any) it had before. This syntax is

---

* Unless automatic exporting has been turned on by **set -a** or **set -o allexport**, in which case all variables that are assigned to will be exported.

† There is an obscure option, **set -k**, that lets you put this type of environment variable definition *anywhere* on the command line, not just at the beginning.

surprisingly useful, but not very widely used; we won't see it much throughout the remainder of this book.

Nevertheless, environment variables are important. Most *.bash_profile* files include definitions of environment variables; the sample built-in *.bash_profile* earlier in this chapter contained six such definitions:

```
PATH=/sbin:/usr/sbin:/bin:/usr/bin:/usr/local/bin
SHELL=/bin/bash
MANPATH=/usr/man:/usr/X11/man
EDITOR=/usr/bin/vi
PS1='\h:\w\$ '
PS2='> '
export EDITOR
```

You can find out which variables are environment variables and what their values are by typing **export** without arguments or by using the **-p** option to the command.

Some environment variable names have been used by so many applications that they have become standard across many shell environments. These variables are not built into *bash*, although some shells, such as the Korn shell, have them as built-ins. Table 3-8 lists the ones you are most likely to come across.

Table 3-8: Standard Variables

Variable	Meaning
COLUMNS	The number of columns your display has
EDITOR	Pathname of your text editor
LINES	The number of lines your display has
SHELL	Pathname of the shell you are running
TERM	The type of terminal that you are using

You may well find that some of these already exist in your own environment, most likely set from the system */etc/profile* file (see Chapter 10). You can define them yourself in your *.bash_profile* and **export** them, as we did earlier.

Terminal types

The variable **TERM** is vitally important for any program that uses your entire screen or window, like a text editor. Such programs include all screen editors (such as *vi* and *emacs*), *more*, and countless third-party applications.

Because users are spending more and more time within programs, and less and less using the shell itself, it is extremely important that your **TERM** is set correctly. It's really your system administrator's job to help you do this (or to do it for you), but in case you need to do it yourself, here are a few guidelines.

The value of **TERM** must be a short character string with lowercase letters that appears as a filename in the *terminfo* database.* This database is a two-tiered directory of files under the root directory */usr/lib/terminfo*. This directory contains subdirectories with single-character names; these in turn contain files of terminal information for all terminals whose names begin with that character. Each file describes how to tell the terminal in question to do certain common things like position the cursor on the screen, go into reverse video, scroll, insert text, and so on. The descriptions are in binary form (i.e., not readable by humans).

Names of terminal description files are the same as that of the terminal being described; sometimes an abbreviation is used. For example, the DEC VT100 has a description in the file */usr/lib/terminfo/v/vt100*. An *xterm* terminal window under the X Window System has a description in */usr/lib/terminfo/x/xterm*.

Sometimes your UNIX software will set up **TERM** incorrectly; this usually happens for X terminals and PC-based UNIX systems. Therefore, you should check the value of **TERM** by typing **echo $TERM** before going any further. If you find that your UNIX system isn't setting the right value for you (especially likely if your terminal is of a different make from that of your computer), you need to find the appropriate value of **TERM** yourself.

The best way to find the **TERM** value—if you can't find a local guru to do it for you—is to guess the *terminfo* name and search for a file of that name under */usr/lib/terminfo* by using *ls*. For example, if your terminal is a Hewlett-Packard 70092, you could try:

```
$ cd /usr/lib/terminfo
$ ls 7/7*
```

If you are successful, you will see something like this:

```
70092   70092A  70092a
```

In this case, the three names are likely to be synonyms for (links to) the same terminal description, so you could use any one as a value of **TERM**. In other words, you could put *any* of these three lines in your *.bash_profile*:

```
TERM=70092
TERM=70092A
TERM=70092a
```

If you aren't successful, *ls* will print an error message, and you will have to make another guess and try again. If you find that *terminfo* contains nothing that resembles your terminal, all is not lost. Consult your terminal's manual to see if the

---

* Versions of UNIX not derived from System V use *termcap*, an older-style database of terminal capabilities that uses the single file */etc/termcap* for all terminal descriptions.

terminal can emulate a more popular model; nowadays the odds for this are excellent.

Conversely, *terminfo* may have several entries that relate to your terminal, for submodels, special modes, etc. If you have a choice of which entry to use as your value of **TERM**, we suggest you test each one out with your text editor or any other screen-oriented programs you use and see which one works best.

The process is much simpler if you are using a windowing system, in which your "terminals" are logical portions of the screen rather than physical devices. In this case, operating system-dependent software was written to control your terminal window(s), so the odds are very good that if it knows how to handle window resizing and complex cursor motion, then it is capable of dealing with simple things like **TERM**. The X Window System, for example, automatically sets **xterm** as its value for **TERM** in an *xterm* terminal window.

Other common variables

Some programs, such as *mail*, need to know what type of editor you would like to use. In most cases they will default to a common editor like *ed* unless you set the **EDITOR** variable to the path of your favorite editor and export it in your *.bash_profile*.

Some programs run shells as subprocesses within themselves (e.g., many mail programs and the *emacs* editor's shell mode); by convention they use the **SHELL** variable to determine which shell to use. **SHELL** is usually set by the process that invokes the login shell; usually *login* or something like *rshd* if you are logged in remotely. *bash* sets it only if it hasn't already been set.

You may have noticed that the value of **SHELL** looks the same as **BASH**. These two variables serve slightly different purposes. **BASH** is set to the pathname of the current shell, whether it is an interactive shell or not. **SHELL**, on the other hand, is set to the name of your login shell, which may be a completely different shell.

COLUMNS and **LINES** are used by screen-oriented editors like *vi*. In most cases a default is used if they are undefined, but if you are having display problems with screen-oriented applications then you should check these variables to see if they are correct.

The Environment File

Although environment variables will always be known to subprocesses, the shell must be explicitly told which other variables, options, aliases, and so on, are to be communicated to subprocesses. The way to do this is to put all such definitions into the *environment file*. *bash*'s default environment file is the *.bashrc* file that we touched on briefly at the beginning of this chapter.

Remember that if you take your definitions out of .*bash_profile* and put them in .*bashrc* you will have to have the line **source** .**bashrc** at the end of your .*bash_profile* so that the definitions become available to the login shell.

The idea of the environment file comes from the C shell's .*cshrc* file. This is reflected in the choice of the name .*bashrc*. The *rc* suffix for initialization files is practically universal throughout the UNIX world.*

As a general rule, you should put as few definitions as possible in .*bash_profile* and as many as possible in your environment file. Because definitions add to rather than take away from an environment, there is little chance that they will cause something in a subprocess not to work properly. (An exception might be name clashes if you go overboard with aliases.)

The only things that really need to be in .*bash_profile* are environment variables and their exports and commands that aren't definitions but actually run or produce output when you log in. Option and alias definitions should go into the environment file. In fact, there are many *bash* users who have tiny .*bash_profile* files, e.g.:

```
stty stop ^S intr ^C erase ^?
date
source .bashrc
```

Although this is a small .*bash_profile*, this user's environment file could be huge.

Customization Hints

You should feel free to try any of the techniques presented in this chapter. The best strategy is to test something out by typing it into the shell during your login session; then if you decide you want to make it a permanent part of your environment, add it to your .*bash_profile*.

A nice, painless way to add to your .*bash_profile* without going into a text editor makes use of the **echo** command and one of *bash*'s editing modes. If you type a customization command in and later decide to add it to your .*bash_profile*, you can recall it via CTRL-P or CTRL-R (in emacs-mode) or j, −, or ? (vi-mode). Let's say the line is:

```
PS1="\u \!--> "
```

After you recall it, edit the line so that it is preceded by an **echo** command, surrounded by *single* quotes, and followed by an I/O redirector that (as you will see

---

* According to the folklore, it stands for "run commands" and has its origins in old DEC operating systems.

in Chapter 7, *Input/Output and Command-Line Processing*) appends the output to
~/.bash_profile:

```
$ echo 'PS1="\u \!--> "' >> ~/.bash_profile
```

Remember that the single quotes are important because they prevent the shell
from trying to interpret things like dollar signs, double quotes, and exclamation
points. Also make sure that you use a double right-caret (>>). A single one will
overwrite the file rather than appending to it.

4

Basic Shell Programming

If you have become familiar with the customization techniques we presented in the previous chapter, you have probably run into various modifications to your environment that you want to make but can't—yet. Shell programming makes these possible.

bash has some of the most advanced programming capabilities of any command interpreter of its type. Although its syntax is nowhere near as elegant or consistent as that of most conventional programming languages, its power and flexibility are comparable. In fact, *bash* can be used as a complete environment for writing software prototypes.*

Some aspects of *bash* programming are really extensions of the customization techniques we have already seen, while others resemble traditional programming language features. We have structured this chapter so that if you aren't a programmer, you can read this chapter and do quite a bit more than you could with the information in the previous chapter. Experience with a conventional programming language like Pascal or C is helpful (though not strictly necessary) for subsequent chapters. Throughout the rest of the book, we will encounter occasional programming problems, called *tasks*, whose solutions make use of the concepts we cover.

Shell Scripts and Functions

A *script*, which is a file that contains shell commands, is a shell program. Your *.bash_profile* and environment files, discussed in the previous chapter, are shell scripts.

---

* An example of this (a compiler for a simple language) is provided in the examples archive for this book. See Appendix E, *Reference Lists*, for instructions on how to obtain the archive.

You can create a script using the text editor of your choice. Once you have created one, there are two ways to run it. One, which we have already covered, is to type **source** *scriptname*. This causes the commands in the script to be read and run as if you typed them in.

The second way to run a script is simply to type its name and hit RETURN, just as if you were invoking a built-in command. This, of course, is the more convenient way. This method makes the script look just like any other UNIX command, and in fact several "regular" commands are implemented as shell scripts (i.e., not as programs originally written in C or some other language), including *spell*, *man* on some systems, and various commands for system administrators. The resulting lack of distinction between "user command files" and "built-in commands" is one factor in UNIX's extensibility and, hence, its favored status among programmers.

You can run a script by typing its name only if the directory where the script is located is in your command search path, or **.** (the current directory) is part of your command search path, i.e., the script's directory path (as discussed in Chapter 3, *Customizing Your Environment*). If these aren't in your path, you must type **.** / *scriptname*, which is really the same thing as typing the script's absolute pathname (see Chapter 1, *bash Basics*).

Before you can invoke the shell script by name, you must also give it "execute" permission. If you are familiar with the UNIX filesystem, you know that files have three types of permissions (read, write, and execute) and that those permissions apply to three categories of user (the file's owner, a *group* of users, and everyone else). Normally, when you create a file with a text editor, the file is set up with read and write permission for you and read-only permission for everyone else.

Therefore you must give your script execute permission explicitly, by using the *chmod* command. The simplest way to do this is to type:

```
$ chmod +x scriptname
```

Your text editor will preserve this permission if you make subsequent changes to your script. If you don't add execute permission to the script and you try to invoke it, the shell will print the message:

```
scriptname: Permission denied
```

But there is a more important difference between the two ways of running shell scripts. While using **source** causes the commands in the script to be run as if they were part of your login session, the "just the name" method causes the shell to do a series of things. First, it runs another copy of the shell as a subprocess; this is called a *subshell*. The subshell then takes commands from the script, runs them, and terminates, handing control back to the parent shell.

Figure 4-1 shows how the shell executes scripts. Assume you have a simple shell script called *alice* that contains the commands *hatter* and *gryphon*. In Figure 4-1.a, typing **source alice** causes the two commands to run in the same shell, just as if you had typed them in by hand. Figure 4-1.b shows what happens when you type just **alice**: the commands run in the subshell while the parent shell waits for the subshell to finish.

You may find it interesting to compare this with the situation in Figure 4-1.c, which shows what happens when you type **alice &**. As you will recall from Chapter 1, the **&** makes the command run in the *background*, which is really just another term for "subprocess." It turns out that the only significant difference between Figure 4-1.c and Figure 4-1.b is that you have control of your terminal or workstation while the command runs—you need not wait until it finishes before you can enter further commands.

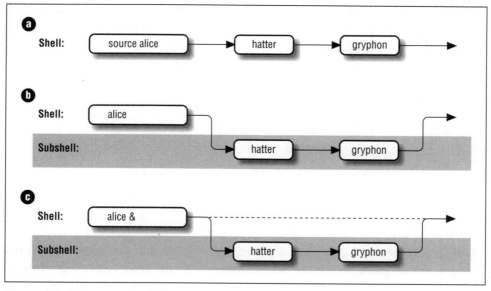

Figure 4-1: Ways to run a shell script

There are many ramifications to using subshells. An important one is that the *export*ed environment variables that we saw in the last chapter (e.g., **TERM**, **EDITOR**, **PWD**) are known in subshells, whereas other shell variables (such as any that you define in your *.bash_profile* without an *export* statement) are not.

Other issues involving subshells are too complex to go into now; see Chapter 7, *Input/Output and Command-Line Processing*, and Chapter 8, *Process Handling*, for more details about subshell I/O and process characteristics, respectively. For now, just bear in mind that a script normally runs in a subshell.

Functions

bash's *function* feature is an expanded version of a similar facility in the System V Bourne shell and a few other shells. A function is sort of a script-within-a-script; you use it to define some shell code by name and store it in the shell's memory, to be invoked and run later.

Functions improve the shell's programmability significantly, for two main reasons. First, when you invoke a function, it is already in the shell's memory; therefore a function runs faster. Modern computers have plenty of memory, so there is no need to worry about the amount of space a typical function takes up. For this reason, most people define as many commonly used functions as possible rather than keep lots of scripts around.

The other advantage of functions is that they are ideal for organizing long shell scripts into modular "chunks" of code that are easier to develop and maintain. If you aren't a programmer, ask one what life would be like without functions (also called *procedures* or *subroutines* in other languages) and you'll probably get an earful.

To define a function, you can use either one of two forms:

```
function functname
{
    shell commands
}
```

or:

```
functname ()
{
    shell commands
}
```

There is no functional difference between the two. We will use both forms in this book. You can also delete a function definition with the command **unset –f** *functname*.

When you define a function, you tell the shell to store its name and definition (i.e., the shell commands it contains) in memory. If you want to run the function later, just type in its name followed by any arguments, as if it were a shell script.

You can find out what functions are defined in your login session by typing **declare –f**. The shell will print not just the names but the definitions of all functions, in alphabetical order by function name. Since this may result in long output, you might want to pipe the output through *more* or redirect it to a file for examination with a text editor. If you just want to see the names of the functions, you can use **declare -F.*** We will look at **declare** in more detail in Chapter 6, *Command-Line Options and Typed Variables.*

Apart from the advantages, there are two important differences between functions and scripts. First, functions do not run in separate processes, as scripts do when you invoke them by name; the "semantics" of running a function are more like those of your *.bash_profile* when you log in or any script when invoked with the **source** command. Second, if a function has the same name as a script or executable program, the function takes precedence.

This is a good time to show the order of precedence for the various sources of commands when you type a command to the shell:

1. Aliases

2. *Keywords* such as **function** and several others, like **if** and **for**, that we will see in Chapter 5, *Flow Control*

3. Functions

4. *Built-ins* like **cd** and **type**

5. Scripts and executable programs, for which the shell searches in the directories listed in the **PATH** environment variable

Thus, an alias takes precedence over a function or a script with the same name. You can, however, change the order of precedence by using the built-ins **command**, **builtin**, and **enable**. This allows you to define functions, aliases, and script files with the same names, and select which one you want to execute. We'll examine this process in more detail in the section on command-line processing in Chapter 7.

If you need to know the exact source of a command, there are options to the **type** built-in command that we saw in Chapter 3. **type** by itself will print how *bash* would interpret the command, based on the search locations listed above. If you had a shell script, a function, and an alias all called *dodo*, **type** would tell you that *dodo*, as an alias, would be used if you typed *dodo*. If you supply more than one argument to **type**, it will print the information for each one in turn.

type has three options that allow you to find specific details of a command. If you want to find out all of the definitions for *dodo* you can use **type -all**. This will produce output similar to the following:

```
$ type -all dodo
dodo is aliased to `echo "Everybody has won, and all must have prizes"'
dodo is a function
dodo ()
```

---

* The **-F** option is not available in versions of *bash* prior to 2.0.

```
{
    echo "Everybody has won, and all must have prizes"
}
dodo is ./dodo
```

It is also possible to restrict the search to commands that are executable files or shell scripts by using the **-path** option. If the command as typed to *bash* executes a file or shell script, the path name of the file is returned; otherwise, nothing is printed.

The default output from **type** is verbose; it will give you the full definition for an alias or function. By using the **-type** option, you can restrict this to a single word descriptor: *alias, keyword, function, builtin,* or *file.* For example:

```
$ type -type bash
file
$ type -type if
keyword
```

The **-type** option can also be used with **-all**.

We will refer mainly to scripts throughout the remainder of this book, but unless we note otherwise, you should assume that whatever we say applies equally to functions.

Shell Variables

bash derives much of its programming functionality from shell variables. We've already seen the basics of variables. To recap briefly: they are named places to store data, usually in the form of character strings, and their values can be obtained by preceding their names with dollar signs ($). Certain variables, called *environment variables,* are conventionally named in all capital letters, and their values are made known (with the **export** statement) to subprocesses.

If you are a programmer, you already know that just about every major programming language uses variables in some way; in fact, an important way of characterizing differences between languages is comparing their facilities for variables.

The chief difference between *bash*'s variable schema and those of conventional languages is that *bash*'s places heavy emphasis on character strings. (Thus it has more in common with a special-purpose language like SNOBOL than a general-purpose one like Pascal.) This is also true of the Bourne shell and the C shell, but *bash* goes beyond them by having additional mechanisms for handling integers explicitly.

Positional Parameters

As we have already seen, you can define values for variables with statements of the form **varname=value**, e.g.:

```
$ hatter=mad
$ echo "$hatter"
mad
```

Some environment variables are predefined by the shell when you log in. There are other built-in variables that are vital to shell programming. We will look at a few of them now and save the others for later.

The most important special, built-in variables are called *positional parameters*. These hold the command-line arguments to scripts when they are invoked. Positional parameters have the names 1, 2, 3, etc., meaning that their values are denoted by **$1**, **$2**, **$3**, etc. There is also a positional parameter 0, whose value is the name of the script (i.e., the command typed in to invoke it).

Two special variables contain all of the positional parameters (except positional parameter 0): * and @. The difference between them is subtle but important, and it's apparent only when they are within double quotes.

"**$***" is a single string that consists of all of the positional parameters, separated by the first character in the environment variable **IFS** (internal field separator), which is a space, TAB, and NEWLINE by default. On the other hand, "**$@**" is equal to "**$1**" "**$2**" ... "**$N**", where *N* is the number of positional parameters. That is, it's equal to *N* separate double-quoted strings, which are separated by spaces. If there are no positional parameters, "**$@**" expands to nothing. We'll explore the ramifications of this difference in a little while.

The variable # holds the number of positional parameters (as a character string). All of these variables are "read-only," meaning that you can't assign new values to them within scripts.

For example, assume that you have the following simple shell script:

```
echo "alice: $@"
echo "$0: $1 $2 $3 $4"
echo "$# arguments"
```

Assume further that the script is called *alice*. Then if you type **alice in wonderland**, you will see the following output:

```
alice: in wonderland
alice: in wonderland
2 arguments
```

In this case, **$3** and **$4** are unset, which means that the shell will substitute the empty (or null) string for them.*

Positional parameters in functions

Shell functions use positional parameters and special variables like * and # in exactly the same way as shell scripts do. If you wanted to define *alice* as a function, you could put the following in your *.bash_profile* or environment file:

```
function alice
{
    echo "alice: $*"
    echo "$0: $1 $2 $3 $4"
    echo "$# arguments"
}
```

You will get the same result if you type **alice in wonderland**.

Typically, several shell functions are defined within a single shell script. Therefore each function will need to handle its own arguments, which in turn means that each function needs to keep track of positional parameters separately. Sure enough, each function has its own copies of these variables (even though functions don't run in their own subshells, as scripts do); we say that such variables are *local* to the function.

However, other variables defined within functions are not local (they are *global*), meaning that their values are known throughout the entire shell script. For example, assume that you have a shell script called *ascript* that contains this:

```
function afunc
{
  echo in function: $0 $1 $2
  var1="in function"
  echo var1: $var1
}

var1="outside function"
echo var1: $var1
echo $0: $1 $2
afunc funcarg1 funcarg2
echo var1: $var1
echo $0: $1 $2
```

If you invoke this script by typing **ascript arg1 arg2**, you will see this output:

```
var1: outside function
ascript: arg1 arg2
in function: ascript funcarg1 funcarg2
```

---

* Unless the option **nounset** is turned on, in which case the shell will return an error message.

```
var1: in function
var1: in function
ascript: arg1 arg2
```

In other words, the function *afunc* changes the value of the variable **var1** from "outside function" to "in function," and that change is known outside the function, while **$1** and **$2** have different values in the function and the main script. Notice that **$0** *doesn't* change because the function executes in the environment of the shell script and **$0** takes the name of the script. Figure 4-2 shows the scope of each variable graphically.

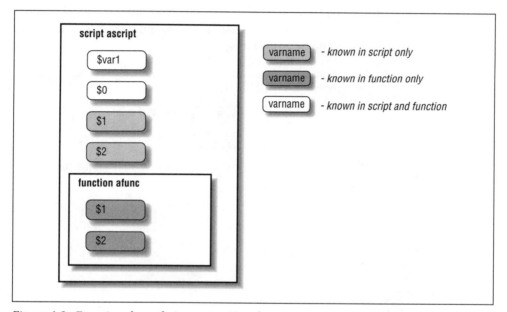

Figure 4-2: Functions have their own positional parameters

Local Variables in Functions

A **local** statement inside a function definition makes the variables involved all become *local* to that function. The ability to define variables that are local to "subprogram" units (procedures, functions, subroutines, etc.) is necessary for writing large programs, because it helps keep subprograms independent of the main program and of each other.

Here is the function from our last example with the variable *var1* made local:

```
function afunc
{
  local var1
  echo in function: $0 $1 $2
```

```
    var1="in function"
    echo var1: $var1
}
```

Now the result of running **ascript arg1 arg2** is:

```
var1: outside function
ascript: arg1 arg2
in function: ascript funcarg1 funcarg2
var1: in function
var1: outside function
ascript: arg1 arg2
```

Figure 4-3 shows the scope of each variable in our new script. Note that **afunc** now has its own, local copy of *var1*, although the original *var1* would still be used by any other functions that **ascript** invokes.

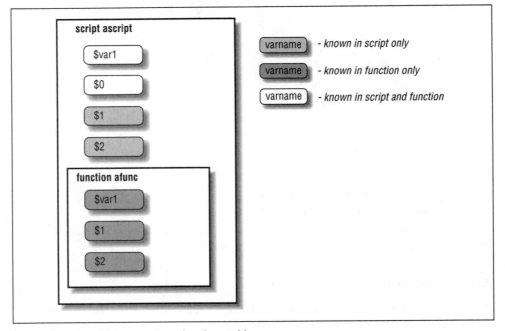

Figure 4-3: Functions can have local variables

Quoting with $@ and $*

Now that we have this background, let's take a closer look at "$@" and "$*". These variables are two of the shell's greatest idiosyncracies, so we'll discuss some of the most common sources of confusion.

- Why are the elements of "**$***" separated by the first character of **IFS** instead of just spaces? To give you output flexibility. As a simple example, let's say you want to print a list of positional parameters separated by commas. This script would do it:

```
IFS=,
echo "$*"
```

Changing **IFS** in a script is risky, but it's probably OK as long as nothing else in the script depends on it. If this script were called *arglist*, then the command **arglist alice dormouse hatter** would produce the output **alice,dormouse,hatter**. Chapters 5 and 10 contain other examples of changing **IFS**.

- Why does "**$@**" act like *N* separate double-quoted strings? To allow you to use them again as separate values. For example, say you want to call a function within your script with the same list of positional parameters, like this:

```
function countargs
{
    echo "$# args."
}
```

Assume your script is called with the same arguments as *arglist* above. Then if it contains the command **countargs** "**$***", the function will print **1 args**. But if the command is **countargs** "**$@**", the function will print **3 args**.

More on Variable Syntax

Before we show the many things you can do with shell variables, we have to point out a simplification we have been making: the syntax of $*varname* for taking the value of a variable is actually the simple form of the more general syntax, ${*varname*}.

Why two syntaxes? For one thing, the more general syntax is necessary if your code refers to more than nine positional parameters: you must use **${10}** for the tenth instead of **$10**. Aside from that, consider the following case where you would like to place an underscore after your user ID:

```
echo $UID_
```

The shell will try to use **UID_** as the name of the variable. Unless, by chance, **$UID_** already exists, this won't print anything (the value being *null* or the empty string, " "). To obtain the desired result, you need to enclose the shell variable in curly brackets:

```
echo ${UID}_
```

It is safe to omit the curly brackets ({}) if the variable name is followed by a character that isn't a letter, digit, or underscore.

String Operators

The curly-bracket syntax allows for the shell's *string operators*. String operators allow you to manipulate values of variables in various useful ways without having to write full-blown programs or resort to external UNIX utilities. You can do a lot with string-handling operators even if you haven't yet mastered the programming features we'll see in later chapters.

In particular, string operators let you do the following:

- Ensure that variables exist (i.e., are defined and have non-null values)
- Set default values for variables
- Catch errors that result from variables not being set
- Remove portions of variables' values that match patterns

Syntax of String Operators

The basic idea behind the syntax of string operators is that special characters that denote operations are inserted between the variable's name and the right curly bracket. Any argument that the operator may need is inserted to the operator's right.

The first group of string-handling operators tests for the existence of variables and allows substitutions of default values under certain conditions. These are listed in Table 4-1.*

Table 4-1: Substitution Operators

Operator	Substitution
${*varname*:-*word*}	If *varname* exists and isn't null, return its value; otherwise return *word*.
Purpose:	Returning a default value if the variable is undefined.
Example:	${count:-0} evaluates to 0 if **count** is undefined.
${*varname*:=*word*}	If *varname* exists and isn't null, return its value; otherwise set it to *word* and then return its value. Positional and special parameters cannot be assigned this way.
Purpose:	Setting a variable to a default value if it is undefined.
Example:	${count:=0} sets **count** to 0 if it is undefined.

---

* The colon (:) in all but the last of these operators is actually optional. If the colon is omitted, then change "exists and isn't null" to "exists" in each definition, i.e., the operator tests for existence only.

Table 4-1: Substitution Operators (continued)

Operator	Substitution
${*varname*:?*message*}	If *varname* exists and isn't null, return its value; otherwise print *varname*: followed by *message*, and abort the current command or script (non-interactive shells only). Omitting *message* produces the default message **parameter null or not set**.
Purpose:	Catching errors that result from variables being undefined.
Example:	{count:?"undefined!"} prints "count: undefined!" and exits if **count** is undefined.
${*varname*:+*word*}	If *varname* exists and isn't null, return *word*; otherwise return null.
Purpose:	Testing for the existence of a variable.
Example:	${count:+1} returns 1 (which could mean "true") if **count** is defined.
${*varname*:*offset*} ${*varname*:*offset:length*}	Performs substring expansion.[a] It returns the substring of $*varname* starting at *offset* and up to *length* characters. The first character in $*varname* is position 0. If *length* is omitted, the substring starts at *offset* and continues to the end of $*varname*. If *offset* is less than 0 then the position is taken from the *end* of $*varname*. If *varname* is @, the *length* is the number of positional parameters starting at parameter *offset*.
Purpose:	Returning parts of a string (substrings or *slices*).
Example:	If **count** is set to *frogfootman*, ${count:4} returns *footman*. ${count:4:4} returns *foot*.

a. The substring expansion operator is not available in versions of *bash* prior to 2.0.

The first of these operators is ideal for setting defaults for command-line arguments in case the user omits them. We'll use this technique in our first programming task.

Task 4-1

You have a large album collection, and you want to write some software to keep track of it. Assume that you have a file of data on how many albums you have by each artist. Lines in the file look like this:

```
5        Depeche Mode
2        Split Enz
3        Simple Minds
1        Vivaldi, Antonio
```

Write a program that prints the *N* highest lines, i.e., the *N* artists by whom you have the most albums. The default for *N* should be 10. The program should take one argument for the name of the input file and an optional second argument for how many lines to print.

By far the best approach to this type of script is to use built-in UNIX utilities, combining them with I/O redirectors and pipes. This is the classic "building-block" philosophy of UNIX that is another reason for its great popularity with programmers. The building-block technique lets us write a first version of the script that is only one line long:

```
sort -nr $1 | head -${2:-10}
```

Here is how this works: the *sort* program sorts the data in the file whose name is given as the first argument (**$1**). The **−n** option tells *sort* to interpret the first word on each line as a number (instead of as a character string); the **−r** tells it to reverse the comparisons, so as to sort in descending order.

The output of *sort* is piped into the *head* utility, which, when given the argument −*N*, prints the first *N* lines of its input on the standard output. The expression **−${2:-10}** evaluates to a dash (−) followed by the second argument if it is given, or to −10 if it's not; notice that the variable in this expression is **2**, which is the second positional parameter.

Assume the script we want to write is called *highest*. Then if the user types **highest myfile**, the line that actually runs is:

```
sort -nr myfile | head -10
```

Or if the user types **highest myfile 22**, the line that runs is:

```
sort -nr myfile | head -22
```

Make sure you understand how the :- string operator provides a default value.

This is a perfectly good, runnable script—but it has a few problems. First, its one line is a bit cryptic. While this isn't much of a problem for such a tiny script, it's not wise to write long, elaborate scripts in this manner. A few minor changes will make the code more readable.

First, we can add comments to the code; anything between # and the end of a line is a comment. At a minimum, the script should start with a few comment lines that indicate what the script does and what arguments it accepts. Second, we can improve the variable names by assigning the values of the positional parameters to regular variables with mnemonic names. Finally, we can add blank lines to space things out; blank lines, like comments, are ignored. Here is a more readable version:

```
#
#        highest filename [howmany]
#
#        Print howmany highest-numbered lines in file filename.
#        The input file is assumed to have lines that start with
#        numbers.  Default for howmany is 10.
#

filename=$1
howmany=${2:-10}

sort -nr $filename | head -$howmany
```

The square brackets around **howmany** in the comments adhere to the convention in UNIX documentation that square brackets denote optional arguments.

The changes we just made improve the code's readability but not how it runs. What if the user were to invoke the script without any arguments? Remember that positional parameters default to null if they aren't defined. If there are no arguments, then **$1** and **$2** are both null. The variable **howmany** (**$2**) is set up to default to 10, but there is no default for **filename** (**$1**). The result would be that this command runs:

```
sort -nr | head -10
```

As it happens, if *sort* is called without a filename argument, it expects input to come from standard input, e.g., a pipe (|) or a user's terminal. Since it doesn't have the pipe, it will expect the terminal. This means that the script will appear to hang! Although you could always hit CTRL-D or CTRL-C to get out of the script, a naive user might not know this.

Therefore we need to make sure that the user supplies at least one argument. There are a few ways of doing this; one of them involves another string operator. We'll replace the line:

```
filename=$1
```

with:

```
filename=${1:?"filename missing."}
```

This will cause two things to happen if a user invokes the script without any arguments: first the shell will print the somewhat unfortunate message:

```
highest: 1: filename missing.
```

to the standard error output. Second, the script will exit without running the remaining code. With a somewhat "kludgy" modification, we can get a slightly better error message.

Consider this code:

```
filename=$1
filename=${filename:?"missing."}
```

This results in the message:

```
highest: filename: missing.
```

(Make sure you understand why.) Of course, there are ways of printing whatever message is desired; we'll find out how in Chapter 5.

Before we move on, we'll look more closely at the three remaining operators in Table 4-1 and see how we can incorporate them into our task solution. The := operator does roughly the same thing as :-, except that it has the "side effect" of setting the value of the variable to the given word if the variable doesn't exist.

Therefore we would like to use := in our script in place of :-, but we can't; we'd be trying to set the value of a positional parameter, which is not allowed. But if we replaced:

```
howmany=${2:-10}
```

with just:

```
howmany=$2
```

and moved the substitution down to the actual command line (as we did at the start), then we could use the := operator:

```
sort -nr $filename | head -${howmany:=10}
```

Using := has the added benefit of setting the value of **howmany** to 10 in case we need it afterwards in later versions of the script.

The operator :+ substitutes a value if the given variable exists and isn't null. Here is how we can use it in our example: Let's say we want to give the user the option of adding a header line to the script's output. If he or she types the option −h, then the output will be preceded by the line:

```
ALBUMS  ARTIST
```

Assume further that this option ends up in the variable **header**, i.e., **$header** is −h if the option is set or null if not. (Later we will see how to do this without disturbing the other positional parameters.)

The following expression yields null if the variable **header** is null, or **ALBUMS ARTIST\n** if it is non-null:

```
${header:+"ALBUMS  ARTIST\n"}
```

This means that we can put the line:

```
echo -e -n ${header:+"ALBUMS  ARTIST\n"}
```

right before the command line that does the actual work. The **−n** option to **echo** causes it *not* to print a LINEFEED after printing its arguments. Therefore this **echo** statement will print nothing—not even a blank line—if **header** is null; otherwise it will print the header line and a LINEFEED (\n). The **−e** option makes **echo** interpret the \n as a LINEFEED rather than literally.

The final operator, substring expansion, returns sections of a string. We can use it to "pick out" parts of a string that are of interest. Assume that our script is able to assign lines of the sorted list, one at a time, to the variable *album_line*. If we want to print out just the album name and ignore the number of albums, we can use substring expansion:

```
echo ${album_line:8}
```

This prints everything from character position 8, which is the start of each album name, onwards.

If we just want to print the numbers and not the album names, we can do so by supplying the length of the substring:

```
echo ${album_line:0:7}
```

Although this example may seem rather useless, it should give you a feel for how to use substrings. When combined with some of the programming features discussed later in the book, substrings can be extremely useful.

Patterns and Pattern Matching

We'll continue refining our solution to Task 4-1 later in this chapter. The next type of string operator is used to match portions of a variable's string value against *patterns*. Patterns, as we saw in Chapter 1, are strings that can contain wildcard characters (*, ?, and [] for character sets and ranges).

Table 4-2 lists *bash*'s pattern-matching operators.

Table 4-2: Pattern-Matching Operators

Operator	Meaning
${*variable#pattern*}	If the pattern matches the beginning of the variable's value, delete the shortest part that matches and return the rest.
${*variable##pattern*}	If the pattern matches the beginning of the variable's value, delete the longest part that matches and return the rest.

Table 4-2: Pattern-Matching Operators (continued)

Operator	Meaning
${*variable%pattern*}	If the pattern matches the end of the variable's value, delete the shortest part that matches and return the rest.
${*variable%%pattern*}	If the pattern matches the end of the variable's value, delete the longest part that matches and return the rest.
${*variable/pattern/string*}	
${*variable//pattern/string*}	The longest match to *pattern* in *variable* is replaced by *string*. In the first form, only the first match is replaced. In the second form, all matches are replaced. If the pattern is begins with a #, it must match at the start of the variable. If it begins with a %, it must match with the end of the variable. If *string* is null, the matches are deleted. If *variable* is @ or *, the operation is applied to each positional parameter in turn and the expansion is the resultant list.[a]

a. The pattern-matching and replacement operator is not available in versions of *bash* prior to 2.0.

These can be hard to remember, so here's a handy mnemonic device: # matches the front because number signs *precede* numbers; % matches the rear because percent signs *follow* numbers.

The classic use for pattern-matching operators is in stripping off components of pathnames, such as directory prefixes and filename suffixes. With that in mind, here is an example that shows how all of the operators work. Assume that the variable **path** has the value */home/cam/book/long.file.name*; then:

```
Expression                Result
${path##/*/}                      long.file.name
${path#/*/}               cam/book/long.file.name
$path               /home/cam/book/long.file.name
${path%.*}               /home/cam/book/long.file
${path%%.*}               /home/cam/book/long
```

The two patterns used here are /*/, which matches anything between two slashes, and .*, which matches a dot followed by anything.

The longest and shortest pattern-matching operators produce the same output unless they are used with the * wildcard operator. As an example, if **filename** had the value **alicece**, then both ${filename%ce} and ${filename%%ce} would produce the result **alice**. This is because **ce** is an *exact* match; for a match to occur, the string *ce* must appear on the end $**filename**. Both the short and long matches will then match the last grouping of *ce* and delete it. If, however, we had used the * wildcard, then ${filename%ce*} would produce **alice** because it matches the shortest occurrence of *ce* followed by anything else. ${filename%%ce*} would return **ali** because it matches the longest occurrence of *ce* followed by anything else; in this case the first and second *ce*.

The next task will incorporate one of these pattern-matching operators.

Task 4-2

You are writing a graphics file conversion utility for use in creating your World Wide Web home page. You want to be able to take a PCX file and convert it to a GIF file for use on the Web page.*

Graphics file conversion utilities are quite common because of the plethora of different graphics formats and file types. They allow you to specify an input file, usually from a range of different formats, and convert it to an output file of a different format. In this case, we want to take a PCX file, which can't be displayed with a Web browser, and convert it to a GIF which can be displayed by nearly all browsers. Part of this process is taking the filename of the PCX file, which ends in *.pcx*, and changing it to one ending in *.gif* for the output file. In essence, you want to take the original filename and strip off the *.pcx*, then append *.gif*. A single shell statement will do this:

```
outfile=${filename%.pcx}.gif
```

The shell takes the filename and looks for .**pcx** on the end of the string. If it is found, .**pcx** is stripped off and the rest of the string is returned. For example, if **filename** had the value **alice.pcx**, the expression **${filename%.pcx}** would return **alice**. The .**gif** is appended to form the desired **alice.gif**, which is then stored in the variable **outfile**.

If **filename** had an inappropriate value (without the .**pcx**) such as **alice.jpg**, the above expression would evaluate to **alice.jpg.gif**: since there was no match, nothing is deleted from the value of **filename**, and .**gif** is appended anyway. Note, however, that if **filename** contained more than one dot (e.g., if it were **alice.1.pcx**—the expression would still produce the desired value **alice.1.gif**).

The next task uses the longest pattern-matching operator.

Task 4-3

You are implementing a filter that prepares a text file for printer output. You want to put the file's name—without any directory prefix—on the "banner" page. Assume that, in your script, you have the pathname of the file to be printed stored in the variable **pathname**.

---

* PCX is a popular graphics file format under Microsoft Windows. GIF (Graphics Interchange Format) is a common graphics format on the Internet and is used to a great extent on Web pages.

Clearly, the objective is to remove the directory prefix from the pathname. The following line will do it:

```
bannername=${pathname##*/}
```

This solution is similar to the first line in the examples shown before. If **pathname** were just a filename, the pattern `*/` (anything followed by a slash) would not match and the value of the expression would be **pathname** untouched. If **pathname** were something like *book/wonderland*, the prefix *book/* would match the pattern and be deleted, leaving just **wonderland** as the expression's value. The same thing would happen if **pathname** were something like */home/cam/book/wonderland*: since the `##` deletes the longest match, it deletes the entire */home/cam/book/*.

If we used `#*/` instead of `##*/`, the expression would have the incorrect value *home/cam/book/wonderland*, because the shortest instance of "anything followed by a slash" at the beginning of the string is just a slash (*/*).

The construct $\${variable\#\#*/}$ is actually equivalent to the UNIX utility *basename*. *basename* takes a pathname as argument and returns the filename only; it is meant to be used with the shell's command substitution mechanism (see the following explanation). *basename* is less efficient than $\${variable\#\#*/}$ because it runs in its own separate process rather than within the shell. Another utility, *dirname*, does essentially the opposite of *basename*: it returns the directory prefix only. It is equivalent to the *bash* expression $\${variable\%/*}$ and is less efficient for the same reason.

The last operator in the table matches patterns and performs substitutions. Task 4–4 is a simple task where it comes in useful.

Task 4-4

The directories in **PATH** can be hard to distinguish when printed out as one line with colon delimiters. You want a simple way to display them, one to a line.

As directory names are separated by colons, the easiest way would be to replace each colon with a LINEFEED:

```
$ echo -e ${PATH//:/'\n'}
/home/cam/bin
/usr/local/bin
/bin
/usr/bin
/usr/X11R6/bin
```

Each occurrence of the colon is replaced by \n. As we saw earlier, the **-e** option allows **echo** to interpret \n as a LINEFEED. In this case we used the second of the two substitution forms. If we'd used the first form, only the first colon would have been replaced with a \n.

Length Operator

There is one remaining operator on variables. It is ${#*varname*}, which returns the length of the value of the variable as a character string. (In Chapter 6, we will see how to treat this and similar values as actual numbers so they can be used in arithmetic expressions.) For example, if **filename** has the value **alice.c**, then ${#**filename**} would have the value 7.

Command Substitution

From the discussion so far, we've seen two ways of getting values into variables: by assignment statements and by the user supplying them as command-line arguments (positional parameters). There is another way: *command substitution*, which allows you to use the standard output of a command as if it were the value of a variable. You will soon see how powerful this feature is.

The syntax of command substitution is:*

```
$(UNIX command)
```

The command inside the parentheses is run, and anything the command writes to standard output is returned as the value of the expression. These constructs can be nested, i.e., the UNIX command can contain command substitutions.

Here are some simple examples:

* The value of **$(pwd)** is the current directory (same as the environment variable **$PWD**).

* The value of **$(ls $HOME)** is the names of all files in your home directory.

* The value of **$(ls $(pwd))** is the names of all files in the current directory.

* To find out detailed information about a command if you don't know where its file resides, type **ls -l $(type -path -all** *command-name***)**. The **-all** option forces **type** to do a pathname look-up and **-path** causes it to ignore keywords, built-ins, etc.

---

* Bourne and C shell users should note that the command substitution syntax of those shells, `*UNIX command*` (with backward quotes, or grave accents), is also supported by *bash* for backward compatibility reasons. However, it is harder to read and less conducive to nesting.

- If you want to edit (with *vi*) every chapter of your book on *bash* that has the phrase "command substitution," assuming that your chapter files all begin with *ch*, you could type:

```
vi $(grep -l 'command substitution' ch*)
```

The –l option to *grep* prints only the names of files that contain matches.

Command substitution, like variable and tilde expansion, is done within double quotes. Therefore, our rule in Chapter 1 and Chapter 3 about using single quotes for strings unless they contain variables will now be extended: "When in doubt, use single quotes, unless the string contains variables or command substitutions, in which case use double quotes."

Command substitution helps us with the solution to the next programming task, which relates to the album database in Task 4-1.

Task 4-5

The file used in Task 4-1 is actually a report derived from a bigger table of data about albums. This table consists of several columns, or *fields*, to which a user refers by names like "artist," "title," "year," etc. The columns are separated by vertical bars (|, the same as the UNIX pipe character). To deal with individual columns in the table, field names need to be converted to field numbers.

Suppose there is a shell function called *getfield* that takes the field name as argument and writes the corresponding field (or column) number on the standard output. Use this routine to help extract a column from the data table.

The *cut* utility is a natural for this task. *cut* is a data filter: it extracts columns from tabular data.* If you supply the numbers of columns you want to extract from the input, *cut* will print only those columns on the standard output. Columns can be character positions or—relevant in this example—fields that are separated by TAB characters or other delimiters.

Assume that the data table in our task is a file called *albums* and that it looks like this:

```
Depeche Mode|Speak and Spell|Mute Records|1981
Depeche Mode|Some Great Reward|Mute Records|1984
Depeche Mode|101|Mute Records|1989
Depeche Mode|Violator|Mute Records|1990
Depeche Mode|Songs of Faith and Devotion|Mute Records|1993
```

---

* Some older BSD-derived systems don't have *cut*, but you can use *awk* instead. Whenever you see a command of the form: cut -f*N* -d*C* *filename*, use this instead: awk -F*C* '{print $*N*}' *filename*.

Here is how we would use *cut* to extract the fourth (year) column:

```
cut -f4 -d\| albums
```

The **-d** argument is used to specify the character used as field delimiter (TAB is the default). The vertical bar must be backslash-escaped so that the shell doesn't try to interpret it as a pipe.

From this line of code and the *getfield* routine, we can easily derive the solution to the task. Assume that the first argument to *getfield* is the name of the field the user wants to extract. Then the solution is:

```
fieldname=$1
cut -f$(getfield $fieldname) -d\| albums
```

If we called this script with the argument **year**, the output would be:

```
1981
1984
1989
1990
1993
. . .
```

Task 4–6 shows another small task that makes use of *cut.*

Task 4-6

Send a mail message to everyone who is currently logged in.

The command *who* tells you who is logged in (as well as which terminal they're on and when they logged in). Its output looks like this:

```
root      tty1        Oct 13 12:05
michael   tty5        Oct 13 12:58
cam       tty23       Oct 13 11:51
kilrath   tty25       Oct 13 11:58
```

The fields are separated by spaces, not TABs. Since we need the first field, we can get away with using a space as the field separator in the *cut* command. (Otherwise we'd have to use the option to *cut* that uses character columns instead of fields.) To provide a space character as an argument on a command line, you can surround it by quotes:

```
$ who | cut -d' ' -f1
```

With the above *who* output, this command's output would look like this:

```
root
michael
cam
kilrath
```

This leads directly to a solution to the task. Just type:

```
$ mail $(who | cut -d' '  -f1)
```

The command **mail root michael cam kilrath** will run and then you can type your message.

Task 4–7 is another task that shows how useful command pipelines can be in command substitution.

Task 4-7
_____

> The **ls** command gives you pattern-matching capability with wildcards, but it doesn't allow you to select files by *modification date*. Devise a mechanism that lets you do this.

Here is a function that allows you to list all files that were last modified on the date you give as argument. Once again, we choose a function for speed reasons. No pun is intended by the function's name:

```
function lsd
{
    date=$1
    ls -l | grep -i "^.\{42\}$date" | cut -c55-
}
```

This function depends on the column layout of the **ls –l** command. In particular, it depends on dates starting in column 42 and filenames starting in column 55. If this isn't the case in your version of UNIX, you will need to adjust the column numbers.*

We use the *grep* search utility to match the date given as argument (in the form *Mon DD*, e.g., **Jan 15** or **Oct 6**, the latter having two spaces) to the output of **ls –l**. This gives us a long listing of only those files whose dates match the argument. The **–i** option to *grep* allows you to use all lowercase letters in the month name, while the rather fancy argument means, "Match any line that contains 41 characters followed by the function argument." For example, typing **lsd 'jan 15'** causes *grep* to search for lines that match any 41 characters followed by **jan 15** (or **Jan 15**).†

The output of *grep* is piped through our ubiquitous friend *cut* to retrieve the filenames only. The argument to *cut* tells it to extract characters in column 55 through the end of the line.

_____

* For example, **ls –l** on SunOS 4.1.x has dates starting in column 33 and filenames starting in column 46.

† Some older BSD-derived versions of UNIX (without System V extensions) do not support the \{*N*\} option. For this example, use 42 periods in a row instead of .\{42\}.

With command substitution, you can use this function with *any* command that accepts filename arguments. For example, if you want to print all files in your current directory that were last modified today, and today is January 15th, you could type:

```
$ lp $(lsd 'jan 15')
```

The output of *lsd* is on multiple lines (one for each filename), but LINEFEEDs are legal field separators for the *lp* command, because the environment variable **IFS** (see earlier in this chapter) contains LINEFEED by default.

Advanced Examples: pushd and popd

We will conclude this chapter with a couple of functions that are already built into *bash* but are useful in demonstrating some of the concepts we have covered in this chapter.*

Task 4-8

> The functions *pushd* and *popd* implement a *stack* of directories that enable you to move to another directory temporarily and have the shell remember where you were. Implement them as shell functions.

We will start by implementing a significant subset of their capabilities and finish the implementation in Chapter 6.

Think of a stack as a spring-loaded dish receptacle in a cafeteria. When you place dishes on the receptacle, the spring compresses so that the top stays at roughly the same level. The dish most recently placed on the stack is the first to be taken when someone wants food; thus, the stack is known as a "last-in, first-out" or *LIFO* structure. Putting something onto a stack is known in computer science parlance as *pushing*, and taking something off the top is called *popping*.

A stack is very handy for remembering directories, as we will see; it can "hold your place" up to an arbitrary number of times. The **cd –** form of the **cd** command does this, but only to one level. For example: if you are in *firstdir* and then you change to *seconddir*, you can type **cd –** to go back. But if you start out in *firstdir*, then change to *seconddir*, and then go to *thirddir*, you can use **cd –** only to go back to *seconddir*. If you type **cd –** again, you will be back in *thirddir*, because it is the previous directory.†

---

* Your copy of *bash* may not have *pushd* and *popd*, since it can be configured without these built-ins.

† Think of **cd –** as a synonym for **cd $OLDPWD**; see the previous chapter.

If you want the "nested" remember-and-change functionality that will take you back to *firstdir*, you need a stack of directories along with the *pushd* and *popd* commands. Here is how these work:

- The first time **pushd** *dir* is called, **pushd** pushes the current directory onto the stack, then **cd**s to *dir* and pushes it onto the stack.

- Subsequent calls to **pushd** *dir* **cd** to *dir* and push *dir* only onto the stack.

- **popd** removes the top directory off the stack, revealing a new top. Then it **cd**s to the new top directory.

For example, consider the series of events in Table 4-3. Assume that you have just logged in, and that you are in your home directory (*/home/you*).

Table 4-3: pushd/popd Example

Command	Stack Contents	Result Directory
pushd lizard	*/home/you/lizard /home/you*	*/home/you/lizard*
pushd /etc	*/etc /home/you/lizard /home/you*	*/etc*
popd	*/home/you/lizard /home/you*	*/home/you/lizard*
popd	*/home/you*	*/home/you*
popd	\<empty\>	(error)

We will implement a stack as an environment variable containing a list of directories separated by spaces.*

Your directory stack should be initialized to the null string when you log in. To do this, put this in your *.bash_profile*:

```
DIR_STACK=""
export DIR_STACK
```

Do *not* put this in your environment file if you have one. The **export** statement guarantees that DIR_STACK is known to all subprocesses; you want to initialize it only once. If you put this code in an environment file, it will get reinitialized in every subshell, which you probably don't want.

Next, we need to implement *pushd* and *popd* as functions. Here are our initial versions:

```
pushd ()
{
    dirname=$1
    DIR_STACK="$dirname ${DIR_STACK:-$PWD' '}"
```

---

* *bash* also maintains a directory stack for the **pushd** and **popd** built-ins, accessible through the environment variable **DIRSTACK**. Unlike our version, however, it is implemented as an *array* (see Chapter 6 for details on arrays).

```
        cd ${dirname:?"missing directory name."}
        echo "$DIR_STACK"
}

popd ()
{
    DIR_STACK=${DIR_STACK#* }
    cd ${DIR_STACK%% *}
    echo "$PWD"
}
```

Notice that there isn't much code! Let's go through the two functions and see how they work, starting with *pushd*. The first line merely saves the first argument in the variable **dirname** for readability reasons.

The second line of the function pushes the new directory onto the stack. The expression **${DIR_STACK:-$PWD' '}** evaluates to **$DIR_STACK** if it is non-null or **$PWD' '** (the current directory and a space) if it is null. The expression within double quotes, then, consists of the argument given, followed by a single space, followed by DIR_STACK or the current directory and a space. The trailing space on the current directory is required for pattern matching in the *popd* function; each directory in the stack is considered to be of the form "*dirname*".

The double quotes in the assignment ensure that all of this is packaged into a single string for assignment back to DIR_STACK. Thus, this line of code handles the special initial case (when the stack is empty) as well as the more usual case (when it's not empty).

The third line's main purpose is to change to the new directory. We use the **:?** operator to handle the error when the argument is missing: if the argument is given, then the expression **${dirname:?"missing directory name."}** evaluates to **$dirname**, but if it is not given, the shell will print the message **pushd: dirname: missing directory name** and exit from the function.

The last line merely prints the contents of the stack, with the implication that the leftmost directory is both the current directory and at the top of the stack. (This is why we chose spaces to separate directories, rather than the more customary colons as in PATH and MAILPATH.)

The *popd* function makes yet another use of the shell's pattern-matching operators. Its first line uses the **#** operator, which tries to delete the shortest match of the pattern "*** **" (anything followed by a space) from the value of DIR_STACK. The result is that the top directory and the space following it are deleted from the stack. This is why we need the space on the end of the first directory pushed onto the stack.

The second line of *popd* uses the pattern-matching operator **%%** to delete the *longest* match to the pattern " *****" (a space followed by anything) from DIR_STACK. This extracts the top directory as an argument to **cd**, but doesn't affect the value of

DIR_STACK because there is no assignment. The final line just prints a confirmation message.

This code is deficient in four ways. First, it has no provision for errors. For example:

- What if the user tries to push a directory that doesn't exist or is invalid?

- What if the user tries *popd* and the stack is empty?

Test your understanding of the code by figuring out how it would respond to these error conditions. The second problem is that if you use *pushd* in a shell script, it will exit everything if no argument is given; ${*varname*: ? *message*} always exits from non-interactive shells. It won't, however, exit an interactive shell from which the function is called. The third deficiency is that it implements only some of the functionality of *bash*'s *pushd* and *popd* commands—albeit the most useful parts. In the next chapter, we will see how to overcome all of these deficiencies.

The fourth problem with the code is that it will not work if, for some reason, a directory name contains a space. The code will treat the space as a separator character. We'll accept this deficiency for now, but you might like to think about how to overcome it in the next few chapters.

In this chapter:
- *if/else*
- *for*
- *case*
- *select*
- *while and until*

5

Flow Control

If you are a programmer, you may have read the last chapter—with its claim at the outset that *bash* has an advanced set of programming capabilities—and wondered where many of the features from conventional languages were. Perhaps the most glaringly obvious "hole" in our coverage thus far concerns *flow control* constructs like **if**, **for**, **while**, and so on.

Flow control gives a programmer the power to specify that only certain portions of a program run, or that certain portions run repeatedly, according to conditions such as the values of variables, whether or not commands execute properly, and others. We call this the ability to control the flow of a program's execution.

Almost every shell script or function that's been shown thus far has had no flow control—they have just been lists of commands to be run! Yet *bash*, like the C and Bourne shells, has all of the flow control abilities you would expect and more; we will examine them in this chapter. We'll use them to enhance the solutions to some of the programming tasks we saw in the last chapter and to solve tasks that we will introduce here.

Although we have attempted to explain flow control so that non-programmers can understand it, we also sympathize with programmers who dread having to slog through yet another *tabula rasa* explanation. For this reason, some of our discussions relate *bash*'s flow-control mechanisms to those that programmers should know already. Therefore you will be in a better position to understand this chapter if you already have a basic knowledge of flow control concepts.

bash supports the following flow control constructs:

if/else
>   Execute a list of statements if a certain condition is/is not true

for

    Execute a list of statements a fixed number of times

while

    Execute a list of statements repeatedly *while* a certain condition holds true

until

    Execute a list of statements repeatedly *until* a certain condition holds true

case

    Execute one of several lists of statements depending on the value of a variable

In addition, *bash* provides a new type of flow-control construct:

select

    Allow the user to select one of a list of possibilities from a menu

We will now cover each of these in detail.

if/else

The simplest type of flow control construct is the *conditional*, embodied in *bash*'s **if** statement. You use a conditional when you want to choose whether or not to do something, or to choose among a small number of things to do, according to the truth or falsehood of *conditions*. Conditions test values of shell variables, characteristics of files, whether or not commands run successfully, and other factors. The shell has a large set of built-in tests that are relevant to the task of shell programming.

The **if** construct has the following syntax:

```
if condition
then
    statements
[elif condition
    then statements...]
[else
    statements]
fi
```

The simplest form (without the **elif** and **else** parts, or *clauses*) executes the *statements* only if the *condition* is true. If you add an **else** clause, you get the ability to execute one set of statements if a condition is true or another set of statements if the condition is false. You can use as many **elif** (a contraction of "else if") clauses as you wish; they introduce more conditions, and thus more choices for which set of statements to execute. If you use one or more **elif**s, you can think of the **else** clause as the "if all *else* fails" part.

Exit Status and Return

Perhaps the only aspect of this syntax that differs from that of conventional languages like C and Pascal is that the "condition" is really a list of statements rather than the more usual Boolean (true or false) expression. How is the truth or falsehood of the condition determined? It has to do with a general UNIX concept that we haven't covered yet: the *exit status* of commands.

Every UNIX command, whether it comes from source code in C, some other language, or a shell script/function, returns an integer code to its calling process—the shell in this case—when it finishes. This is called the exit status. 0 is *usually* the OK exit status, while anything else (1 to 255) *usually* denotes an error.*

if checks the exit status of the *last* statement in the list following the **if** keyword. The list is usually just a single statement. If the status is 0, the condition evaluates to true; if it is anything else, the condition is considered false. The same is true for each condition attached to an **elif** statement (if any).

This enables us to write code of the form:

```
if command ran successfully
then
    normal processing
else
    error processing
fi
```

More specifically, we can now improve on the *pushd* function that we saw in the last chapter:

```
pushd ()
{
    dirname=$1
    DIR_STACK="$dirname ${DIR_STACK:-$PWD' '}"
    cd ${dirname:?"missing directory name."}
    echo $DIR_STACK
}
```

This function requires a valid directory as its argument. Let's look at how it handles error conditions: if no argument is given, the third line of code prints an error message and exits. This is fine.

However, the function reacts deceptively when an argument is given that isn't a valid directory. In case you didn't figure it out when reading the last chapter, here is what happens: the **cd** fails, leaving you in the same directory you were in. This

---

* Because this is a convention and not a "law," there are exceptions. For example, *diff* (find differences between two files) returns 0 for "no differences," 1 for "differences found," or 2 for an error such as an invalid filename argument.

is also appropriate. But the second line of code has pushed the bad directory onto the stack anyway, and the last line prints a message that leads you to believe that the push was successful. Even placing the **cd** before the stack assignment won't help because it doesn't exit the function if there is an error.

We need to prevent the bad directory from being pushed and to print an error message. Here is how we can do this:

```
pushd ()
{
  dirname=$1
  if cd ${dirname:?"missing directory name."}     # if cd was successful
  then
      DIR_STACK="$dirname ${DIR_STACK:-$PWD' '}" # push the directory
      echo $DIR_STACK
  else
      echo still in $PWD.                          # else do nothing
  fi
}
```

The call to **cd** is now inside an **if** construct. If **cd** is successful, it will return 0; the next two lines of code are run, finishing the *pushd* operation. But if the **cd** fails, it returns with exit status 1, and *pushd* will print a message saying that you haven't gone anywhere.

Notice that in providing the check for a bad directory, we have slightly altered the way *pushd* functions. The stack will now always start out with two copies of the first directory pushed onto it. That is because **$PWD** is expanded after the new directory has been changed to. We'll fix this in the next section.

You can usually rely on built-in commands and standard UNIX utilities to return appropriate exit statuses, but what about your own shell scripts and functions? For example, what if you wrote a **cd** function that overrides the built-in command?

Let's say you have the following code in your *.bash_profile*.

```
cd ()
{
    builtin cd "$@"
    echo "$OLDPWD --> $PWD"
}
```

The function *cd* simply changes directories and prints a message saying where you were and where you are now. Because functions have higher priority than most built-in commands in the shell's order of command look-up, we need to make sure that the built-in **cd** is called, otherwise the shell will enter an endless loop of calling the function, known as *infinite recursion*.

The **builtin** command allows us to do this. **builtin** tells the shell to use the built-in command and ignore any function of that name. Using **builtin** is easy; you just give it the name of the built-in you want to execute and any parameters you want to pass. If you pass in the name of something which isn't a built-in command, **builtin** will display an appropriate message. For example: **builtin: alice: not a shell builtin**.

We want this function to return the same exit status that the built-in **cd** returns. The problem is that the exit status is reset by every command, so it "disappears" if you don't save it immediately. In this function, the built-in **cd**'s exit status disappears when the **echo** statement runs (and sets its own exit status).

Therefore, we need to save the status that **cd** sets and use it as the entire function's exit status. Two shell features we haven't seen yet provide the way. First is the special shell variable **?**, whose value (**$?**) is the exit status of the last command that ran. For example:

```
cd baddir
echo $?
```

causes the shell to print **1**, while the following command causes it to print **0**:

```
cd gooddir
echo $?
```

So, to save the exit status we need to assign the value of **?** to a variable with the line **es=$?** right after the **cd** is done.

Return

The second feature we need is the statement **return** *N*, which causes the surrounding function to exit with exit status *N*. *N* is actually optional; it defaults to the exit status of the last command. Functions that finish without a **return** statement (i.e., every one we have seen so far) return whatever the last statement returns. **return** can only be used inside functions, and shell scripts that have been executed with **source**. In contrast, the statement **exit** *N* exits the entire script, no matter how deeply you are nested in functions.

Getting back to our example: if the call to the built-in **cd** were last in our *cd* function, it would behave properly. Unfortunately, we really need the assignment statement where it is. Therefore we need to save **cd**'s exit status and return it as the function's exit status. Here is how to do it:

```
cd ()
{
    builtin cd "$@"
    es=$?
    echo "$OLDPWD --> $PWD"
    return $es
}
```

The second line saves the exit status of **cd** in the variable **es**; the fourth returns it as the function's exit status. We'll see a substantial **cd** "wrapper" in Chapter 7.

Exit statuses aren't very useful for anything other than their intended purpose. In particular, you may be tempted to use them as "return values" of functions, as you would with functions in C or Pascal. That won't work; you should use variables or command substitution instead to simulate this effect.

Combinations of Exit Statuses

One of the more obscure parts of *bash* syntax allows you to combine exit statuses logically, so that you can test more than one thing at a time.

The syntax *statement1* **&&** *statement2* means, "execute *statement1*, and if its exit status is 0, execute *statement2*." The syntax *statement1* || *statement2* is the converse: it means, "execute *statement1*, and if its exit status is *not* 0, execute *statement2*." At first, these look like "if/then" and "if not/then" constructs, respectively. But they are really intended for use within conditions of **if** constructs—as C programmers will readily understand.

It's much more useful to think of these constructs as "and" and "or," respectively. Consider this:

```
if statement1 && statement2
then
    ...
fi
```

In this case, *statement1* is executed. If it returns a 0 status, then presumably it ran without error. Then *statement2* runs. The **then** clause is executed if *statement2* returns a 0 status. Conversely, if *statement1* fails (returns a non-zero exit status), then *statement2* doesn't even run; the last statement that actually ran was *statement1*, which failed—so the **then** clause doesn't run, either. Taken all together, it's fair to conclude that the **then** clause runs if *statement1* and *statement2* both succeeded.

Similarly, consider this:

```
if statement1 || statement2
then
    ...
fi
```

If *statement1* succeeds, then *statement2* does *not* run. This makes *statement1* the last statement, which means that the **then** clause runs. On the other hand, if *statement1* fails, then *statement2* runs, and whether the **then** clause runs or not depends on the success of *statement2*. The upshot is that the **then** clause runs if *statement1* or *statement2* succeeds.

bash also allows you to reverse the return status of a statement with the use of !, the logical "not". Preceding a statement with ! will cause it to return 0 if it fails and 1 if it succeeds. We'll see an example of this at the end of this chapter.

As a simple example of testing exit statuses, assume that we need to write a script that checks a file for the presence of two words and just prints a message saying whether *either* word is in the file or not. We can use *grep* for this: it returns exit status 0 if it found the given string in its input, non-zero if not:

```
filename=$1
word1=$2
word2=$3

if grep $word1 $filename || grep $word2 $filename
then
     echo "$word1 or $word2 is in $filename."
fi
```

The **then** clause of this code runs if either *grep* statement succeeds. Now assume that we want the script to say whether the input file contains *both* words. Here's how to do it:

```
filename=$1
word1=$2
word2=$3

if grep $word1 $filename && grep $word2 $filename
then
     echo "$word1 and $word2 are both in $filename."
fi
```

We'll see more examples of these logical operators later in this chapter.

Condition Tests

Exit statuses are the only things an **if** construct can test. But that doesn't mean you can check only whether commands ran properly. The shell provides a way of testing a variety of conditions with the [...] construct.*

You can use the construct to check many different attributes of a file (whether it exists, what type of file it is, what its permissions and ownership are, etc.), compare two files to see which is newer, and do comparisons on strings.

[*condition*] is actually a statement just like any other, except that the only thing it does is return an exit status that tells whether *condition* is true. (The spaces after

---

* The built-in command **test** is synonymous with [...]. For example, to test the equivalence of two strings you can either put [*string1* = *string2*] or **test** *string1* = *string2*.

the opening bracket "[" and before the closing bracket "]" are required.) Thus it fits within the **if** construct's syntax.

String comparisons

The square brackets ([]) surround expressions that include various types of *operators*. We will start with the string comparison operators, listed in Table 5-1. (Notice that there are no operators for "greater than or equal" or "less than or equal" comparisons.) In the table, *str1* and *str2* refer to expressions with a string value.

Table 5-1: String Comparison Operators

Operator	True if . . .
str1 = *str2*[a]	*str1* matches *str2*
str1 != *str2*	*str1* does not match *str2*
str1 < *str2*	*str1* is less than *str2*
str1 > *str2*	*str1* is greater than *str2*
−n *str1*	*str1* is not null (has length greater than 0)
−z *str1*	*str1* is null (has length 0)

a. Note that there is only one equal sign (=). This is a common source of error.

We can use one of these operators to improve our *popd* function, which reacts badly if you try to pop and the stack is empty. Recall that the code for *popd* is:

```
popd ()
{
    DIR_STACK=${DIR_STACK#* }
    cd ${DIR_STACK%% *}
    echo "$PWD"
}
```

If the stack is empty, then **$DIR_STACK** is the null string, as is the expression **${DIR_STACK%% }**. This means that you will change to your home directory; instead, we want *popd* to print an error message and do nothing.

To accomplish this, we need to test for an empty stack, i.e., whether **$DIR_STACK** is null or not. Here is one way to do it:

```
popd ()
{
    if [ -n "$DIR_STACK" ]; then
        DIR_STACK=${DIR_STACK#* }
        cd ${DIR_STACK%% *}
        echo "$PWD"
    else
        echo "stack empty, still in $PWD."
    fi
}
```

In the condition, we have placed the **$DIR_STACK** in double quotes, so that when it is expanded it is treated as a single word. If you don't do this, the shell will expand **$DIR_STACK** to individual words and the test will complain that it was given too many arguments.

There is another reason for placing **$DIR_STACK** in double quotes, which will become important later on: sometimes the variable being tested will expand to nothing, and in this example the test will become [-n], which returns **true**. Surrounding the variable in double quotes ensures that even if it expands to nothing, there will be an empty string as an argument (i.e., [-n ""]).

Also notice that instead of putting **then** on a separate line, we put it on the same line as the **if** after a semicolon, which is the shell's standard statement separator character.

We could have used operators other than **−n**. For example, we could have used **−z** and switched the code in the **then** and **else** clauses.

While we're cleaning up code we wrote in the last chapter, let's fix up the error handling in the *highest* script (Task 4-1). The code for that script was:

```
filename=${1:?"filename missing."}
howmany=${2:-10}
sort -nr $filename | head -$howmany
```

Recall that if you omit the first argument (the filename), the shell prints the message **highest: 1: filename missing**. We can make this better by substituting a more standard "usage" message. While we are at it, we can also make the command more in line with conventional UNIX commands by requiring a dash before the optional argument.

```
if [ -z "$1" ]; then
    echo 'usage: highest filename [-N]'
else
  filename=$1
  howmany=${2:--10}
  sort -nr $filename | head $howmany
fi
```

Notice that we have moved the dash in front of **$howmany** inside the parameter expansion **${2:--10}**.

It is considered better programming style to enclose all of the code in the **if-then-else**, but such code can get confusing if you are writing a long script in which you need to check for errors and bail out at several points along the way. Therefore, a more usual style for shell programming follows.

```
if [ -z "$1" ]; then
    echo 'usage: highest filename [-N]'
    exit 1
fi

filename=$1
howmany=${2:--10}
sort -nr $filename | head $howmany
```

The **exit** statement informs any calling program whether it ran successfully or not.

As an example of the = operator, we can add to the graphics utility that we touched on in Task 4-2. Recall that we were given a filename ending in *.pcx* (the original graphics file), and we needed to contruct a filename that was the same but ended in *.gif* (the output file). It would be nice to be able to convert several other types of formats to GIF files so that we could use them on a Web page. Some common types we might want to convert besides PCX include XPM (X PixMap), TGA (Targa), TIFF (Tagged Image File Format), and JPEG (Joint Photographics Expert Group).

We won't attempt to perform the actual manipulations needed to convert one graphics format to another ourselves. Instead we'll use some tools that are freely available on the Internet, conversion utilities from the NetPBM archive and from the Independent JPEG Group.*

Don't worry about the details of how these utilities work; all we want to do is create a shell frontend that processes the filenames and calls the correct conversion utilities. At this point it is sufficient to know that each conversion utility takes a filename as an argument and sends the results of the conversion to standard output. To reduce the number of conversion programs necessary to convert between the thirty or so different graphics formats it supports, NetPBM has its own format: a Portable Anymap file, also called a PNM, with extensions format has a utility to convert to and from this "central" PNM format.

The frontend script we are developing should first choose the correct conversion utility based on the filename extension, and then convert the resulting PNM file into a GIF:

```
filename=$1
extension=${filename##*.}
ppmfile=${filename%.*}.ppm
outfile=${filename%.*}.gif
```

---

* NetPBM is a portable graphics conversion utility package derived from another package written in the late '80s by Jef Poskanzer, called PBMplus. It is freely available from many FTP sites including *ftp://ftp.x.org/contrib/utilities/netpbm-1mar1994.tar.gz*. NetPBM doesn't include any conversion utilities for handling JPEG files (JPEG, like GIF, is a popular graphics format for Web pages) but the necessary utilities, which are *cjpeg* and *djpeg*, are available from the Independent JPEG Group at *ftp://ftp.uu.net/graphics/jpeg/*.

```
if [ -z $filename ]; then
    echo "procfile: No file specified"
    exit 1
fi

if [ $extension = gif ]; then
    exit 0
elif [ $extension = tga ]; then
    tgatoppm $filename > $ppmfile
elif [ $extension = xpm ]; then
    xpmtoppm $filename > $ppmfile
elif [ $extension = pcx ]; then
    pcxtoppm $filename > $ppmfile
elif [ $extension = tif ]; then
    tifftopnm $filename > $ppmfile
elif [ $extension = jpg ]; then
    djpeg $filename > $ppmfile
else
    echo "procfile: $filename is an unknown graphics file."
    exit 1
fi

ppmquant -quiet 256 $ppmfile | ppmtogif -quiet > $outfile

rm $ppmfile
```

Recall from the previous chapter that the expression **${filename%.*}** deletes the extension from **filename**; **${filename##*.}** deletes the basename and keeps the extension.

Once the correct conversion is chosen, the script runs the utility and writes the output to a temporary file. The second to last line takes the temporary file, performs some magic, and then converts it to a GIF.* The temporary file is then removed. Notice that if the original file was a GIF we just exit without having to do any processing.

This script has a few problems. We'll look at improving it later in this chapter.

File attribute checking

The other kind of operator that can be used in conditional expressions checks a file for certain properties. There are 20 such operators. We will cover those of most general interest here; the rest refer to arcana like sticky bits, sockets, and file descriptors, and thus are of interest only to systems hackers. Refer to Appendix B, *Reference Lists*, for the complete list. Table 5-2 lists those that we will examine.

---

* **ppmquant** *quantizes* the image. Some of the input formats have a higher number of colors than GIF's maximum of 256 colors, so we have to compress the colors down to 256 or fewer. This is one good reason why GIF shouldn't be used for "real world" images, e.g., photographs of people or landscapes. However, for the purposes of this and future examples, we'll stick with the GIF format.

Table 5-2: File Attribute Operators

Operator	True if ...
-d *file*	*file* exists and is a directory
-e *file*	*file* exists
-f *file*	*file* exists and is a regular file (i.e., not a directory or other special type of file)
-r *file*	You have read permission on *file*
-s *file*	*file* exists and is not empty
-w *file*	You have write permission on *file*
-x *file*	You have execute permission on *file*, or directory search permission if it is a directory
-O *file*	You own *file*
-G *file*	*file*'s group ID matches yours (or one of yours, if you are in multiple groups).
file1 **-nt** *file2*	*file1* is newer than *file2*[a]
file1 **-ot** *file2*	*file1* is older than *file2*

a. Specifically, the **-nt** and **-ot** operators compare *modification times* of two files.

Before we get to an example, you should know that conditional expressions inside [and] can also be combined using the logical operators **&&** and **||**, just as we saw with plain shell commands, in the previous section entitled "Combinations of Exit Statuses." For example:

```
if [ condition ] && [ condition ]; then
```

It's also possible to combine shell commands with conditional expressions using logical operators, like this:

```
if command && [ condition ]; then
    ...
```

You can also negate the truth value of a conditional expression by preceding it with an exclamation point (!), so that ! *expr* evaluates to true only if *expr* is false. Furthermore, you can make complex logical expressions of conditional operators by grouping them with parentheses (which must be "escaped" with backslashes to prevent the shell from treating them specially), and by using two logical operators we haven't seen yet: **-a** (AND) and **-o** (OR).

The **-a** and **-o** operators are similar to the **&&** and **||** operators used with exit statuses. However, unlike those operators, **-a** and **-o** are only available inside a **test** conditional expression.

Here is how we would use two of the file operators, a logical operator, and a string operator to fix the problem of duplicate stack entries in our *pushd* function. Instead of having **cd** determine whether the argument given is a valid directory—

i.e., by returning with a bad exit status if it's not—we can do the checking ourselves. Here is the code:

```
pushd ()
{
    dirname=$1
    if [ -n "$dirname" ] && [ \( -d "$dirname" \) -a \
            \( -x "$dirname" \) ]; then
        DIR_STACK="$dirname ${DIR_STACK:-$PWD' '}"
        cd $dirname
        echo "$DIR_STACK"
    else
        echo "still in $PWD."
    fi
}
```

The conditional expression evaluates to true only if the argument **$1** is not null
(**–n**), a directory (**–d**) *and* the user has permission to change to it (**–x**).* Notice
that this conditional handles the case where the argument is missing (**$dirname** is
null) first; if it is, the rest of the condition is *not* executed. This is important
because, if we had just put:

```
if [ \( -n "$dirname"\) -a  \( -d "$dirname" \) -a \
        \( -x "$dirname" \) ]; then
```

the second condition, if null, would cause **test** to complain and the function would
exit prematurely.

Here is a more comprehensive example of the use of file operators.

Task 5-1

Write a script that prints essentially the same information as **ls –l** but in a more
user-friendly way.

Although this task requires relatively long-winded code, it is a straightforward
application of many of the file operators:

```
if [ ! -e "$1" ]; then
    echo "file $1 does not exist."
    exit 1
fi
if [ -d "$1" ]; then
    echo -n "$1 is a directory that you may "
    if [ ! -x "$1" ]; then
        echo -n "not "
    fi
```

---

* Remember that the same permission flag that determines execute permission on a regular file determines search permission on a directory. This is why the **–x** operator checks both things depending on
file type.

```
        echo "search."
elif [ -f "$1" ]; then
        echo "$1 is a regular file."
else
        echo "$1 is a special type of file."
fi
if [ -O "$1" ]; then
        echo 'you own the file.'
else
        echo 'you do not own the file.'
fi
if [ -r "$1" ]; then
        echo 'you have read permission on the file.'
fi
if [ -w "$1" ]; then
        echo 'you have write permission on the file.'
fi
if [ -x "$1" -a ! -d "$1" ]; then
        echo 'you have execute permission on the file.'
fi
```

We'll call this script *fileinfo*. Here's how it works:

- The first conditional tests if the file given as argument does *not* exist (the exclamation point is the "not" operator; the spaces around it are required). If the file does not exist, the script prints an error message and exits with error status.

- The second conditional tests if the file is a directory. If so, the first *echo* prints part of a message; remember that the **–n** option tells *echo* not to print a LINEFEED at the end. The inner conditional checks if you do *not* have search permission on the directory. If you don't have search permission, the word "not" is added to the partial message. Then, the message is completed with "search." and a LINEFEED.

- The **elif** clause checks if the file is a regular file; if so, it prints a message.

- The **else** clause accounts for the various special file types on recent UNIX systems, such as sockets, devices, FIFO files, etc. We assume that the casual user isn't interested in details of these.

- The next conditional tests to see if the file is owned by you (i.e., if its owner ID is the same as your login ID). If so, it prints a message saying that you own it.

- The next two conditionals test for your read and write permission on the file.

- The last conditional checks if you can execute the file. It checks to see if you have execute permission and that the file is *not* a directory. (If the file were a directory, execute permission would really mean directory search permission.) In this test we haven't used any brackets to group the tests and have relied on *operator precedence*. Simply put, operator precedence is the order in which the shell processes the operators. This is exactly the same concept as arithmetic precedence in mathematics, where multiply and divide are done before addition and subtraction. In our case, [−x "$1" −a ! −d "$1"] is equivalent to [\(−x "$1" \) −a \(! −d "$1" \)]. The file tests are done first, followed by any negations (!) and followed by the AND and OR tests.

As an example of *fileinfo*'s output, assume that you do an **ls −l** of your current directory and it contains these lines:

```
-rwxr-xr-x   1 cam      users        2987 Jan 10 20:43 adventure
-rw-r--r--   1 cam      users          30 Jan 10 21:45 alice
-r--r--r--   1 root     root        58379 Jan 11 21:30 core
drwxr-xr-x   2 cam      users        1024 Jan 10 21:41 dodo
```

alice and *core* are regular files, *dodo* is a directory, and *adventure* is a shell script. Typing **fileinfo adventure** produces this output:

```
adventure is a regular file.
you own the file.
you have read permission on the file.
you have write permission on the file.
you have execute permission on the file.
```

Typing **fileinfo alice** results in this:

```
alice is a regular file.
you own the file.
you have read permission on the file.
you have write permission on the file.
```

Finally, typing **fileinfo dodo** results in this:

```
dodo is a directory that you may search.
you own the file.
you have read permission on the file.
you have write permission on the file.
```

Typing **fileinfo core** produces this:

```
core is a regular file.
you do not own the file.
you have read permission on the file.
```

Integer Conditionals

The shell also provides a set of *arithmetic* tests. These are different from *character string* comparisons like < and >, which compare *lexicographic* values of strings,[*] not numeric values. For example, "6" is greater than "57" lexicographically, just as

---

[*] "Lexicographic order" is really just "dictionary order."

"p" is greater than "ox," but of course the opposite is true when they're compared as integers.

The integer comparison operators are summarized in Table 5-3.

Table 5-3: Arithmetic Test Operators

Test	Comparison
−lt	Less than
−le	Less than or equal
−eq	Equal
−ge	Greater than or equal
−gt	Greater than
−ne	Not equal

You'll find these to be of the most use in the context of the integer variables we'll see in the next chapter. They're necessary if you want to combine integer tests with other types of tests within the same conditional expression.

However, the shell has a separate syntax for conditional expressions that involve integers only. It's considerably more efficient, so you should use it in preference to the arithmetic test operators listed above. Again, we'll cover the shell's integer conditionals in the next chapter.

for

The most obvious enhancement we could make to the previous script is the ability to report on multiple files instead of just one. Tests like **−e** and **−d** take only single arguments, so we need a way of calling the code once for each file given on the command line.

The way to do this—indeed, the way to do many things with *bash*—is with a looping construct. The simplest and most widely applicable of the shell's looping constructs is the **for** loop. We'll use **for** to enhance *fileinfo* soon.

The **for** loop allows you to repeat a section of code a fixed number of times. During each time through the code (known as an *iteration*), a special variable called a *loop variable* is set to a different value; this way each iteration can do something slightly different.

The **for** loop is somewhat, but not entirely, similar to its counterparts in conventional languages like C and Pascal. The chief difference is that the shell's **for** loop doesn't let you specify a number of times to iterate or a range of values over which to iterate; instead, it only lets you give a fixed list of values. In other words, you can't do anything like this Pascal-type code, which executes *statements* 10 times:

```
for x := 1 to 10 do
begin
    statements...
end
```

(You need the **while** construct, which we'll see soon, to construct this type of loop. You also need the ability to do integer arithmetic, which we will see in Chapter 6, *Command-Line Options and Typed Variables*.)

However, the **for** loop is ideal for working with arguments on the command line and with sets of files (e.g., all files in a given directory). We'll look at an example of each of these. But first, we'll show the syntax for the **for** construct:

```
for name [in list]
do
    statements that can use $name...
done
```

The *list* is a list of names. (If **in** *list* is omitted, the list defaults to "$@", i.e., the quoted list of command-line arguments, but we'll always supply the **in** *list* for the sake of clarity.) In our solutions to the following task, we'll show two simple ways to specify lists.

Task 5-2

Task 4-4 used pattern matching and substitution to list the directories in **PATH**, one to a line. Unfortunately, old versions of *bash* don't have that particular pattern operator. Write a general shell script, *listpath*, that prints each directory in **PATH**, one per line. In addition, have it print out information about each directory, such as the permissions and the modification times.

The easiest way to do this is by changing the **IFS** variable we saw in Chapter 4:

```
IFS=:

for dir in $PATH
do
    ls -ld $dir
done
```

This sets the **IFS** to be a colon, which is the separator used in **PATH**. The **for** loop then loops through, setting **dir** to each of the colon delimited fields in **PATH**. *ls* is used to print out the directory name and associated information. The **−l** parameter specifies the "long" format and the **−d** tells ls to show only the directory itself and not its contents.

In using this you might see an error generated by *ls* saying, for example, **ls: /usr/TeX/bin: No such file or directory**. It indicates that a directory in **PATH** doesn't exist. We can modify the *listpath* script to check the **PATH** variable for nonexistent directories by adding some of the tests we saw earlier;

```
IFS=:

for dir in $PATH; do
    if [ -z "$dir" ]; then dir=.; fi

    if ! [ -e "$dir" ]; then
        echo "$dir doesn't exist"
    elif ! [ -d "$dir" ]; then
        echo "$dir isn't a directory"
    else
        ls -ld $dir
    fi
done
```

This time, as the script loops, we first check to see if the length of **$dir** is zero (caused by having a value of :: in the **PATH**). If it is, we set it to the current directory. Then we check to see if the directory *doesn't* exist. If it doesn't, we print out an appropriate message. Otherwise we check to see if the file is not a directory. If it isn't, we say so.

The foregoing illustrated a simple use of **for**, but it's much more common to use **for** to iterate through a list of command-line arguments. To show this, we can enhance the *fileinfo* script above to accept multiple arguments. First, we write a bit of "wrapper" code that does the iteration:

```
for filename in "$@" ; do
    finfo "$filename"
    echo
done
```

Next, we make the original script into a function called *finfo*:*

```
finfo ()
{
    if [ ! -e "$1" ]; then
        print "file $1 does not exist."
        return 1
    fi
    ...
}
```

The complete script consists of the **for** loop code and the above function, in either order; good programming style dictates that the function definition should go first.

---

* A function can have the same name as a script; however, this isn't good programming practice.

The *fileinfo* script works as follows: in the **for** statement, `"$@"` is a list of all positional parameters. For each argument, the body of the loop is run with **filename** set to that argument. In other words, the function *finfo* is called once for each value of **$filename** as its first argument (**$1**). The call to *echo* after the call to *finfo* merely prints a blank line between sets of information about each file.

Given a directory with the same files as the earlier example, typing **fileinfo** * would produce the following output:

```
adventure is a regular file.
you own the file.
you have read permission on the file.
you have write permission on the file.
you have execute permission on the file.

alice is a regular file.
you own the file.
you have read permission on the file.
you have write permission on the file.

core is a regular file.
you do not own the file.
you have read permission on the file.

dodo is a directory that you may search.
you own the file.
you have read permission on the file.
you have write permission on the file.
```

Here is a programming task that exploits the other major use of **for**.

Task 5-3

It is possible to print out all of the directories below a given one by using the **–R** option of *ls*. Unfortunately, this doesn't give much idea about the directory structure because it prints all the files and directories line by line. Write a script that performs a recursive directory listing and produces output that gives an idea of the structure for a small number of subdirectories.

We'll probably want output that looks something like this:

```
.
    adventure
            aaiw
                    dodo
                    duchess
                    hatter
                    march_hare
                    queen
                    tarts
            biog
```

```
            ttlg
                    red_queen
                    tweedledee
                    tweedledum
        lewis.carroll
```

Each column represents a directory level. Entries below and to the right of an entry are files and directories under that directory. Files are just listed with no entries to their right. This example shows that the directory *adventure* and the file *lewis.carroll* are in the current directory; the directories *aaiw* and *ttlg*, and the file *biog* are under *adventure*, etc. To make life simple, we'll use TABs to line the columns up and ignore any "bleed over" of filenames from one column into an adjacent one.

We need to be able to traverse the directory hierarchy. To do this easily we'll use a programming technique known as *recursion*. Recursion is simply referencing something from itself; in our case, calling a piece of code from itself. For example, consider this script, *tracedir*, in your home directory:

```
file=$1
echo $file

if [ -d "$file" ]; then
    cd $file
    ~/tracedir $(ls)
    cd ..
fi
```

First we copy and print the first argument. Then we test to see if it is a directory. If it is, we **cd** to it and call the script again with an argument of the files in that directory. This script is recursive; when the first argument is a directory, a new shell is invoked and a new script is run on the new directory. The old script waits until the new script returns, then the old script executes a **cd** back up one level and exits. This happens in each invocation of the *tracedir* script. The recursion will stop only when the first argument isn't a directory.

Running this on the directory structure listed above with the argument *adventure* will produce:

```
adventure
aaiw
dodo
```

dodo is a file and the script exits.

This script has a few problems, but it is the basis for the solution to this task. One major problem with the script is that it is very inefficient. Each time the script is called, a new shell is created. We can improve on this by making the script into a function, because (as you probably remember from Chapter 4, *Basic Shell*

Programming) functions are part of the shell they are started from. We also need a way to set up the TAB spacing. The easiest way is to have an initializing script or function and call the recursive routine from that. Let's look at this routine.

```
recls ()
{
    singletab="\t"

    for tryfile in "$@"; do
        echo $tryfile
        if [ -d "$tryfile" ]; then
            thisfile=$tryfile
            recdir $(command ls $tryfile)
        fi
    done

    unset dir singletab tab
}
```

First, we set up a variable to hold the TAB character for the **echo** command (Chapter 7, *Input/Output and Command-Line Processing*, explains all of the options and formatting commands you can use with **echo**). Then we loop through each argument supplied to the function and print it out. If it is a directory, we call our recursive routine, supplying the list of files with *ls*. We have introduced a new command at this point: **command**. **command** is a shell built-in that disables function and alias look-up. In this case, it is used to make sure that the *ls* command is one from your command search path, PATH, and not a function (for further information on **command**, see Chapter 7). After it's all over, we clean up by unsetting the variables we have used.

Now we can expand on our earlier shell script.

```
recdir ()
{
    tab=$tab$singletab

    for file in "$@"; do
        echo -e $tab$file
        thisfile=$thisfile/$file

        if [ -d "$thisfile" ]; then
            recdir $(command ls $thisfile)
        fi

        thisfile=${thisfile%/*}
    done

    tab=${tab%\t}
}
```

Each time it is called, *recdir* loops through the files it is given as arguments. For each one it prints the filename and then, if the file is a directory, calls itself with arguments set to the contents of the directory. There are two details that have to be taken care of: the number of TABs to use, and the pathname of the "current" directory in the recursion.

Each time we go down a level in the directory hierarchy we want to add a TAB character, so we append a TAB to the variable **tab** every time we enter *recdir*. Likewise, when we exit *recdir* we are moving up a directory level, so we remove the TAB when we leave the function. Initially, **tab** is not set, so the first time *recdir* is called, **tab** will be set to one TAB. If we recurse into a lower directory, *recdir* will be called again and another TAB will be appended. Remember that **tab** is a global variable, so it will grow and shrink in TABs for every entry and exit of *recdir*. The −e option to **echo** tells it to recognize escaped formatting characters, in our case the TAB character, \t.

In this version of the recursive routine we haven't used **cd** to move between directories. That means that an **ls** of a directory will have to be supplied with a relative path to files further down in the hierarchy. To do this, we need to keep track of the directory we are currently examining. The initialization routine sets the variable **thisfile** to the directory name each time a directory is found while looping. This variable is then used in the recursive routine to keep the relative pathname of the current file being examined. On each iteration of the loop, **thisfile** has the current filename appended to it, and at the end of the loop the filename is removed.

You might like to think of ways to modify the behavior and improve the output of this code. Here are some programming challenges:

1. In the current version, there is no way to determine if *biog* is a file or a directory. An empty directory looks no different to a file in the listing. Change the output so it appends a / to each directory name when it displays it.

2. Modify the code so that it only recurses down a maximum of eight subdirectories (which is about the maximum before the lines overflow the right-hand side of the screen). Hint: think about how TABs have been implemented.

3. Change the output so it includes dashed lines and adds a blank line after each directory, thus:

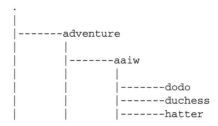

```
|         |          |-------march_hare
|         |          |-------queen
|         |          |-------tarts
|         |
|         |-------biog
...
```

Hint: You'll need at least two other variables that contain the characters "|" and "-".

case

The next flow-control construct we will cover is **case**. While the **case** statement in Pascal and the similar **switch** statement in C can be used to test simple values like integers and characters, *bash*'s **case** construct lets you test strings against patterns that can contain wildcard characters. Like its conventional-language counterparts, **case** lets you express a series of if-then-else type statements in a concise way.

The syntax of **case** is as follows:

```
case expression in
    pattern1 )
        statements ;;
    pattern2 )
        statements ;;
    ...
  esac
```

Any of the *pattern*s can actually be several patterns separated by pipe characters (|). If *expression* matches one of the patterns, its corresponding statements are executed. If there are several patterns separated by pipe characters, the expression can match any of them in order for the associated statements to be run. The patterns are checked in order until a match is found; if none is found, nothing happens.

This construct should become clearer with an example. Let's revisit our solution to Task 4-2 and the additions to it presented earlier in this chapter, our graphics utility. Remember that we wrote some code that processed input files according to their suffixes (*.pcx* for PCX format, *.jpg* for JPEG format, etc.).

We can improve upon this solution in two ways. Firstly, we can use a **for** loop to allow multiple files to be processed one at a time; secondly, we can use the **case** construct to streamline the code:

```
for filename in "$@"; do
    ppmfile=${filename%.*}.ppm

    case $filename in
        *.gif ) exit 0 ;;
```

```
          *.tga ) tgatoppm $filename > $ppmfile ;;

          *.xpm ) xpmtoppm $filename > $ppmfile ;;

          *.pcx ) pcxtoppm $filename > $ppmfile ;;

          *.tif ) tifftopnm $filename > $ppmfile ;;

          *.jpg ) djpeg $filename > $ppmfile ;;

              * ) echo "procfile: $filename is an unknown graphics file."
                  exit 1 ;;
      esac

      outfile=${ppmfile%.ppm}.new.gif

      ppmquant -quiet 256 $ppmfile | ppmtogif -quiet > $outfile
      rm $ppmfile

  done
```

The **case** construct in this code does the same thing as the **if** statements that we saw in the earlier version. It is, however, clearer and easier to follow.

The first six patterns in the **case** statement match the various file extensions that we wish to process. The last pattern matches anything that hasn't already been matched by the previous statements. It is essentially a catchall and is analogous to the **default** case in C.

There is another slight difference to the previous version; we have moved the pattern matching and replacement inside the added **for** loop that processes all of the command-line arguments. Each time we pass through the loop, we want to create a temporary and final file with a name based on the name in the current command-line argument.

We'll return to this example in Chapter 6, when we further develop the script and discuss how to handle dash options on the command line. In the meantime, here is a task that requires that we use **case**.

Task 5-4

Write a function that implements the Korn shell's **cd** *old new*. **cd** takes the pathname of the current directory and tries to find the string *old*. If it finds it, it substitutes *new* and attempts to change to the resulting directory.

We can implement this by using a **case** statement to check the number of arguments and the built-in **cd** command to do the actual change of directory.

Here is the code:*

```
cd()
{
    case "$#" in
        0 | 1)  builtin cd $1 ;;
        2     )  newdir=$(echo $PWD | sed -e "s:$1:$2:g")
                 case "$newdir" in
                     $PWD)   echo "bash: cd: bad substitution" >&2 ;
                         return 1 ;;
                     *  )    builtin cd "$newdir" ;;
                 esac ;;
        *     )  echo "bash: cd: wrong arg count" 1>&2 ; return 1 ;;
    esac
}
```

The **case** statement in this task tests the number of arguments to our **cd** command against three alternatives.

For zero or one arguments, we want our **cd** to work just like the built-in one. The first alternative in the **case** statement does this. It includes something we haven't used so far; the pipe symbol between the **0** and **1** means that either pattern is an acceptable match. If the number of arguments is either of these, the built-in **cd** is executed.

The next alternative is for two arguments, which is where we'll add the new functionality to **cd**. The first thing that has to be done is finding and replacing the old string with the new one. We use *sed* to perform this operation on the current directory, **s:$1:$2:g**, meaning globally substitute string **$2** for string **$1**. The result is then assigned to **newdir**. If the substitution didn't take place, the pathname will be unchanged. We'll use this fact in the next few lines.

Another **case** statement chooses between performing the **cd** or reporting an error because the new directory is unchanged. If *sed* is unable to find the *old* string, it leaves the pathname untouched. The ***** alternative is a catchall for anything other than the current pathname (caught by the first alternative).

You might notice one small problem with this code: if your old and new strings are the same you'll get **bash:: cd: bad substitution**. It should just leave you in the same directory with no error message, but because the directory path doesn't change, it uses the first alternative in the inner **case** statement. The problem lies in knowing if *sed* has performed a substitution or not. You might like to think about ways to fix this problem (hint: you could use *grep* to check whether the pathname has the *old* string in it).

---

* To make the function a little clearer, we've used some advanced I/O redirection. I/O redirection is covered in Chapter 7.

The last alternative in the outer **case** statement prints an error message if there are more than two arguments.

select

All of the flow-control constructs we have seen so far are also available in the Bourne shell, and the C shell has equivalents with different syntax. Our next construct, **select**, is available only in the Korn shell and *bash*;* moreover, it has no analogy in conventional programming languages.

select allows you to generate simple menus easily. It has concise syntax, but it does quite a lot of work. The syntax is:

```
select name [in list]
do
    statements that can use $name...
done
```

This is the same syntax as **for** except for the keyword **select**.

And like **for**, you can omit the **in** *list* and it will default to "$@", i.e., the list of quoted command-line arguments. Here is what **select** does:

- Generates a menu of each item in *list*, formatted with numbers for each choice
- Prompts the user for a number
- Stores the selected choice in the variable *name* and the selected number in the built-in variable **REPLY**
- Executes the statements in the body
- Repeats the process forever (but see below for how to exit)

Here is a task that adds another command to our *pushd* and *popd* utilities.

Task 5-5

> Write a function that allows the user to select a directory from a list of directories currently in the *pushd* directory stack. The selected directory is moved to the front of the stack and it becomes the current working directory.

The display and selection of directories is best handled by using **select**. We can start off with something along the lines of:†

---

* **select** is not available in *bash* versions prior to 1.14.

† Versions of *bash* prior to 1.14.3 have a serious bug with **select**. These versions will crash if the **select** list is empty. In this case, surround **select**s with a test for a null list.

```
selectd ()
{
    PS3='directory? '
    select selection in $DIR_STACK; do
        if [ $selection ]; then
            #statements that manipulate the stack...
            break
        else
            echo 'invalid selection.'
        fi
    done
}
```

If you type **DIR_STACK="/usr /home /bin"** and execute this function, you'll see:

```
1) /usr
2) /home
3) /bin
directory?
```

The built-in shell variable **PS3** contains the prompt string that **select** uses; its default value is the not particularly useful "#? ". So the first line of the above code sets it to a more relevant value.

The **select** statement constructs the menu from the list of choices. If the user enters a valid number (from 1 to the number of directories), then the variable **selection** is set to the corresponding value; otherwise it is null. (If the user just presses RETURN, the shell prints the menu again.)

The code in the loop body checks if **selection** is non-null. If so, it executes the statements we will add in a short while; then the **break** statement exits the **select** loop. If **selection** is null, the code prints an error message and repeats the menu and prompt.

The **break** statement is the usual way of exiting a **select** loop. Actually (like its analog in C), it can be used to exit any surrounding control structure we've seen so far (except **case**, where the double semicolons act like **break**) as well as the **while** and **until** we will see soon. We haven't introduced **break** until now because it is considered bad coding style to use it to exit a loop. However, it can make code easier to read if used judiciously. *break* is necessary for exiting **select** when the user makes a valid choice.*

Now we'll add the missing pieces to the code:

```
selectd ()
{
    PS3='directory? '
```

---

* A user can also type CTRL-D (for end-of-input) to get out of a **select** loop. This gives the user a uniform way of exiting, but it doesn't help the shell programmer much.

```
        dirstack=" $DIR_STACK "

    select selection in $dirstack; do
        if [ $selection ]; then
            DIR_STACK="$selection${dirstack%% $selection *}"
            DIR_STACK="$DIR_STACK ${dirstack##* $selection }"
            DIR_STACK=${DIR_STACK% }
            cd $selection
            break
        else
            echo 'invalid selection.'
        fi
    done
}
```

The first two lines initialize environment variables. **dirstack** is a copy of **DIR_STACK** with spaces appended at the beginning and end so that each directory in the list is of the form *space directory space*. This form simplifies the code when we come to manipulating the directory stack.

The **select** and **if** statements are the same as in our initial function. The new code inside the **if** uses *bash*'s pattern-matching capability to manipulate the directory stack.

The first statement sets **DIR_STACK** to **selection**, followed by **dirstack** with everything from **selection** to the end of the list removed. The second statement adds everything in the list from the directory following **selection** to the end of **DIR_STACK**. The next line removes the trailing space that was appended at the start. To complete the operation, a **cd** is performed to the new directory, followed by a **break** to exit the **select** code.

As an example of the list manipulation performed in this function, consider a **DIR_STACK** set to */home /bin /usr2*. In this case, **dirstack** would become */home /bin /usr2*. Typing *selectd* would result in:

```
$ selectd
1) /home
2) /bin
3) /usr2
directory?
```

After selecting */bin* from the list, the first statement inside the *if* section sets **DIR_STACK** to */bin* followed by **dirstack** with everything from */bin* onwards removed, i.e., */home*.

The second statement then takes **DIR_STACK** and appends everything in **dirstack** following */bin* (i.e., */usr2*) to it. The value of **DIR_STACK** becomes */bin /home /usr2*. The trailing space is removed in the next line.

while and until

The remaining two flow control constructs *bash* provides are **while** and **until**. These are similar; they both allow a section of code to be run repetitively while (or until) a certain condition becomes true. They also resemble analogous constructs in Pascal (**while/do** and **repeat/until**) and C (**while** and **do/until**).

while and **until** are actually most useful when combined with features we will see in the next chapter, such as integer arithmetic, input/output of variables, and command-line processing. Yet we can show a useful example even with what we have covered so far.

The syntax for **while** is:

```
while condition
do
    statements...
done
```

For **until**, just substitute **until** for **while** in the above example. As with **if**, the *condition* is really a list of *statements* that are run; the exit status of the last one is used as the value of the condition. You can use a conditional with **test** here, just as you can with **if**.

Note that the *only* difference between **while** and **until** is the way the condition is handled. In **while**, the loop executes as long as the condition is true; in **until**, it runs as long as the condition is false. The **until** condition is checked at the *top* of the loop, *not* at the bottom as it is in analogous constructs in C and Pascal.

The result is that you can convert any **until** into a **while** by simply negating the condition. The only place where **until** might be more meaningful is something like this:

```
until command; do
    statements...
done
```

The meaning of this is essentially, "Do *statements* until *command* runs correctly." This is not a likely contingency.

Here is an earlier task that can be rewritten using a **while**.

Task 5-6

Reimplement Task 5-2 without the use of the **IFS** variable.

We can use the **while** construct and pattern matching to traverse the **PATH** list:

```
path=$PATH:

while [ $path ]; do
    ls -ld ${path%%:*}
    path=${path#*:}
done
```

The first line copies **PATH** to a temporary copy, **path**, and appends a colon to it. Normally colons are used only between directories in **PATH**; adding one to the end makes the code simple.

Inside the **while** loop we display the directory with *ls* as we did in Task 5-2. **path** is then updated by removing the first directory pathname and colon (which is why we needed to append the colon in the first line of the script). The **while** will keep looping until **$path** expands to nothing (the empty string ""), which occurs once the last directory in **path** has been listed.

Here is another task that is a good candidate for **until**.

Task 5-7
_____

Write a script that attempts to copy a file to a directory and, if it fails, waits five seconds, then tries again, continuing until it succeeds.

Here is the code:

```
until cp $1 $2; do
    echo 'Attempt to copy failed. waiting...'
    sleep 5
done
```

This is a fairly simple use of **until**. First, we use the *cp* command to perform the copy for us. If it can't perform the copy for any reason, it will return with a non-zero exit code. We set our **until** loop so that if the result of the copy is *not* 0 then the script prints a message and waits five seconds.

As we said earlier, an **until** loop can be converted to a **while** by the use of the ! operator:

```
while ! cp $1 $2; do
    echo 'Attempt to copy failed. waiting...'
    sleep 5
done
```

In our opinion, you'll seldom need to use **until**; therefore, we'll use **while** throughout the rest of this book. We'll see further use of the **while** construct in Chapter 7.

6

Command-Line Options and Typed Variables

You should have a healthy grasp of shell programming techniques now that you have gone through the previous chapters. What you have learned up to this point enables you to write many non-trivial, useful shell scripts and functions.

Still, you may have noticed some remaining gaps in the knowledge you need to write shell code that behaves like the UNIX commands you are used to. In particular, if you are an experienced UNIX user, it might have occurred to you that none of the example scripts shown so far have the ability to handle *options* preceded by a dash (-) on the command line. And if you program in a conventional language like C or Pascal, you will have noticed that the only type of data that we have seen in shell variables is character strings; we haven't seen how to do arithmetic, for example.

These capabilities are certainly crucial to the shell's ability to function as a useful UNIX programming language. In this chapter, we will show how *bash* supports these and related features.

Command-Line Options

We have already seen many examples of the *positional parameters* (variables called 1, 2, 3, etc.) that the shell uses to store the command-line arguments to a shell script or function when it runs. We have also seen related variables like * (for the string of all arguments) and # (for the number of arguments).

Indeed, these variables hold all of the information on the user's command-line. But consider what happens when options are involved. Typical UNIX commands have the form *command [-options] args*, meaning that there can be 0 or more options. If a shell script processes the command **teatime alice hatter**, then $1 is "alice" and **$2** is "hatter". But if the command is **teatime −o alice hatter**, then **$1** is −o, **$2** is "alice", and **$3** is "hatter".

You might think you could write code like this to handle it:

```
if [ $1 = -o ]; then
    code that processes the -o option
    1=$2
    2=$3
fi

normal processing of $1 and $2...
```

But this code has several problems. First, assignments like **1=$2** are illegal because positional parameters are read-only. Even if they were legal, another problem is that this kind of code imposes limitations on how many arguments the script can handle—which is very unwise. Furthermore, if this command had several possible options, the code to handle all of them would get very messy very quickly.

shift

Luckily, the shell provides a way around this problem. The command **shift** performs the function of:

```
    1=$2
    2=$3
    ...
```

for every argument, regardless of how many there are. If you supply a numeric argument to **shift**, it will shift the arguments that many times over; for example, **shift 3** has this effect:

```
    1=$4
    2=$5
    ...
```

This leads immediately to some code that handles a single option (call it −o) and arbitrarily many arguments:

```
if [ $1 = -o ]; then
    process the -o option
    shift
fi
normal processing of arguments...
```

After the **if** construct, **$1**, **$2**, etc., are set to the correct arguments.

We can use **shift** together with the programming features we have seen so far to implement simple option schemes. However, we will need additional help when things get more complex. The **getopts** built-in command, which we will introduce later, provides this help.

shift by itself gives us enough power to implement the *−N* option to the *highest* script we saw in Chapter 4, *Basic Shell Programming* (Task 4-1). Recall that this script takes an input file that lists artists and the number of albums you have by them. It sorts the list and prints out the *N* highest numbers, in descending order. The code that does the actual data processing is:

```
filename=$1
howmany=${2:-10}
sort -nr $filename | head -$howmany
```

Our original syntax for calling this script was **highest** *filename* [−*N*], where *N* defaults to 10 if omitted. Let's change this to a more conventional UNIX syntax, in which options are given before arguments: **highest** [−*N*] *filename*. Here is how we would write the script with this syntax:

```
if [ -n "$(echo $1 | grep '^-[0-9][0-9]*$')" ]; then
    howmany=$1
    shift
elif [ -n "$(echo $1 | grep '^-')" ]; then
    print 'usage: highest [-N] filename'
    exit 1
else
    howmany="-10"
fi

filename=$1
sort -nr $filename | head $howmany
```

This uses the *grep* search utility to test if **$1** matches the appropriate pattern. To do this we provide the regular expression ^-[0-9][0-9]*$ to *grep*, which is interpreted as "an initial dash followed by a digit, optionally followed by one or more digits." If a match is found then *grep* will return the match and the test will be true, otherwise *grep* will return nothing and processing will pass to the **elif** test. Notice that we have enclosed the regular expression in single quotes to stop the shell from interpreting the **$** and *, and pass them through to *grep* unmodified.

If **$1** doesn't match, we test to see if it's an option at all, i.e., if it matches the pattern − followed by anything else. If it does, then it's invalid; we print an error message and exit with error status. If we reach the final (**else**) case, we assume that **$1** is a filename and treat it as such in the ensuing code. The rest of the script processes the data as before.

We can extend what we have learned so far to a general technique for handling multiple options. For the sake of concreteness, assume that our script is called *alice* and we want to handle the options −**a**, −**b**, and −**c**:

```
while [ -n "$(echo $1 | grep '-')" ]; do
    case $1 in
        -a ) process option -a ;;
```

```
        -b ) process option -b ;;
        -c ) process option -c ;;
        *  ) echo 'usage: alice [-a] [-b] [-c] args...'
             exit 1
    esac
    shift
done
```

normal processing of arguments...

This code checks **$1** repeatedly as long as it starts with a dash (-). Then the **case** construct runs the appropriate code depending on which option **$1** is. If the option is invalid—i.e., if it starts with a dash but isn't **−a**, **−b**, or **−c**—then the script prints a usage message and returns with an error exit status.

After each option is processed, the arguments are shifted over. The result is that the positional parameters are set to the actual arguments when the **while** loop finishes.

Notice that this code is capable of handling options of arbitrary length, not just one letter (e.g., **−adventure** instead of **−a**).

Options with Arguments

We need to add one more ingredient to make option processing really useful. Recall that many commands have options that take their *own* arguments. For example, the *cut* command, on which we relied heavily in Chapter 4, accepts the option **−d** with an argument that determines the field delimiter (if it is not the default TAB). To handle this type of option, we just use another **shift** when we are processing the option.

Assume that, in our *alice* script, the option **−b** requires its own argument. Here is the modified code that will process it:

```
while [ -n "$(echo $1 | grep '-')" ]; do
    case $1 in
        -a ) process option -a ;;
        -b ) process option -b
             $2 is the option's argument
             shift ;;
        -c ) process option -c ;;
        *  ) echo 'usage: alice [-a] [-b barg] [-c] args...'
             exit 1
    esac
    shift
done
```

normal processing of arguments...

getopts

So far, we have a complete, but constrained, way of handling command-line options. The above code does not allow a user to combine arguments with a single dash, e.g., **−abc** instead of **−a −b −c**. It also doesn't allow one to specify arguments to options without a space in between, e.g., **−barg** in addition to **−b arg**.*

The shell provides a built-in way to deal with multiple complex options without these constraints. The built-in command **getopts**† can be used as the condition of the **while** in an option-processing loop. Given a specification of which options are valid and which require their own arguments, it sets up the body of the loop to process each option in turn.

getopts takes two arguments. The first is a string that can contain letters and colons. Each letter is a valid option; if a letter is followed by a colon, the option requires an argument. **getopts** picks options off the command line and assigns each one (without the leading dash) to a variable whose name is **getopts**'s second argument. As long as there are options left to process, **getopts** will return exit status 0; when the options are exhausted, it returns exit status 1, causing the **while** loop to exit.

getopts does a few other things that make option processing easier; we'll encounter them as we examine how to use **getopts** in this example:

```
while getopts ":ab:c" opt; do
    case $opt in
        a  ) process option -a ;;
        b  ) process option -b
             $OPTARG is the option's argument ;;
        c  ) process option -c ;;
        \? ) echo 'usage: alice [-a] [-b barg] [-c] args...'
             exit 1
    esac
done
shift $(($OPTIND - 1))

normal processing of arguments...
```

The call to **getopts** in the **while** condition sets up the loop to accept the options **−a**, **−b**, and **−c**, and specifies that **−b** takes an argument. (We will explain the : that starts the option string in a moment.) Each time the loop body is executed, it will have the latest option available, without a dash (–), in the variable **opt**.

---

* Although most UNIX commands allow this, it is actually contrary to the Command Syntax Standard Rules in *intro* of the *User's Manual*.

† **getopts** replaces the external command *getopt*, used in Bourne shell programming; **getopts** is better integrated into the shell's syntax and runs more efficiently. C programmers will recognize **getopts** as very similar to the standard library routine *getopt*.

If the user types an invalid option, **getopts** normally prints an unfortunate error message (of the form **cmd: getopts: illegal option — o**) and sets **opt** to ?. However if you begin the option letter string with a colon, **getopts** won't print the message.* We recommend that you specify the colon and provide your own error message in a case that handles ?, as above.

We have modified the code in the **case** construct to reflect what **getopts** does. But notice that there are no more **shift** statements inside the **while** loop: **getopts** does not rely on **shifts** to keep track of where it is. It is unnecessary to shift arguments over until **getopts** is finished, i.e., until the **while** loop exits.

If an option has an argument, **getopts** stores it in the variable **OPTARG**, which can be used in the code that processes the option.

The one **shift** statement left is after the **while** loop. **getopts** stores in the variable **OPTIND** the number of the next argument to be processed; in this case, that's the number of the first (non-option) command-line argument. For example, if the command line were **alice −ab rabbit**, then $OPTIND would be "3". If it were **alice −a −b rabbit**, then $OPTIND would be "4".

The expression **$(($OPTIND - 1))** is an arithmetic expression (as we'll see later in this chapter) equal to **$OPTIND** minus 1. This value is used as the argument to **shift**. The result is that the correct number of arguments are shifted out of the way, leaving the "real" arguments as **$1**, **$2**, etc.

Before we continue, now is a good time to summarize everything **getopts** does:

1. Its first argument is a string containing all valid option letters. If an option requires an argument, a colon follows its letter in the string. An initial colon causes **getopts** not to print an error message when the user gives an invalid option.

2. Its second argument is the name of a variable that will hold each option letter (without any leading dash) as it is processed.

3. If an option takes an argument, the argument is stored in the variable **OPTARG**.

4. The variable **OPTIND** contains a number equal to the next command-line argument to be processed. After **getopts** is done, it equals the number of the first "real" argument.

The advantages of **getopts** are that it minimizes extra code necessary to process options and fully supports the standard UNIX option syntax (as specified in *intro* of the *User's Manual*).

---

* You can also turn off the **getopts** messages by setting the environment variable **OPTERR** to 0. We will continue to use the colon method in this book.

As a more concrete example, let's return to our graphics utility (Task 4-2). So far, we have given our script the ability to process various types of graphics files such as PCX files (ending with *.pcx*), JPEG files (*.jpg*), XPM files (*.xpm*), etc. As a reminder, here is what we have coded in the script so far:

```
filename=$1

if [ -z $filename ]; then
    echo "procfile: No file specified"
    exit 1
fi

for filename in "$@"; do
    ppmfile=${filename%.*}.ppm

    case $filename in
        *.gif ) exit 0 ;;

        *.tga ) tgatoppm $filename > $ppmfile ;;

        *.xpm ) xpmtoppm $filename > $ppmfile ;;

        *.pcx ) pcxtoppm $filename > $ppmfile ;;

        *.tif ) tifftopnm $filename > $ppmfile ;;

        *.jpg ) djpeg $filename > $ppmfile ;;

            * ) echo "procfile: $filename is an unknown graphics file."
                exit 1 ;;
    esac

    outfile=${ppmfile%.ppm}.new.gif

    ppmquant -quiet 256 $ppmfile | ppmtogif -quiet > $outfile
    rm $ppmfile

done
```

This script works quite well, in that it will convert the various different graphics files that we have lying around into GIF files suitable for our Web page. However, NetPBM has a whole range of useful utilities besides file converters that we could use on the images. It would be nice to be able to select some of them from our script.

Things we might wish to do to the images for our Web page include changing the size and placing a border around them. We want to make the script as flexible as possible; we will want to change the size of the resulting images and we might not want a border around every one of them, so we need to be able to specify to the script what it should do. This is where the command-line option processing will come in useful.

We can change the size of an image by using the NetPBM utility *pnmscale*. You'll recall from the last chapter that the NetPBM package has its own format called PNM, the Portable Anymap. The fancy utilities we'll be using to change the size and add borders work on PNM's. Fortunately, our script already converts the various formats we give it into PNM's (actually PPM's in our script, which are full-color instances of PNM's). Besides a PNM file, *pnmscale* also requires some arguments telling it how to scale the image.* There are various different ways to do this, but the one we'll choose is *–xysize* which takes a horizontal and a vertical size in pixels for the final image.†

The other utility we'll need is *pnmmargin* which places a colored border around an image. It takes as arguments the width of the border in pixels, and the color of the border.

Our graphics utility will need some options to reflect the ones we have just seen: **–s** *size* will specify a size into which the final image will fit (minus any border), **–w** *width* will specify the width of the border around the image, and **–c** *color-name* will specify the color of the border.

Here is the code for the script *procimage* that includes the option processing:

```
# Set up the defaults
size=320
width=1
colour="-color black"
usage="Usage: $0 [-s N] [-w N] [-c S] imagefile..."

while getopts ":s:w:c:" opt; do
    case $opt in
       s ) size=$OPTARG ;;
       w ) width=$OPTARG ;;
       c ) colour="-color $OPTARG" ;;
       \? ) echo $usage
            exit 1 ;;
    esac
done

shift $(($OPTIND - 1))

if [ -z "$@" ]; then
    echo $usage
    exit 1
fi
```

---

* We'll also need the *–quiet* option, which you may already have noticed as an option to the *ppmquant* and *ppmtogif* utilities. *–quiet* suppresses diagnostic output from some NetPBM utilities.

† Actually, *–xysize* fits the image into a box defined by its arguments without changing the *aspect ratio* of the image, i.e., without stretching the image horizontally or vertically. For example, if you had an image of size 200 by 100 pixels and you processed it with *pnmscale –xysize 100 100*, you'd end up with an image of size 100 by 50 pixels.

```
# Process the input files
for filename in "$*"; do
    ppmfile=${filename%.*}.ppm

    case $filename in
        *.gif ) giftopnm $filename > $ppmfile ;;

        *.tga ) tgatoppm $filename > $ppmfile ;;

        *.xpm ) xpmtoppm $filename > $ppmfile ;;

        *.pcx ) pcxtoppm $filename > $ppmfile ;;

        *.tif ) tifftopnm $filename > $ppmfile ;;

        *.jpg ) djpeg $filename > $ppmfile ;;

            * ) echo "$0: Unknown filetype '${filename##*.}'"
                exit 1;;
    esac

    outfile=${ppmfile%.ppm}.new.gif
    pnmscale -quiet -xysize $size $size $ppmfile |
        pnmmargin $colour $width |
        ppmquant -quiet 256 | ppmtogif -quiet > $outfile

    rm $ppmfile

done
```

The first several lines of this script initialize variables used as default settings. The defaults set the image size to 320 pixels and a black border of width 1 pixel.

The **while**, **getopts**, and **case** constructs process the options in the same way as in the previous example. The code for the first three options assigns the respective argument to a variable (replacing the default value). The last option is a catchall for any invalid options.

The rest of the code works in much the same way as in the previous example except that we have added the *pnmscale* and *pnmmargin* utilities to the processing pipeline.

The script also now generates a different filename; it appends *.new.gif* to the basename. This allows us to process a GIF file as input, applying scaling and borders, and write it out without destroying the original file.

This version doesn't address every issue, e.g., what if we don't want any scaling to be performed? We'll return to this script and develop it further in the next chapter.

Typed Variables

So far we've seen how *bash* variables can be assigned textual values. Variables can also have other attributes, including being *read only* and being of type *integer*.

You can set variable attributes with the **declare** built-in.* Table 6-1 summarizes the available options with **declare**.† A − turns the option on, while + turns it off.

Table 6-1: Declare Options

Option	Meaning
−a	The variables are treated as arrays
−f	Use function names only
−F	Display function names without definitions
−i	The variables are treated as integers
−r	Makes the variables read-only
−x	Marks the variables for export via the environment

Typing **declare** on its own displays the values of all variables in the environment. The −f option limits this display to the function names and definitions currently in the environment. −F limits it further by displaying only the function names.

The −a option declares *arrays*—a variable type that we haven't seen yet, but will be discussed shortly.

The −i option is used to create an integer variable, one that holds numeric values and can be used in and modified by arithmetic operations. Consider this example:

```
$ val1=12 val2=5
$ result1=val*val2
$ echo $result1
val1*val2
$
$ declare -i val3=12 val4=5
$ declare -i result2
$ result2=val3*val4
$ echo $result2
60
```

In the first example, the variables are ordinary shell variables and the result is just the string "val1*val2". In the second example, all of the variables have been declared as type *integer*. The variable **result** contains the result of the arithmetic computation twelve multiplied by five. Actually, we didn't need to declare **val3** and **val4** as type integer. Anything being assigned to **result2** is interpreted as an arithmetic statement and evaluation is attempted.

---

* The **typeset** built-in is synonymous with **declare** but is considered obsolete.

† The −a and −F options are not available in *bash* prior to version 2.0.

The **−x** option to **declare** operates in the same way as the **export** built-in that we saw in Chapter 3, *Customizing Your Environment.* It allows the listed variables to be exported outside the current shell environment.

The **−r** option creates a read-only variable, one that cannot have its value changed by subsequent assignment statements.

A related built-in is **readonly** *name* ... which operates in exactly the same way as **declare −r**. **readonly** has four options: **−f**, which makes **readonly** interpret the name arguments as function names rather than variable names, **-n**, which removes the read-only property from the names, **−p**, which makes the built-in print a list of all read-only names, and **-a**, which interprets the name arguments as arrays.

Lastly, variables **declare**d in a function are local to that function, just like using **local** to declare them.

Integer Variables and Arithmetic

The expression **$(($OPTIND − 1))** in the last graphics utility example shows another way that the shell can do integer arithmetic. As you might guess, the shell interprets words surrounded by **$((** and **))** as arithmetic expressions.* Variables in arithmetic expressions do *not* need to be preceded by dollar signs, though it is not wrong to do so.

Arithmetic expressions are evaluated inside double quotes, like tildes, variables, and command substitutions. We're *finally* in a position to state the definitive rule about quoting strings: When in doubt, enclose a string in single quotes, unless it contains tildes or any expression involving a dollar sign, in which case you should use double quotes.

For example, the *date* command on System V-derived versions of UNIX accepts arguments that tell it how to format its output. The argument **+%j** tells it to print the day of the year, i.e., the number of days since December 31st of the previous year.

We can use **+%j** to print a little holiday anticipation message:

```
echo "Only $(( (365-$(date +%j)) / 7 )) weeks until the New Year"
```

We'll show where this fits in the overall scheme of command-line processing in Chapter 7, *Input/Output and Command-Line Processing.*

The arithmetic expression feature is built into *bash*'s syntax, and was available in the Bourne shell (most versions) only through the external command *expr*. Thus it

---

* You can also use the older form **$[...]**, but we don't recommend this because it will be phased out in future versions of *bash*.

is yet another example of a desirable feature provided by an external command being better integrated into the shell. **getopts**, as we have already seen, is another example of this design trend.

bash arithmetic expressions are equivalent to their counterparts in the C language.* Precedence and associativity are the same as in C. Table 6-2 shows the arithmetic operators that are supported. Although some of these are (or contain) special characters, there is no need to backslash-escape them, because they are within the $((. . .)) syntax.

Table 6-2: Arithmetic Operators

Operator	Meaning
+	Plus
−	Minus
*	Multiplication
/	Division (with truncation)
%	Remainder
<<	Bit-shift left
>>	Bit-shift right
&	Bitwise and
|	Bitwise or
~	Bitwise not
!	Bitwise not
^	Bitwise exclusive or

Parentheses can be used to group subexpressions. The arithmetic expression syntax also (as in C) supports relational operators as "truth values" of 1 for true and 0 for false. Table 6-3 shows the relational operators and the logical operators that can be used to combine relational expressions.

Table 6-3: Relational Operators

Operator	Meaning
<	Less than
>	Greater than
<=	Less than or equal to
>=	Greater than or equal to
==	Equal to
!=	Not equal to

---

* The assignment forms of these operators are also permitted. For example, $((x += 2)) adds 2 to **x** and stores the result back in **x**.

Table 6-3: Relational Operators (continued)

Operator	Meaning
&&	Logical and
||	Logical or

For example, $((3 > 2))$ has the value 1; $(((3 > 2) \|\| (4 <= 1)))$ also has the value 1, since at least one of the two subexpressions is true.

The shell also supports base *N* numbers, where *N* can be from 2 to 36. The notation *B#N* means "*N* base *B*". Of course, if you omit the *B#*, the base defaults to 10.

Arithmetic Conditionals

In Chapter 5, *Flow Control,* we saw how to compare strings by the use of [. . .] notation (or with the **test** built-in). Arithmetic conditions can also be tested in this way. However, the tests have to be carried out with their own operators. These are shown in Table 6-4.

Table 6-4: Test Relational Operators

Operator	Meaning
−lt	Less than
−gt	Greater than
−le	Less than or equal to
−ge	Greater than or equal to
−eq	Equal to
−ne	Not equal to

As with string comparisons, the arithmetic test returns a result of true or false; 0 if true, 1 otherwise. So, for example, [3 −gt 2] produces exit status 0, as does [\(3 −gt 2 \) \|\| \(4 −le 1 \)], but [\(3 −gt 2 \) && \(4 −le 1 \)] has exit status 1 since the second subexpression isn't true.

In these examples we have had to escape the parentheses and pass them to **test** as separate arguments. As you can see, the result can look rather unreadable if there are many parentheses.

Another way to make arithmetic tests is to use the $((. . .)) form to encapsulate the condition. For example: [$(((3 > 2) && (4 <= 1))) = 1]. This evaluates the conditionals and then compares the resulting value to 1 (true).*

---

* Note that the truth values returned by $((. . .)) are 1 for true, 0 for false—the reverse of the **test** and exit statuses.

There is an even neater and more efficient way of performing an arithmetic test: by using the ((...)) construct.* This returns an exit status of 0 if the expression is true, and 1 otherwise.

The above expression using this construct becomes: (((3 > 2) && (4 <= 1))). This example returns with an exit status of 1 because, as we said, the second subexpression is false.

Arithmetic Variables and Assignment

As we saw earlier, you can define integer variables by using **declare**. You can also evaluate arithmetic expressions and assign them to variables with the use of **let**. The syntax is:

```
let intvar=expression
```

It is not necessary (because it's actually redundant) to surround the expression with $((and)) in a **let** statement. **let** doesn't create a variable of type integer; it only causes the expression following the assignment to be interpreted as an arithmetic one. As with any variable assignment, there must not be any space on either side of the equal sign (=). It is good practice to surround expressions with quotes, since many characters are treated as special by the shell (e.g., *, #, and parentheses); furthermore, you must quote expressions that include whitespace (spaces or TABs). See Table 6-5 for examples.

Table 6-5: Sample Integer Expression Assignments

Assignment let x=	Value $x
1+4	5
'1 + 4'	5
'(2+3) * 5'	25
'2 + 3 * 5'	17
'17 / 3'	5
'17 % 3'	2
'1<<4'	16
'48>>3'	6
'17 & 3'	1
'17 | 3'	19
'17 ^ 3'	18

---

* ((...)) is not available in versions of *bash* prior to 2.0.

Task 6-1

Here is a small task that makes use of integer arithmetic. Write a script called *ndu* that prints a summary of the disk space usage for each directory argument (and any subdirectories), both in terms of bytes, and kilobytes or megabytes (whichever is appropriate).

Here is the code:

```
for dir in ${*:-.}; do
    if [ -e $dir ]; then
        result=$(du -s $dir | cut -f 1)
        let total=$result*1024

        echo -n "Total for $dir = $total bytes"

        if [ $total -ge 1048576 ]; then
            echo " ($((total/1048576)) Mb)"
        elif [ $total -ge 1024 ]; then
            echo " ($((total/1024)) Kb)"
        fi
    fi
done
```

To obtain the disk usage of files and directories, we can use the UNIX utility *du*. The default output of *du* is a list of directories with the amount of space each one uses, and looks something like this:

```
6          ./toc
3          ./figlist
6          ./tablist
1          ./exlist
1          ./index/idx
22         ./index
39         .
```

If you don't specify a directory to *du*, it will use the current directory (.). Each directory and subdirectory is listed along with the amount of space it uses. The grand total is given in the last line.

The amount of space used by each directory and all the files in it is listed in terms of blocks. Depending on the UNIX system you are running on, one block can represent 512 or 1024 bytes. Each file and directory uses at least one block. Even if a file or directory is empty, it is still allocated a block of space in the filesystem.

In our case, we are only interested in the total usage, given on the last line of *du*'s output. To obtain only this line, we can use the −s option of *du*. Once we have the line, we want only the number of blocks and can throw away the directory name. For this we use our old friend *cut* to extract the first field.

Once we have the total, we can multiply it by the number of bytes in a block (1024 in this case) and print the result in terms of bytes. We then test to see if the total is greater than the number of bytes in one megabyte (1048576 bytes, which is 1024 × 1024) and if it is, we can print how many megabytes it is by dividing the total by this large number. If not, we see if it can be expressed in kilobytes, otherwise nothing is printed.

We need to make sure that any specified directories exist, otherwise *du* will print an error message and the script will fail. We do this by using the test for file or directory existence (–e) that we saw in Chapter 5 before calling *du*.

To round out this script, it would be nice to imitate *du* as closely as possible by providing for multiple arguments. To do this, we wrap the code in a **for** loop. Notice how parameter substitution has been used to specify the current directory if no arguments are given.

As a bigger example of integer arithmetic, we will complete our emulation of the *pushd* and *popd* functions (Task 4-8). Remember that these functions operate on **DIR_STACK**, a stack of directories represented as a string with the directory names separated by spaces. *bash's pushd* and *popd* take additional types of arguments, which are:

- **pushd +n** takes the *n*th directory in the stack (starting with 0), rotates it to the top, and **cd**s to it.

- **pushd** without arguments, instead of complaining, swaps the two top directories on the stack and **cd**s to the new top.

- **popd +n** takes the *n*th directory in the stack and just deletes it.

The most useful of these features is the ability to get at the *n*th directory in the stack. Here are the latest versions of both functions:

```
pushd ()
{
    dirname=$1   if [ -n $dirname ] && [ \( -d $dirname \) -a
            \( -x $dirname \) ]; then
        DIR_STACK="$dirname ${DIR_STACK:-$PWD' '}"
        cd $dirname
        echo "$DIR_STACK"
    else
        echo "still in $PWD."
    fi
}

popd ()
{
    if [ -n "$DIR_STACK" ]; then
        DIR_STACK=${DIR_STACK#* }
```

```
            cd ${DIR_STACK%% *}
            echo "$PWD"
        else
            echo "stack empty, still in $PWD."
        fi
    }
```

To get at the *n*th directory, we use a **while** loop that transfers the top directory to a temporary copy of the stack *n* times. We'll put the loop into a function called *getNdirs* that looks like this:

```
getNdirs ()
{
    stackfront=''
    let count=0
    while [ $count -le $1 ]; do
        target=${DIR_STACK%${DIR_STACK#* }}
        stackfront="$stackfront$target"
        DIR_STACK=${DIR_STACK#$target}
        let count=count+1
    done

    stackfront=${stackfront%$target}
}
```

The argument passed to *getNdirs* is the *n* in question. The variable **target** contains the directory currently being moved from **DIR_STACK** to a temporary stack, **stackfront**. **target** will contain the *n*th directory and **stackfront** will have all of the directories above (and including) **target** when the loop finishes. **stackfront** starts as null; **count**, which counts the number of loop iterations, starts as 0.

The first line of the loop body copies the first directory on the stack to **target**. The next line appends **target** to **stackfront** and the following line removes **target** from the stack **${DIR_STACK#$target}**. The last line increments the counter for the next iteration. The entire loop executes *n*+1 times, for values of **count** from 0 to *N*.

When the loop finishes, the directory in **$target** is the *n*th directory. The expression **${stackfront%$target}** removes this directory from **stackfront** so that **stackfront** will contain the first *n*−1 directories. Furthermore, **DIR_STACK** now contains the "back" of the stack, i.e., the stack *without* the first *n* directories. With this in mind, we can now write the code for the improved versions of *pushd* and *popd*:

```
pushd ()
{
    if [ $(echo $1 | grep '^+[0-9][0-9]*$') ]; then

        # case of pushd +n: rotate n-th directory to top
        let num=${1#+}
        getNdirs $num
```

```
                DIR_STACK="$target$stackfront$DIR_STACK"
                cd $target
                echo "$DIR_STACK"

        elif [ -z "$1" ]; then
                # case of pushd without args; swap top two directories
                firstdir=${DIR_STACK%% *}
                DIR_STACK=${DIR_STACK#* }
                seconddir=${DIR_STACK%% *}
                DIR_STACK=${DIR_STACK#* }
                DIR_STACK="$seconddir $firstdir $DIR_STACK"
                cd $seconddir

        else
                # normal case of pushd dirname
                dirname=$1
                if [ \( -d $dirname \) -a \( -x $dirname \) ]; then
                    DIR_STACK="$dirname ${DIR_STACK:-$PWD" "}"
                    cd $dirname
                    echo "$DIR_STACK"
                else
                    echo still in "$PWD."
                fi
        fi
}

popd ()
{
    if [ $(echo $1 | grep '^+[0-9][0-9]*$') ]; then

        # case of popd +n: delete n-th directory from stack
        let num=${1#+}
        getNdirs $num
        DIR_STACK="$stackfront$DIR_STACK"
        cd ${DIR_STACK%% *}
        echo "$PWD"

    else

        # normal case of popd without argument
        if [ -n "$DIR_STACK" ]; then
            DIR_STACK=${DIR_STACK#* }
            cd ${DIR_STACK%% *}
            echo "$PWD"
        else
            echo "stack empty, still in $PWD."
        fi
    fi
}
```

These functions have grown rather large; let's look at them in turn. The **if** at the beginning of *pushd* checks if the first argument is an option of the form +*N*. If so, the first body of code is run. The first **let** simply strips the plus sign (+) from the argument and assigns the result—as an integer—to the variable **num**. This, in turn, is passed to the *getNdirs* function.

The next assignment statement sets **DIR_STACK** to the new ordering of the list. Then the function **cds** to the new directory and prints the current directory stack.

The **elif** clause tests for no argument, in which case *pushd* should swap the top two directories on the stack. The first four lines of this clause assign the top two directories to **firstdir** and **seconddir**, and delete these from the stack. Then, as above, the code puts the stack back together in the new order and **cds** to the new top directory.

The **else** clause corresponds to the usual case, where the user supplies a directory name as argument.

popd works similarly. The **if** clause checks for the +*N* option, which in this case means "delete the *n*th directory." A **let** extracts the *N* as an integer; the *getNdirs* function puts the first *n* directories into **stackfront**. Finally, the stack is put back together with the *n*th directory missing, and a *cd* is performed in case the deleted directory was the first in the list.

The **else** clause covers the usual case, where the user doesn't supply an argument.

Before we leave this subject, here are a few exercises that should test your understanding of this code:

1. Implement *bash*'s *dirs* command and the options **+n** and **−l**. *dirs* by itself displays the list of currently remembered directories (those in the stack). The **+n** option prints out the *n*th directory (starting at 0) and the **−l** option produces a long listing; any tildes (˜) are replaced by the full pathname.

2. Modify the *getNdirs* function so that it checks for *N* exceeding the number of directories in the stack and exits with an appropriate error message if true.

3. Modify *pushd*, *popd*, and *getNdirs* so that they use variables of type **integer** in the arithmetic expressions.

4. Change *getNdirs* so that it uses *cut* (with command substitution), instead of the **while** loop, to extract the first *N* directories. This uses less code but runs more slowly because of the extra processes generated.

5. *bash*'s versions of *pushd* and *popd* also have a −*N* option. In both cases −*N* causes the *n*th directory from the right-hand side of the list to have the operation performed on it. As with +*N*, it starts at 0. Add this functionality.

6. Use *getNdirs* to reimplement the *selectd* function from the last chapter.

Arrays

The *pushd* and *popd* functions use a string variable to hold a list of directories and manipulate the list with the string pattern-matching operators. Although this is quite efficient for adding or retrieving items at the beginning or end of the string, it becomes cumbersome when attempting to access items that are anywhere else, e.g., obtaining item *N* with the *getNdirs* function. It would be nice to be able to specify the number, or *index*, of the item and retrieve it. Arrays allow us to do this.*

An array is like a series of slots that hold values. Each slot is known as an *element*, and each element can be accessed via a numerical index. An array element can contain a string or a number, and you can use it just like any other variable. The indices for arrays start at 0 and continue up to a very large number.† So, for example, the fifth element of array **names** would be **names[4]**. Indices can be any valid arithmetic expression that evaluates to a number greater than or equal to 0.

There are several ways to assign values to arrays. The most straightforward way is with an assignment, just like any other variable:

```
names[2]=alice
names[0]=hatter
names[1]=duchess
```

This assigns **hatter** to element **0**, **duchess** to element **1**, and **alice** to element **2** of the array **names**.

Another way to assign values is with a compound assignment:

```
names=([2]=alice [0]=hatter [1]=duchess)
```

This is equivalent to the first example and is convenient for initializing an array with a set of values. Notice that we didn't have to specify the indices in numerical order. In fact, we don't even have to supply the indices if we reorder our values slightly:

```
names=(hatter duchess alice)
```

bash automatically assigns the values to consecutive elements starting at 0. If we provide an index at some point in the compound assignment, the values get assigned consecutively from that point on, so:

```
names=(hatter [5]=duchess alice)
```

assigns **hatter** to element **0**, **duchess** to element **5**, and **alice** to element **6**.

---

* Support for arrays is not available in versions of *bash* prior to 2.0.

† Actually, up to 599147937791. That's almost six hundred billion, so yes, it's pretty large.

An array is created automatically by any assignment of these forms. To explicitly create an empty array, you can use the -a option to **declare**. Any attributes that you set for the array with **declare** (e.g., the read-only attribute) apply to the entire array. For example, the statement **declare -ar names** would create a read-only array called **names**. Every element of the array would be read-only.

An element in an array may be referenced with the syntax ${*array*[*i*]}. So, from our last example above, the statement **echo ${names[5]}** would print the string "duchess". If no index is supplied, array element 0 is assumed.

You can also use the special indices @ and *. These return all of the values in the array and work in the same way as for the positional parameters; when the array reference is within double quotes, using * expands the reference to one word consisting of all the values in the array separated by the first character of the **IFS** variable, while @ expands the values in the array to separate words. When unquoted, both of them expand the values of the array to separate words. Just as with positional parameters, this is useful for iterating through the values with a **for** loop:

```
for i in "${names[@]}"; do
    echo $i
done
```

Any array elements which are unassigned don't exist; they default to null strings if you explicitly reference them. Therefore, the previous looping example will print out only the assigned elements in the array **names**. If there were three values at indexes 1, 45, and 1005, only those three values would be printed.

A useful operator that you can use with arrays is #, the length operator that we saw in Chapter 4. To find out the length of any element in the array, you can use ${#*array*[*i*]}. Similarly, to find out how many values there are in the array, use * or @ as the index. So, for **names=(hatter [5]=duchess alice)**, ${#names[5]} has the value 7, and ${#names[@]} has the value 3.

Reassigning to an existing array with a compound array statement replaces the old array with the new one. All of the old values are lost, even if they were at different indices to the new elements. For example, if we reassigned **names** to be (**[100]=tweedledee tweedledum**), the values **hatter**, **duchess**, and **alice** would disappear.

You can destroy any element or the entire array by using the **unset** built-in. If you specify an index, that particular element will be unset. **unset names[100]**, for instance, would remove the value at index **100**; **tweedledee** in the example above. However, unlike assignment, if you don't specify an index the *entire* array is unset, not just element 0. You can explicitly specify unsetting the entire array by using * or @ as the index.

Let's now look at a simple example that uses arrays to match user IDs to account names on the system. The code takes a user ID as an argument and prints the name of the account plus the number of accounts currently on the system:

```
for i in $(cut -f 1,3 -d: /etc/passwd) ; do
    array[${i#*:}]=${i%:*}
done

echo "User ID $1 is ${array[$1]}."
echo "There are currently ${#array[@]} user accounts on the system."
```

We use *cut* to create a list from fields 1 and 3 in the */etc/passwd* file. Field 1 is the account name and field 3 is the user ID for the account. The script loops through this list using the user ID as an index for each array element and assigns each account name to that element. The script then uses the supplied argument as an index into the array, prints out the value at that index, and prints the number of existing array values.

Some of the environment variables in *bash* are arrays; **DIRSTACK** functions as a stack for the *pushd* and *popd* built-ins, **BASH_VERSINFO** is an array of version information for the current instance of the shell, and **PIPESTATUS** is an array of exit status values for the last foreground pipe that was executed.

We'll see a further use of arrays when we build a *bash* debugger in Chapter 9.

To end this chapter, here are some problems relating to what we've just covered:

1. Improve the account ID script so that it checks whether the argument is a number. Also, add a test to print an appropriate message if the user ID doesn't exist.

2. Make the script print out the username (field 5) as well. Hint: this isn't as easy as it sounds. A username can have spaces in it, causing the **for** loop to iterate on each part of the name.

3. As mentioned earlier, the built-in versions of *pushd* and *popd* use an array to implement the stack. Change the *pushd*, *popd*, and *getNdirs* code that we developed in this chapter so that it uses arrays.

7

Input/Output and Command-Line Processing

The past few chapters have gone into detail about various shell programming techniques, mostly focused on the flow of data and control through shell programs. In this chapter, we switch the focus to two related topics. The first is the shell's mechanisms for doing file-oriented input and output. We present information that expands on what you already know about the shell's basic I/O redirectors.

Second, we'll "zoom in" and talk about I/O at the line and word level. This is a fundamentally different topic, since it involves moving information between the domains of files/terminals and shell variables. **echo** and command substitution are two ways of doing this that we've seen so far.

Our discussion of line and word I/O will lead into a more detailed explanation of how the shell processes command lines. This information is necessary so that you can understand exactly how the shell deals with *quotation*, and so that you can appreciate the power of an advanced command called **eval**, which we will cover at the end of the chapter.

I/O Redirectors

In Chapter 1, *bash Basics*, you learned about the shell's basic I/O redirectors: >, <, and |. Although these are enough to get you through 95% of your UNIX life, you should know that *bash* supports many other redirectors. Table 7-1 lists them, including the three we've already seen. Although some of the rest are broadly useful, others are mainly for systems programmers.

Table 7-1: I/O Redirectors

Redirector	Function
cmd1 | *cmd2*	Pipe; take standard output of *cmd1* as standard input to *cmd2*
> *file*	Direct standard output to *file*
< *file*	Take standard input from *file*
>> *file*	Direct standard output to *file*; append to *file* if it already exists
>| *file*	Force standard output to *file* even if **noclobber** is set
n>| *file*	Force output to *file* from file descriptor *n* even if **noclobber** is set
<> *file*	Use *file* as both standard input and standard output
n<> *file*	Use *file* as both input and output for file descriptor *n*
<< *label*	Here-document; see text
n> *file*	Direct file descriptor *n* to *file*
n< *file*	Take file descriptor *n* from *file*
n>> *file*	Direct file descriptor *n* to *file*; append to *file* if it already exists
n>&	Duplicate standard output to file descriptor *n*
n<&	Duplicate standard input from file descriptor *n*
n>&*m*	File descriptor *n* is made to be a copy of the output file descriptor
n<&*m*	File descriptor *n* is made to be a copy of the input file descriptor
&>*file*	Directs standard output and standard error to *file*
<&–	Close the standard input
>&–	Close the standard output
n>&–	Close the output from file descriptor *n*
n<&–	Close the input from file descriptor *n*

Notice that some of the redirectors in Table 7-1 contain a digit *n*, and that their descriptions contain the term *file descriptor*; we'll cover that in a little while.

The first two new redirectors, >> and >\|, are simple variations on the standard output redirector >. The >> appends to the output file (instead of overwriting it) if it already exists; otherwise it acts exactly like >. A common use of >> is for adding a line to an initialization file (such as *.bashrc* or *.mailrc*) when you don't want to bother with a text editor. For example:

```
$ cat >> .bashrc
  alias cdmnt='mount -t iso9660 /dev/sbpcd /cdrom'
  ^D
```

As we saw in Chapter 1, *cat* without an argument uses standard input as its input. This allows you to type the input and end it with CTRL-D on its own line. The **alias** line will be appended to the file *.bashrc* if it already exists; if it doesn't, the file is created with that one line.

Recall from Chapter 3, *Customizing Your Environment*, that you can prevent the shell from overwriting a file with > *file* by typing **set –o noclobber**. >\| overrides **noclobber**—it's the "Do it anyway, dammit!" redirector.

The redirector <> is mainly meant for use with device files (in the */dev* directory), i.e., files that correspond to hardware devices such as terminals and communication lines. Low-level systems programmers can use it to test device drivers; otherwise, it's not very useful.

Here-documents

The << *label* redirector essentially forces the input to a command to be the shell's standard input, which is read until there is a line that contains only *label*. The input in between is called a *here-document*. Here-documents aren't very interesting when used from the command prompt. In fact, it's the same as the normal use of standard input except for the label. We could use a here-document to simulate the *mail* facility. When you send a message to someone with the *mail* utility, you end the message with a dot (.). The body of the message is saved in a file, *msgfile*:

```
$ cat >> msgfile << .
> this is the text of
> our message.
> .
```

Here-documents are meant to be used from within shell scripts; they let you specify "batch" input to programs. A common use of here-documents is with simple text editors like *ed*. Task 7–1 is a programming task that uses a here-document in this way.

Task 7-1

The s *file* command in *mail* saves the current message in *file*. If the message came over a network (such as the Internet), then it has several header lines prepended that give information about network routing. Write a shell script that deletes the header lines from the file.

We can use *ed* to delete the header lines. To do this, we need to know something about the syntax of mail messages; specifically, that there is always a blank line between the header lines and the message text. The *ed* command 1,/^[]*$/d does the trick: it means, "Delete from line 1 until the first blank line." We also need the *ed* commands **w** (write the changed file) and **q** (quit). Here is the code that solves the task:

```
ed $1 << EOF
1,/^[ ]*$/d
w
q
EOF
```

The shell does parameter (variable) substitution and command substitution on text in a here-document, meaning that you can use shell variables and commands to customize the text. A good example of this is the *bashbug* script, which sends a bug report to the *bash* maintainer (see Chapter 11, *bash for Your System*). Here is a stripped-down version:

```
MACHINE="i586"
OS="linux-gnu"
CC="gcc"
CFLAGS=" -DPROGRAM='bash' -DHOSTTYPE='i586' -DOSTYPE='linux-gnu' \
    -DMACHTYPE='i586-pc-linux-gnu' -DSHELL -DHAVE_CONFIG_H   -I. \
    -I. -I./lib -g -O2"
RELEASE="2.01"
PATCHLEVEL="0"
RELSTATUS="release"
MACHTYPE="i586-pc-linux-gnu"

TEMP=/tmp/bbug.$$

case "$RELSTATUS" in
alpha*|beta*)   BUGBASH=chet@po.cwru.edu ;;
*)              BUGBASH=bug-bash@prep.ai.mit.edu ;;
esac

BUGADDR="${1-$BUGBASH}"

UN=
if (uname) >/dev/null 2>&1; then
        UN=`uname -a`
fi

cat > $TEMP <<EOF
From: ${USER}
To: ${BUGADDR}
Subject: [50 character or so descriptive subject here (for reference)]

Configuration Information [Automatically generated, do not change]:
Machine: $MACHINE
OS: $OS
Compiler: $CC
Compilation CFLAGS: $CFLAGS
uname output: $UN
Machine Type: $MACHTYPE

bash Version: $RELEASE
Patch Level: $PATCHLEVEL
Release Status: $RELSTATUS

Description:
        [Detailed description of the problem, suggestion, or complaint.]

Repeat-By:
        [Describe the sequence of events that causes the problem
        to occur.]
```

```
Fix:
        [Description of how to fix the problem.  If you don't know a
        fix for the problem, don't include this section.]
EOF

vi $TEMP

mail $BUGADDR < $TEMP
```

The first eight lines are generated when *bashbug* is installed. The shell will then substitute the appropriate values for the variables in the text whenever the script is run.

The redirector **<<** has two variations. First, you can prevent the shell from doing parameter and command substitution by surrounding the *label* in single or double quotes. In the above example, if you used the line **cat > $TEMP <<'EOF'**, then text like **$USER** and **$MACHINE** would remain untouched (defeating the purpose of this particular script).

The second variation is **<<-**, which deletes leading TABs (but not blanks) from the here-document and the label line. This allows you to indent the here-document's text, making the shell script more readable:

```
cat > $TEMP <<-EOF
        From: ${USER}
        To: ${BUGADDR}
        Subject: [50 character or so descriptive subject here]

        Configuration Information [Automatically generated,
            do not change]:
        Machine: $MACHINE
        OS: $OS
        Compiler: $CC
        Compilation CFLAGS: $CFLAGS
        ...
    EOF
```

Make sure you are careful when choosing your *label* so that it doesn't appear as an actual input line.

File Descriptors

The next few redirectors in Table 7-1 depend on the notion of a *file descriptor*. Like the device files used with **<>**, this is a low-level UNIX I/O concept that is of interest only to systems programmers—and then only occasionally. You can get by with a few basic facts about them; for the whole story, look at the entries for *read()*, *write()*, *fcntl()*, and others in Section 2 of the UNIX manual. You might wish to refer to *UNIX Power Tools* by Jerry Peek, Tim O'Reilly, and Mike Loukides (published by O'Reilly & Associates).

File descriptors are integers starting at 0 that refer to particular streams of data associated with a process. When a process starts, it usually has three file descriptors open. These correspond to the three *standards*: standard input (file descriptor 0), standard output (1), and standard error (2). If a process opens additional files for input or output, they are assigned to the next available file descriptors, starting with 3.

By far the most common use of file descriptors with *bash* is in saving standard error in a file. For example, if you want to save the error messages from a long job in a file so that they don't scroll off the screen, append **2>** *file* to your command. If you also want to save standard output, append **>** *file1* **2>** *file2*.

This leads to another programming task.

Task 7-2

> You want to start a long job in the background (so that your terminal is freed up) and save both standard output and standard error in a single log file. Write a script that does this.

We'll call this script *start*. The code is very terse:

```
"$@" > logfile 2>&1 &
```

This line executes whatever command and parameters follow **start**. (The command cannot contain pipes or output redirectors.) It sends the command's standard output to *logfile*.

Then, the redirector **2>&1** says, "send standard error (file descriptor 2) to the same place as standard output (file descriptor 1)." Since standard output is redirected to *logfile*, standard error will go there too. The final **&** puts the job in the background so that you get your shell prompt back.

As a small variation on this theme, we can send both standard output and standard error into a *pipe* instead of a file: *command* **2>&1 |** ... does this. (Make sure you understand why.) Here is a script that sends both standard output and standard error to the logfile (as above) and to the terminal:

```
"$@" 2>&1 | tee logfile &
```

The command *tee* takes its standard input and copies it to standard output *and* the file given as argument.

These scripts have one shortcoming: you must remain logged in until the job completes. Although you can always type **jobs** (see Chapter 1) to check on progress, you can't leave your terminal until the job finishes, unless you want to risk a breach of security.* We'll see how to solve this problem in the next chapter.

The other file-descriptor-oriented redirectors (e.g., <&*n*) are usually used for reading input from (or writing output to) more than one file at the same time. We'll see an example later in this chapter. Otherwise, they're mainly meant for systems programmers, as are <&– (force standard input to close) and >&– (force standard output to close).

Before we leave this topic, we should just note that 1> is the same as >, and 0< is the same as <. If you understand this, then you probably know all you need to know about file descriptors.

String I/O

Now we'll zoom back in to the string I/O level and examine the **echo** and **read** statements, which give the shell I/O capabilities that are more analogous to those of conventional programming languages.

echo

As we've seen countless times in this book, **echo** simply prints its arguments to standard output. Now we'll explore the command in greater detail.

Options to echo

echo accepts a few dash options, listed in Table 7-2.

Table 7-2: echo Options

Option	Function
–e	Turns on the interpretation of backslash-escaped characters
–E	Turns off the interpretation of backslash-escaped character on systems where this mode is the default
–n	Omit the final newline (same as the \c escape sequence)

echo escape sequences

echo accepts a number of *escape sequences* that start with a backslash.† These are similar to the escape sequences recognized by **echo** and the C language; they are listed in Table 7-3.

---

* Don't put it past people to come up to your unattended terminal and cause mischief!

† You must use a double backslash if you don't surround the string that contains them with quotes; otherwise, the shell itself "steals" a backslash before passing the arguments to **echo**.

These sequences exhibit fairly predictable behavior, except for **\f**: on some displays, it causes a screen clear, while on others it causes a line feed. It ejects the page on most printers. **\v** is somewhat obsolete; it usually causes a line feed.

Table 7-3: echo Escape Sequences

Sequence	Character Printed
\a	ALERT or CTRL-G (bell)
\b	BACKSPACE or CTRL-H
\c	Omit final NEWLINE
\E	Escape character[a]
\f	FORMFEED or CTRL-L
\n	NEWLINE (not at end of command) or CTRL-J
\r	RETURN (ENTER) or CTRL-M
\t	TAB or CTRL-I
\v	VERTICAL TAB or CTRL-K
\n	ASCII character with octal (base-8) value *n*, where *n* is 1 to 3 digits
\\	Single backslash

a. Not available in versions of *bash* prior to 2.0.

The **\n** sequence is even more device-dependent and can be used for complex I/O, such as cursor control and special graphics characters.

read

The other half of the shell's string I/O facilities is the **read** command, which allows you to read values *into* shell variables. The basic syntax is:

```
read var1 var2...
```

This statement takes a line from the standard input and breaks it down into words delimited by any of the characters in the value of the environment variable **IFS** (see Chapter 4, *Basic Shell Programming*; these are usually a space, a TAB, and NEWLINE). The words are assigned to variables *var1*, *var2*, etc. For example:

```
$ read character1 character2
alice duchess
$ echo $character1
alice
$ echo $character2
duchess
```

If there are more words than variables, then excess words are assigned to the last variable. If you omit the variables altogether, the entire line of input is assigned to the variable **REPLY**.

You may have identified this as the "missing ingredient" in the shell programming capabilities we have seen thus far. It resembles input statements in conventional languages, like its namesake in Pascal. So why did we wait this long to introduce it?

Actually, **read** is sort of an "escape hatch" from traditional shell programming philosophy, which dictates that the most important unit of data to process is a *text file*, and that UNIX utilities such as *cut, grep, sort*, etc., should be used as building blocks for writing programs.

read, on the other hand, implies line-by-line processing. You could use it to write a shell script that does what a pipeline of utilities would normally do, but such a script would inevitably look like:

```
while (read a line) do
    process the line
    print the processed line
end
```

This type of script is usually much slower than a pipeline; furthermore, it has the same form as a program someone might write in C (or some similar language) that does the same thing *much* faster. In other words, if you are going to write it in this line-by-line way, there is no point in writing a shell script.

Reading lines from files

Nevertheless, shell scripts with **read** are useful for certain kinds of tasks. One is when you are reading data from a file small enough so that efficiency isn't a concern (say a few hundred lines or less), and it's *really necessary* to get bits of input into shell variables.

Consider the case of a UNIX machine that has terminals that are hardwired to the terminal lines of the machine. It would be nice if the TERM environment variable was set to the correct terminal type when a user logged in.

One way to do this would be to have some code that sets the terminal information when a user logs in. This code would presumably reside in */etc/profile*, the system-wide initialization file that *bash* runs before running a user's *.bash_profile*. If the terminals on the system change over time—as surely they must—then the code would have to be changed. It would be better to store the information in a file and change just the file instead.

Assume we put the information in a file whose format is typical of such UNIX "system configuration" files: each line contains a device name, a TAB, and a **TERM** value.

We'll call the file */etc/terms*, and it would typically look something like this:

```
console          console
tty01            wy60
tty03            vt100
tty04            vt100
tty07            wy85
tty08            vt100
```

The values on the left are terminal lines and those on the right are the terminal types that **TERM** can be set to. The terminals connected to this system are a Wyse 60 (wy60), three VT100s (vt100), and a Wyse 85 (wy85). The machines' master terminal is the console, which has a **TERM** value of **console**.

We can use **read** to get the data from this file, but first we need to know how to test for the end-of-file condition. Simple: **read**'s exit status is 1 (i.e., non-zero) when there is nothing to read. This leads to a clean **while** loop:

```
TERM=vt100        # assume this as a default
line=$(tty)
while read dev termtype; do
    if [ $dev = $line ]; then
        TERM=$termtype
        echo "TERM set to $TERM."
        break
    fi
done
```

The **while** loop reads each line of the input into the variables **dev** and **termtype**. In each pass through the loop, the **if** looks for a match between **$dev** and the user's tty (**$line**, obtained by command substitution from the *tty* command). If a match is found, **TERM** is set, a message is printed, and the loop exits; otherwise **TERM** remains at the default setting of **vt100**.

We're not quite done, though: this code reads from the standard input, not from */etc/terms*! We need to know how to redirect input to *multiple commands*. It turns out that there are a few ways of doing this.

I/O redirection and multiple commands

One way to solve the problem is with a *subshell*, as we'll see in the next chapter. This involves creating a separate process to do the reading. However, it is usually more efficient to do it in the same process; *bash* gives us four ways of doing this.

The first, which we have seen already, is with a function:

```
findterm () {
    TERM=vt100        # assume this as a default
    line=$(tty)
    while read dev termtype; do
        if [ $dev = $line ]; then
```

```
                    TERM=$termtype
                    echo "TERM set to $TERM."
                    break;
            fi
        done
    }


    findterm < /etc/terms
```

A function acts like a script in that it has its own set of standard I/O descriptors, which can be redirected in the line of code that calls the function. In other words, you can think of this code as if *findterm* were a script and you typed **findterm <** **/etc/terms** on the command line. The **read** statement takes input from */etc/terms* a line at a time, and the function runs correctly.

The second way is to simplify this slightly by placing the redirection at the end of the function:

```
findterm () {
    TERM=vt100        # assume this as a default
    line=$(tty)
    while read dev termtype; do
        if [ $dev = $line ]; then
            TERM=$termtype
            echo "TERM set to $TERM."
            break;
        fi
    done
} < /etc/terms
```

Whenever *findterm* is called, it takes its input from */etc/terms*.

The third way is by putting the I/O redirector at the end of the loop, like this:

```
TERM=vt100          # assume this as a default
line=$(tty)
while read dev termtype; do
    if [ $dev = $line ]; then
        TERM=$termtype
        echo "TERM set to $TERM."
        break;
    fi
done < /etc/terms
```

You can use this technique with any flow-control construct, including **if...fi**, **case...esac**, **select...done**, and **until...done**. This makes sense because these are all *compound statements* that the shell treats as single commands for these purposes. This technique works fine—the **read** command reads a line at a time—as long as all of the input is done within the compound statement.

Command blocks

But if you want to redirect I/O to or from an arbitrary group of commands without creating a separate process, you need to use a construct that we haven't seen yet. If you surround some code with { and }, the code will behave like a function that has no name. This is another type of compound statement. In accordance with the equivalent concept in the C language, we'll call this a *command block*.

What good is a block? In this case, it means that the code within the curly brackets ({}) will take standard I/O descriptors just as we described in the last block of code. This construct is appropriate for the current example because the code needs to be called only once, and the entire script is not really large enough to merit breaking down into functions. Here is how we use a block in the example:

```
{
    TERM=vt100        # assume this as a default
    line=$(tty)
    while read dev termtype; do
        if [ $dev = $line ]; then
            TERM=$termtype
            echo "TERM set to $TERM."
            break;
        fi
    done
} < /etc/terms
```

To help you understand how this works, think of the curly brackets and the code inside them as if they were one command, i.e.:

```
{ TERM=vt100; line=$(tty); while ... } < /etc/terms;
```

Configuration files for system administration tasks like this one are actually fairly common; a prominent example is */etc/hosts*, which lists machines that are accessible in a TCP/IP network. We can make */etc/terms* more like these standard files by allowing comment lines in the file that start with #, just as in shell scripts. This way */etc/terms* can look like this:

```
#
# System Console is console
console          console
#
# Cameron's line has a Wyse 60
tty01            wy60
...
```

We can handle comment lines by modifying the **while** loop so that it ignores lines begining with #. We can place a *grep* in the test:

```
if [ -z "$(echo $dev | grep ^#)" ]  && [ $dev = $line ]; then
    ...
```

As we saw in Chapter 5, *Flow Control,* the **&&** combines the two conditions so that *both* must be true for the entire condition to be true.

As another example of command blocks, consider the case of creating a standard algebraic notation frontend to the *dc* command. *dc* is a UNIX utility that simulates a Reverse Polish Notation (RPN) calculator:*

```
{ while read line; do
    echo "$(alg2rpn $line)"
  done
} | dc
```

We'll assume that the actual conversion from one notation to the other is handled by a function called *alg2rpn.* It takes a line of standard algebraic notation as an argument and prints the RPN equivalent on the standard output. The **while** loop reads lines and passes them through the conversion function, until an EOF is typed. Everything is executed inside the command block and the output is piped to the *dc* command for evaluation.

Reading user input

The other type of task to which **read** is suited is prompting a user for input. Think about it: we have hardly seen any such scripts so far in this book. In fact, the only ones were the modified solutions to Task 5-4, which involved **select**.

As you've probably figured out, **read** can be used to get user input into shell variables.

We can use **echo** to prompt the user, like this:

```
echo -n 'terminal? '
read TERM
echo "TERM is $TERM"
```

Here is what this looks like when it runs:

```
terminal? wy60
TERM is wy60
```

However, shell convention dictates that prompts should go to standard *error,* not standard output. (Recall that **select** prompts to standard error.) We could just use file descriptor 2 with the output redirector we saw earlier in this chapter:

```
echo -n 'terminal? ' >&2
read TERM
echo TERM is $TERM
```

---

* If you have ever owned a Hewlett-Packard calculator you will be familiar with RPN. We'll discuss RPN further in one of the exercises at the end of this chapter.

We'll now look at a more complex example by showing how Task 5-5 would be done if **select** didn't exist. Compare this with the code in Chapter 5:

```
echo 'Select a directory:'
done=false

while [ $done = false ]; do
    do=true
    num=1
    for direc in $DIR_STACK; do
        echo $num $direc
        num=$((num+1))
    done
    echo -n 'directory? '
    read REPLY

    if [ $REPLY -lt $num ] && [ $REPLY -gt 0 ]; then
        set - $DIR_STACK

        #statements that manipulate the stack...

        break
    else
        echo 'invalid selection.'
    fi
done
```

The **while** loop is necessary so that the code repeats if the user makes an invalid choice. **select** includes the ability to construct multicolumn menus if there are many choices, and better handling of null user input.

Before leaving **read**, we should note that it has four options: **-a**, **-e**, **-p**, and **-r**.* The first of these options allows you to read values into an array. Each successive item read in is assigned to the given array starting at index 0. For example:

```
$ read -a people
alice duchess dodo
$ echo ${people[2]}
dodo
$
```

In this case, the array **people** now contains the items *alice, duchess,* and *dodo.*

The option **-e** can be used only with scripts run from interactive shells. It causes *readline* to be used to gather the input line, which means that you can use any of the *readline* editing features that we looked at in Chapter 2.

The **-p** option followed by a string argument prints the string before reading input. We could have used this in the earlier examples of **read**, where we printed

---

* **-a**, **-e**, and **-p** are not available in versions of *bash* prior to 2.0.

out a prompt before doing the read. For example, the directory selection script could have used **read –p 'directory? ' REPLY**.

read lets you input lines that are longer than the width of your display by providing a backslash (\) as a continuation character, just as in shell scripts. The **–r** option overrides this, in case your script reads from a file that may contain lines that happen to end in backslashes. **read –r** also preserves any other escape sequences the input might contain. For example, if the file *hatter* contains this line:

```
A line with a\n escape sequence
```

Then **read –r aline** will include the backslash in the variable **aline**, whereas without the **–r**, **read** will "eat" the backslash. As a result:

```
$ read -r aline < hatter
$ echo -e "$aline"
A line with a
  escape sequence
$
```

However:

```
$ read aline < hatter
$ echo -e "$aline"
A line with an escape sequence
$
```

Command-Line Processing

We've seen how the shell uses **read** to process input lines: it deals with single quotes (' '), double quotes (" "), and backslashes (\); it separates lines into words, according to delimiters in the environment variable **IFS**; and it assigns the words to shell variables. We can think of this process as a subset of the things the shell does when processing *command lines*.

We've touched upon command-line processing throughout this book; now is a good time to make the whole thing explicit. Each line that the shell reads from the standard input or a script is called a *pipeline*; it contains one or more *commands* separated by zero or more pipe characters (|). For each pipeline it reads, the shell breaks it up into commands, sets up the I/O for the pipeline, then does the following for each command (Figure 7-1):

1. Splits the command into *tokens* that are separated by the fixed set of *metacharacters*: SPACE, TAB, NEWLINE, ;, (,), <, >, |, and **&**. Types of tokens include *words*, *keywords*, I/O redirectors, and semicolons.

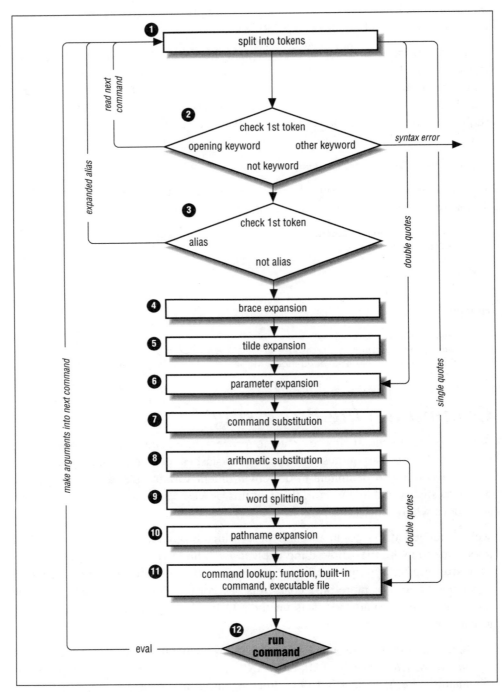

Figure 7-1: Steps in command-line processing

2. Checks the first token of each command to see if it is a *keyword* with no quotes or backslashes. If it's an opening keyword, such as **if** and other control-structure openers, **function**, **{**, or **(**, then the command is actually a *compound command*. The shell sets things up internally for the compound command, reads the next command, and starts the process again. If the keyword isn't a compound command opener (e.g., is a control-structure "middle" like **then**, **else**, or **do**, an "end" like **fi** or **done**, or a logical operator), the shell signals a syntax error.

3. Checks the first word of each command against the list of *aliases*. If a match is found, it substitutes the alias's definition and *goes back to Step 1*; otherwise, it goes on to Step 4. This scheme allows *recursive* aliases (see Chapter 3). It also allows aliases for keywords to be defined, e.g., **alias aslongas=while** or **alias procedure=function**.

4. Performs *brace expansion*. For example, **a{b,c}** becomes **ab ac**.

5. Substitutes the user's home directory (**$HOME**) for *tilde* if it is at the beginning of a word.* Substitutes *user*'s home directory for `~user`.

6. Performs *parameter (variable) substitution* for any expression that starts with a dollar sign (**$**).

7. Does *command substitution* for any expression of the form **$(*string*)**.

8. Evaluates *arithmetic expressions* of the form **$((*string*))**.

9. Takes the parts of the line that resulted from parameter, command, and arithmetic substitution and splits them into words again. This time it uses the characters in **$IFS** as delimiters instead of the set of metacharacters in Step 1.

10. Performs *pathname expansion*, a.k.a. *wildcard expansion*, for any occurrences of *****, **?**, and **[/]** pairs.

11. Uses the first word as a command by looking up its source according to the rest of the list in Chapter 4, i.e., as a *function* command, then as a *built-in*, then as a file in any of the directories in **$PATH**.

12. Runs the command after setting up I/O redirection and other such things.

That's a lot of steps—and it's not even the whole story! But before we go on, an example should make this process clearer. Assume that the following command has been run:

```
alias ll="ls -l"
```

---

* Two obscure variations on this: the shell substitutes the current directory (**$PWD**) for `~+` and the previous directory (**$OLDPWD**) for `~-`.

Further assume that a file exists called *.hist537* in user **alice**'s home directory, which is */home/alice*, and that there is a double-dollar-sign variable **$$** whose value is **2537** (we'll see what this special variable is in the next chapter).

Now let's see how the shell processes the following command:

```
ll $(type -path cc) ~alice/.*$(($$%1000))
```

Here is what happens to this line:

1. `ll $(type -path cc) ~alice/.*$(($$%1000))`
   Splitting the input into words.

2. `ll` is not a keyword, so Step 2 does nothing.

3. `ls -l $(type -path cc) ~alice/.*$(($$%1000))`
   Substituting **ls -l** for its alias "ll". The shell then repeats Steps 1 through 3; Step 2 splits the **ls -l** into two words.

4. `ls -l $(type -path cc) ~alice/.*$(($$%1000))`
   This step does nothing.

5. `ls -l $(type -path cc) /home/alice/.*$(($$%1000))`
   Expanding ~**alice** into */home/alice*.

6. `ls -l $(type -path cc) /home/alice/.*$((2537%1000))`
   Substituting **2537** for **$$**.

7. `ls -l /usr/bin/cc /home/alice/.*$((2537%1000))`
   Doing command substitution on "type -path cc".

8. `ls -l /usr/bin/cc /home/alice/.*537`
   Evaluating the arithmetic expression **2537%1000**.

9. `ls -l /usr/bin/cc /home/alice/.*537`
   This step does nothing.

10. `ls -l /usr/bin/cc /home/alice/.hist537`
    Substituting the filename for the wildcard expression `.*537`.

11. The command **ls** is found in */usr/bin*.

12. */usr/bin/ls* is run with the option −l and the two arguments.

Although this list of steps is fairly straightforward, it is not the whole story. There are still five ways to *modify* the process: quoting; using **command**, **builtin**, or **enable**; and using the advanced command **eval**.

Quoting

You can think of quoting as a way of getting the shell to skip some of the 12 steps above. In particular:

- Single quotes (' ') bypass *everything* through Step 10—including aliasing. All characters inside a pair of single quotes are untouched. You can't have single quotes inside single quotes—not even if you precede them with backslashes.*

- Double quotes (" ") bypass Steps 1 through 4, plus steps 9 and 10. That is, they ignore pipe characters, aliases, tilde substitution, wildcard expansion, and splitting into words via delimiters (e.g., blanks) inside the double quotes. Single quotes inside double quotes have no effect. But double quotes do allow parameter substitution, command substitution, and arithmetic expression evaluation. You can include a double quote inside a double-quoted string by preceding it with a backslash (\). You must also backslash-escape **$**, ` (the archaic command substitution delimiter), and \ itself.

Table 7-4 has simple examples to show how these work; they assume the statement **person=hatter** was run and user **alice**'s home directory is */home/alice*.

If you are wondering whether to use single or double quotes in a particular shell programming situation, it is safest to use single quotes unless you specifically need parameter, command, or arithmetic substitution.

Table 7-4: Examples of Quoting Rules

Expression	Value
$person	hatter
"$person"	hatter
\$person	$person
'$person'	$person
"'$person'"	'hatter'
~alice	/home/alice
"~alice"	~alice
'~alice'	~alice

command, builtin, and enable

Before moving on to the last part of the command-line processing cycle, we'll take a look at the command lookup order that we touched on in Chapter 4 and how it can be altered with several shell built-ins.

The default order for command lookup is functions, followed by built-ins, with scripts and executables last. There are three built-ins that you can use to override this order: **command**, **builtin**, and **enable**.

---

* However, as we saw in Chapter 1, *bash Basics*, '\'' (i.e., single quote, backslash, single quote, single quote) acts pretty much like a single quote in the middle of a single-quoted string; e.g., 'abc'\''def' evaluates to abc'def.

command removes alias and function lookup.* Only built-ins and commands found in the search path are executed. This is useful if you want to create functions that have the same name as a shell built-in or a command in the search path and you need to call the original command from the function. For instance, we might want to create a function called *cd* that replaces the standard **cd** command with one that does some fancy things and then executes the built-in **cd**:

```
cd ()
{
    #Some fancy things
    command cd
}
```

In this case we avoid plunging the function into a recursive loop by placing **command** in front of **cd**. This ensures that the built-in **cd** is called and not the function.

command has some options, listed in Table 7-5.

Table 7-5: command Options

Option	Description
–p	Use a default value for **PATH**
–v	Prints the command or pathname used to invoke the command
–V	A more verbose description than with –v
–	Turns off further option checking

The **–p** option is a default path which guarantees that the command lookup will find all of the standard UNIX utilities.† In this case, **command** will ignore the directories in your **PATH**.

builtin is very similar to **command** but is more restrictive. It looks up only built-in commands, ignoring functions and commands found in **PATH**. We could have replaced **command** with **builtin** in the **cd** example above.

The last command enables and disables shell built-ins—it is called **enable**. Disabling a built-in allows a shell script or executable of the same name to be run without giving a full pathname. Consider the problem many beginning UNIX shell programmers have when they name a script *test*. Much to their surprise, executing **test** usually results in nothing, because the shell is executing the built-in **test**, rather than the shell script. Disabling the built-in with **enable** overcomes this.‡

---

* **command** removes alias lookup as a side effect. Because the first argument of **command** is no longer the first word that *bash* parses, it is not subjected to alias lookup.

† Unless *bash* has been compiled with a brain-dead value for the default. See Chapter 11 for how to change the default value.

‡ Note that the wrong *test* may still be run. If your current directory is the last in **PATH** you'll probably execute the system file *test*. *test* is not a good name for a program.

Table 7-6 lists the options available with **enable**.* Some options are for working with *dynamically loadable* built-ins. See Appendix C, *Loadable Built-Ins*, for details on these options, and how to create and load your own built-in commands.

Table 7-6: enable Options

Option	Description
−a	Displays every built-in and whether it is enabled or not
−d	Delete a built-in loaded with −f
−f *filename*	Loads a new built-in from the shared-object *filename*
−n	Disables a built-in or displays a list of disabled built-ins
−p	Displays a list of all of the built-ins
−s	Restricts the output to POSIX "special" built-ins

Of these options, −n is the most useful; it is used to disable a built-in. **enable** without an option enables a built-in. More than one built-in can be given as arguments to **enable**, so **enable −n pushd popd dirs** would disable the **pushd**, **popd**, and **dirs** built-ins.†

You can find out what built-ins are currently enabled and disabled by using the command on its own, or with the −p option; **enable** or **enable −p** will list all enabled built-ins, and **enable −n** will list all disabled built-ins. To get a complete list with their current status, you can use **enable −a**.

The −s option restricts the output to POSIX 'special' built-ins. These are :, ., **source**, **break**, **continue**, **eval**, **exec**, **exit**, **export**, **readonly**, **return**, **set**, **shift**, **trap**, and **unset**.

eval

We have seen that quoting lets you skip steps in command-line processing. Then there's the **eval** command, which lets you go through the process again. Performing command-line processing twice may seem strange, but it's actually very powerful: it lets you write scripts that create command strings on the fly and then pass them to the shell for execution. This means that you can give scripts "intelligence" to modify their own behavior as they are running.

The **eval** statement tells the shell to take **eval**'s arguments and run them through the command-line processing steps all over again. To help you understand the implications of **eval**, we'll start with a trivial example and work our way up to a situation in which we're constructing and running commands on the fly.

---

* The −d, −f, −p, and −s options are not available in versions of *bash* prior to 2.0.

† Be careful—it is possible to disable **enable** (**enable −n enable**). There is a compile-time option that allows **builtin** to act as an escape-hatch. For more details, see Chapter 11.

eval ls passes the string **ls** to the shell to execute; the shell prints a list of files in the current directory. Very simple; there is nothing about the string **ls** that needs to be sent through the command-processing steps twice. But consider this:

```
listpage="ls | more"
$listpage
```

Instead of producing a paginated file listing, the shell will treat | and **more** as arguments to *ls*, and *ls* will complain that no files of those names exist. Why? Because the pipe character "appears" in Step 6 when the shell evaluates the variable, *after* it has actually looked for pipe characters. The variable's expansion isn't even parsed until Step 9. As a result, the shell will treat | and **more** as arguments to *ls*, so that *ls* will try to find files called | and *more* in the current directory!

Now consider **eval $listpage** instead of just **$listpage**. When the shell gets to the last step, it will run the command **eval** with arguments **ls**, |, and **more**. This causes the shell to go back to Step 1 with a line that consists of these arguments. It finds | in Step 2 and splits the line into two commands, *ls* and *more*. Each command is processed in the normal (and in both cases trivial) way. The result is a paginated list of the files in your current directory.

Now you may start to see how powerful **eval** can be. It is an advanced feature that requires considerable programming cleverness to be used most effectively. It even has a bit of the flavor of artificial intelligence, in that it enables you to write programs that can "write" and execute other programs.* You probably won't use **eval** for everyday shell programming, but it's worth taking the time to understand what it can do.

As a more interesting example, we'll revisit Task 4-1, the very first task in the book. In it, we constructed a simple pipeline that sorts a file and prints out the first *N* lines, where *N* defaults to 10. The resulting pipeline was:

```
sort -nr $1 | head -${2:-10}
```

The first argument specified the file to sort; **$2** is the number of lines to print.

Now suppose we change the task just a bit so that the default is to print the *entire file* instead of 10 lines. This means that we don't want to use *head* at all in the default case. We could do this in the following way:

```
if [ -n "$2" ]; then
    sort -nr $1 | head -$2
else
    sort -nr $1
fi
```

---

* You could actually do this without **eval**, by **echo**ing commands to a temporary file and then "sourcing" that file with . *filename*. But that is *much* less efficient.

In other words, we decide which pipeline to run according to whether **$2** is null. But here is a more compact solution:

```
eval sort -nr \$1 ${2:+"| head -\$2"}
```

The last expression in this line evaluates to the string | **head –\$2** if **$2** exists (is not null); if **$2** is null, then the expression is null too. We backslash-escape dollar signs (**\$**) before variable names to prevent unpredictable results if the variables' values contain special characters like **>** or **|**. The backslash effectively puts off the variables' evaluation until the **eval** command itself runs. So the entire line is either:

```
eval sort -nr \$1 | head -\$2
```

if **$2** is given, or:

```
eval sort -nr \$1
```

if **$2** is null. Once again, we can't just run this command without **eval** because the pipe is "uncovered" after the shell tries to break the line up into commands. **eval** causes the shell to run the correct pipeline when **$2** is given.

Next, we'll revisit Task 7-2 from earlier in this chapter, the *start* script that lets you start a command in the background and save its standard output and standard error in a logfile. Recall that the one-line solution to this task had the restriction that the command could not contain output redirectors or pipes. Although the former doesn't make sense when you think about it, you certainly would want the ability to start a pipeline in this way.

eval is the obvious way to solve this problem:

```
eval "$@" > logfile 2>&1 &
```

The only restriction that this imposes on the user is that pipes and other such special characters be quoted (surrounded by quotes or preceded by backslashes).

Here's a way to apply **eval** in conjunction with various other interesting shell programming concepts.

Task 7-3

Implement the core of the *make* utility as a shell script.

make is known primarily as a programmer's tool, but it seems as though someone finds a new use for it every day. Without going into too much extraneous detail, *make* basically keeps track of multiple files in a particular project, some of which depend on others (e.g., a document depends on its word processor input file(s)). It makes sure that when you change a file, all of the other files that depend on it are processed.

For example, assume you're using the *troff* word processor to write a book. You have files for the book's chapters called *ch1.t*, *ch2.t*, and so on; the *troff* output for these files are *ch1.out*, *ch2.out*, etc. You run commands like **troff ch*N*.t > ch*N*.out** to do the processing. While you're working on the book, you tend to make changes to several files at a time.

In this situation, you can use *make* to keep track of which files need to be reprocessed, so that all you need to do is type **make**, and it will figure out what needs to be done. You don't need to remember to reprocess the files that have changed.

How does *make* do this? Simple: it compares the *modification times* of the input and output files (called *sources* and *targets* in *make* terminology), and if the input file is newer, then *make* reprocesses it.

You tell *make* which files to check by building a file called *makefile* that has constructs like this:

```
target : source1 source2 ...
        commands to make target
```

This essentially says, "For *target* to be up to date, it must be newer than all of the *sources*. If it's not, run the *commands* to bring it up to date." The *commands* are on one or more lines that must start with TABs: e.g., to make *ch7.out*:

```
ch7.out : ch7.t
        troff ch7.t > ch7.out
```

Now suppose that we write a shell function called *makecmd* that reads and executes a single construct of this form. Assume that the *makefile* is read from standard input. The function would look like the following code.

```
makecmd ()
{
    read target colon sources
    for src in $sources; do
        if [ $src -nt $target ]; then
            while read cmd && [ $(grep \t* $cmd) ]; do
                echo "$cmd"
                eval ${cmd#\t}
            done
            break
        fi
    done
}
```

This function reads the line with the target and sources; the variable **colon** is just a placeholder for the :. Then it checks each source to see if it's newer than the target, using the **−nt** file attribute test operator that we saw in Chapter 5. If the source is newer, it reads, prints, and executes the commands until it finds a line that doesn't start with a TAB or it reaches end-of-file. (The real *make* does more than this; see the exercises at the end of this chapter.) After running the commands (which are stripped of the initial TAB), it breaks out of the **for** loop, so that it doesn't run the commands more than once.

As a final example of **eval**, we'll look again at *procimage*, the graphics utility that we developed in the last three chapters. Recall that one of the problems with the script as it stands is that it performs the process of scaling and bordering regardless of whether you want them. If no command-line options are present, a default size, border width, and border color are used. Rather than invent some if **then** logic to get around this, we'll look at how you can dynamically build a pipeline of commands in the script; those commands that aren't needed simply disappear when the time comes to execute them. As an added bonus, we'll add another capability to our script: *image enhancement.*

Looking at the *procimage* script you'll notice that the NetPBM commands form a nice pipeline; the output of one operation becomes the input to the next, until we end up with the final image. If it weren't for having to use a particular conversion utility, we could reduce the script to the following pipeline (ignoring options for now):

```
cat $filename | convertimage | pnmscale | pnmmargin | ppmquant | \
    ppmtogif > $outfile
```

Or, better yet:

```
convertimage $filename | pnmscale | pnmmargin | ppmquant | ppmtogif \
    > $outfile
```

As we've already seen, this is equivalent to:

```
eval convertimage $filename | pnmscale | pnmmargin | ppmquant | \
    ppmtogif > $outfile
```

And knowing what we do about how **eval** operates, we can transform this into:

```
eval "convertimage" $filename " | pnmscale" " | pnmmargin" \
    " | ppmquant" " | ppmtogif" > $outfile
```

And thence to:

```
convert='convertimage'
scale=' | pnmscale'
border=' | pnmmargin'
standardise=' | ppmquant | ppmtogif'

eval $convert $filename $scale $border $standardise > $outfile
```

Now consider what happens when we don't want to scale the image. We do this:

```
scale=""

while getopts ":s:w:c:" opt; do
    case $opt in
        s  ) scale=' | pnmscale' ;;

    ...

    eval $convert $filename $scale $border $standardise > $outfile
```

In this code fragment, **scale** is set to a default of the empty string. If **–s** is not given on the command line, then the final line evaluates with **$scale** as the empty string and the pipeline will "collapse" into:

```
$convert $filename $border $standardise > $outfile
```

Using this principle, we can modify the previous version of the *procimage* script and produce a pipeline version. For each input file we need to construct and run a pipeline based upon the options given on the command line. Here is the new version:

```
# Set up the defaults
width=1
colour='-color grey'
usage="Usage: $0 [-s N] [-w N] [-c S] imagefile..."

# Initialise the pipeline components
standardise=' | ppmquant -quiet 256 | ppmtogif -quiet'

while getopts ":s:w:c:" opt; do
    case $opt in
        s  ) size=$OPTARG
             scale=' | pnmscale -quiet -xysize $size $size' ;;
        w  ) width=$OPTARG
             border=' | pnmmargin $colour $width' ;;
        c  ) colour="-color $OPTARG"
             border=' | pnmmargin $colour $width' ;;
        \? ) echo $usage
             exit 1 ;;
    esac
done

shift $(($OPTIND - 1))

if [ -z "$@" ]; then
    echo $usage
    exit 1
fi

# Process the input files
for filename in "$@"; do
```

```
        case $filename in
            *.gif ) convert=giftopnm  ;;

            *.tga ) convert=tgatoppm  ;;

            *.xpm ) convert=xpmtoppm  ;;

            *.pcx ) convert=pcxtoppm  ;;

            *.tif ) convert=tifftopnm  ;;

            *.jpg ) convert=djpeg ;;

                * ) echo "$0: Unknown filetype '${filename##*.}'"
                    exit 1;;
        esac

        outfile=${filename%.*}.new.gif

        eval $convert $filename $scale $border $standardise > $outfile

    done
```

This version has been simplified somewhat from the previous one in that it no longer needs a temporary file to hold the converted file. It is also a lot easier to read and understand. To show how easy it is to add further processing to the script, we'll now add one more NetPBM utility.

You might have noticed that when you reduced an image in size it appeared to get a little less sharp. NetPBM provides a utility to enhance an image and make it sharper: *pnmnlfilt*. This utility is an image filter that samples the image and can enhance edges in the image (it can also smooth the image if given the appropriate values). It takes two parameters that tell it how much to enhance the image. For the purposes of our script, we'll just choose some optimal values and provide an option to switch enhancement on and off in the script.

To put the new capability in place all we have to do is add the new option (−S) to the **getopts case** statement, update the usage line, and add a new variable to the pipeline. Here is the new code:

```
# Set up the defaults
width=1
colour='-color grey'
usage="Usage: $0 [-S] [-s N] [-w N] [-c S] imagefile..."

# Initialise the pipeline components
standardise=' | ppmquant -quiet 256 | ppmtogif -quiet'

while getopts ":Ss:w:c:" opt; do
    case $opt in
      S  ) sharpness=' | pnmnlfilt -0.7 0.45' ;;
```

```
    s ) size=$OPTARG
        scale=' | pnmscale -quiet -xysize $size $size' ;;
    w ) width=$OPTARG
        border=' | pnmmargin $colour $width' ;;
    c ) colour="-color $OPTARG"
        border=' | pnmmargin $colour $width' ;;
    \? ) echo $usage
        exit 1 ;;
    esac
done

shift $(($OPTIND - 1))

if [ -z "$@" ]; then
    echo $usage
    exit 1
fi

# Process the input files
for filename in "$@"; do
    case $filename in
        *.gif ) convert=giftopnm  ;;

        *.tga ) convert=tgatoppm  ;;

        *.xpm ) convert=xpmtoppm  ;;

        *.pcx ) convert=pcxtoppm  ;;

        *.tif ) convert=tifftopnm ;;

        *.jpg ) convert=djpeg ;;

        * ) echo "$0: Unknown filetype '${filename##*.}'"
            exit 1;;
    esac

    outfile=${filename%.*}.new.gif

    eval $convert $filename $scale $border $sharpness $standardise \
        > $outfile

done
```

We could go on forever with increasingly complex examples of **eval**, but we'll set-
tle for concluding the chapter with a few exercises. The questions in Exercise 3
are really more like items on the menu of food for thought.

1. Here are a couple of ways to enhance *procimage*, the graphics utility:

    a. Add an option, **−q**, that allows the user to turn on and off the printing of
       diagnostic information from the NetPBM utilities. You'll need to map **−q** to

the **–quiet** option of the utilities. Also, add your own diagnostic output for those utilities that don't print anything, e.g., the format conversions.

b. Add an option that allows the user to specify the *order* that the NetPBM processes take place, i.e., whether enhancing the image comes before bordering, or bordering comes before resizing. Rather than using an **if** construct to make the choice amongst hard-coded orders, construct a string dynamically which will look similar to this:

```
"eval $convert $filename $scale $border $sharpness
    $standardise > $outfile"
```

You'll then need **eval** to evaluate this string.

2. The function *makecmd* in the solution to Task 7-3 represents an oversimplification of the real *make*'s functionality. *make* actually checks file dependencies recursively, meaning that a *source* on one line in a *makefile* can be a *target* on another line. For example, the book chapters in the example could themselves depend on some figures in separate files that were made with a graphics package.

a. Write a function called **readtargets** that goes through the *makefile* and stores all of the targets in a variable or temporary file.

b. *makecmd* merely checks to see if any of the sources are newer than the given target. It should really be a recursive routine that looks like this:

```
function makecmd ()
{
    target=$1
    get sources for $target
    for each source src; do
        if $src is also a target in this makefile then
            makecmd $src
        fi
        if [ $src -nt $target ]; then
            run commands to make target
            return
        fi
    done
}
```

Implement this.

c. Write the "driver" script that turns the *makecmd* function into a full *make* program. This should make the target given as argument, or if none is given, the first target listed in the makefile.

d. The above *makecmd* still doesn't do one important thing that the real *make* does: allow for "symbolic" targets that aren't files. These give *make* much of the power that makes it applicable to such an incredible variety of situations. Symbolic targets always have a modification time of 0, so that *make* always runs the commands to make them. Modify *makecmd* so that it allows for symbolic targets. (Hint: the crux of this problem is to figure out how to get a file's modification time. This is quite difficult.)

3. Here are some problems that really test your knowledge of **eval** and the shell's command-line processing rules. Solve these and you're a true *bash* hacker!

a. Advanced shell programmers sometimes use a little trick that includes **eval**: using the *value* of a variable as the *name* of another variable. In other words, you can give a shell script control over the *names* of variables to which it assigns values. The latest version of *bash* has this built in in the form of ${!*varname*}, where *varname* contains the name of another variable that will be the target of the operation. This is known as *indirect expansion*. How would you do this using *only* **eval**?

(Hint: if **$object** equals "person", and **$person** is "alice", then you might think that you could type **echo $$object** and get the response **alice**. This doesn't actually work, but it's on the right track.)

b. You could use the above technique together with other **eval** tricks to implement new control structures for the shell. For example, see if you can write a script that emulates the behavior of a **for** loop in a conventional language like C or Pascal, i.e., a loop that iterates a fixed number of times, with a loop variable that steps from 1 to the number of iterations (or, for C fans, 0 to iterations−1). Call your script **loop** to avoid clashes with the keywords **for** and **do**.

c. The **pushd**, **popd**, and **dirs** functions that we built up in previous chapters can't handle directories with spaces in their names (because DIR_STACK uses a space as a delimiter). Use **eval** to overcome this limitation.

(Hint: use **eval** to implement an array. Each array element is called *array1*, *array2*, ... *arrayn*, and each array element contains a directory name.)

d. (The following doesn't have that much to do with the material in this chapter *per se*, but it is a classic programming exercise:)

Write the function *alg2rpn* used in the section on *command blocks*. Here's how to do this: Arithmetic expressions in algebraic notation have the form *expr op expr*, where each *expr* is either a number or another expression (perhaps in parentheses), and *op* is +, −, ×, /, or % (remainder). In RPN, expressions have the form *expr expr op*. For example: the algebraic expression 2+3 is 2 3 + in RPN; the RPN equivalent of (2+3) × (9−5) is 2 3 + 9 5 − ×. The main advantage of RPN is that it obviates the need for parentheses and operator precedence rules (e.g., × is evaluated before +). The *dc* program accepts standard RPN, but each expression should have "p" appended to it, which tells *dc* to print its result; e.g., the first example above should be given to *dc* as 2 3 + p.

e. You need to write a routine that converts algebraic notation to RPN. This should be (or include) a function that calls itself (a *recursive* function) whenever it encounters a subexpression. It is especially important that this function keep track of where it is in the input string and how much of the string it "eats up" during its processing. (Hint: make use of the pattern-matching operators discussed in Chapter 4, to ease the task of parsing input strings.)

To make your life easier, don't worry about operator precedence for now; just convert to RPN from left to right: e.g., treat 3+4×5 as (3+4)×5 and 3×4+5 as (3×4)+5. This makes it possible for you to convert the input string on the fly, i.e., without having to read in the whole thing before doing any processing.

f. Enhance your solution to the previous exercise so that it supports operator precedence in the "usual" order: ×, /, % (remainder) +, −. For example, treat 3+4×5 as 3+(4×5) and 3×4+5 as (3×4)+5.

g. Here is something else to really test your skills; write a graphics utility script, *index*, that takes a list of image files, reduces them in size and creates an "index" image. An index image is comprised of thumbnail-sized versions of the original images, placed neatly in columns and rows, and with a caption underneath (usually the name of the original file).

Besides the list of files, you'll need some options, including the number of columns to create and the size of the thumbnail images. You might also like to include an option to specify the gap between each image.

The new NetPBM utilities you'll need are *pbmtext* and *pnmcat*. You'll also need our old favorites *pnmscale, ppmquant,* and one or more of the conversion utilities, depending upon whether you decide to take in various formats (as we did for *procimage*) and what output format you decide on.

pbmtext takes as an argument some text and converts the text into a PNM bitmap. *pnmcat* is a little more complex. Like *cat*, it concatenates things; in this case, images. You can specify as many PNM files as you like as arguments and *pnmcat* will put them together into one long image. By using the −lr and −tb options, you can specify whether you want the images to be placed one after the other going from left to right, or from top to bottom. The first option to *pnmcat* is the background color. It can be either −**black** for a black background, or −**white** for a white background. We suggest −**white** to match the *pbmtext* black text on a white background.

You'll need to take each file, run the filename through *pbmtext*, and use *pnmcat* to place it underneath a scaled down version of the original image. Then you'll need to continue doing this for each file and use *pnmcat* to connect them together. In addition, you'll have to keep tabs on how many columns you have completed and when to start a new row. Note that you'll need to build up the rows individually and use *pnmcat* to connect them together. *pnmcat* won't do this for you automatically.

8

Process Handling

The UNIX operating system built its reputation on a small number of concepts, all of which are simple yet powerful. We've seen most of them by now: standard input/output, pipes, text-filtering utilities, the tree-structured file system, and so on. UNIX also gained notoriety as the first small-computer operating system to give each user control over more than one process. We call this capability *user-controlled multitasking*.

If UNIX is the only operating system that you're familiar with, you might be surprised to learn that several other major operating systems have been sadly lacking in this area. For example, Microsoft's MS-DOS, for IBM PC compatibles, has no multitasking at all, let alone user-controlled multitasking. IBM's own VM/CMS system for large mainframes handles multiple users but gives them only one process each. DEC's VAX/VMS has user-controlled multitasking, but it is limited and difficult to use. The latest generation of small-computer operating systems, such as Apple's Macintosh OS System 7, IBM's OS/2 Version 2, and Microsoft's Windows NT, finally include user-controlled multitasking at the operating-system level.[*]

But if you've gotten this far in this book, you probably don't think that multitasking is a big deal. You're probably used to the idea of running a process in the background by putting an ampersand (&) at the end of the command line. You have also seen the idea of a *subshell* in Chapter 4, *Basic Shell Programming*, when we showed how shell scripts run.

In this chapter, we will cover most of *bash*'s features that relate to multitasking and process handling in general. We say "most" because some of these features are,

---

[*] Programs like Apple's Multifinder and Microsoft Windows work *on top of* the operating system (Mac OS Version 6 and MS-DOS, respectively) to give the user limited multitasking.

like the file descriptors we saw in the previous chapter, of interest only to low-level systems programmers.

We'll start out by looking at certain important primitives for identifying processes and for controlling them during login sessions and within shell scripts. Then we will move out to a higher-level perspective, looking at ways to get processes to communicate with each other. We'll look in more detail at concepts we've already seen, like pipes and subshells.

Don't worry about getting bogged down in low-level technical details about UNIX. We will provide only the technical information that is necessary to explain higher-level features, plus a few other tidbits designed to pique your curiosity. If you are interested in finding out more about these areas, refer to your UNIX Programmer's Manual or a book on UNIX internals that pertains to your version of UNIX. You might also find *UNIX Power Tools* (published by O'Reilly & Associates) of value.

We strongly recommend that you try out the examples in this chapter. The behavior of code that involves multiple processes is not as easy to understand on paper as most of the other examples in this book.

Process IDs and Job Numbers

UNIX gives all processes numbers, called *process IDs*, when they are created. You will notice that when you run a command in the background by appending **&** to it, the shell responds with a line that looks like this:

```
$ alice &
[1] 93
```

In this example, 93 is the process ID for the **alice** process. The [1] is a *job number* assigned by the shell (not the operating system). What's the difference? Job numbers refer to background processes that are currently running under your shell, while process IDs refer to all processes currently running on the entire system, for all users. The term *job* basically refers to a command line that was invoked from your shell.

If you start up additional background jobs while the first one is still running, the shell will number them 2, 3, etc. For example:

```
$ duchess &
[2] 102
$ hatter &
[3] 104
```

Clearly, 1, 2, and 3 are easier to remember than 93, 102, and 104!

The shell includes job numbers in messages it prints when a background job completes, like this:*

```
[1]+   Done              alice
```

We'll explain what the plus sign means soon. If the job exits with non-zero status (see Chapter 5, *Flow Control*), the shell will indicate the exit status:†

```
[1]+   Exit 1            alice
```

The shell prints other types of messages when certain abnormal things happen to background jobs; we'll see these later in this chapter.

Job Control

Why should you care about process IDs or job numbers? Actually, you could probably get along fine through your UNIX life without ever referring to process IDs (unless you use a windowing workstation—as we'll see soon). Job numbers are more important, however: you can use them with the shell commands for *job control*.‡

You already know the most obvious way of controlling a job: create one in the background with &. Once a job is running in the background, you can let it run to completion, bring it into the *foreground*, or send it a message called a *signal*.

Foreground and Background

The built-in command **fg** brings a background job into the foreground. Normally this means that the job will have control of your terminal or window and therefore will be able to accept your input. In other words, the job will begin to act as if you typed its command without the &.

If you have only one background job running, you can use **fg** without arguments, and the shell will bring that job into the foreground. But if you have several jobs running in the background, the shell will pick the one that you put into the background most recently. If you want some other job put into the foreground, you need to use the job's command name, preceded by a percent sign (%), or you can

---

* The messages are, by default, printed before the next prompt is displayed so as not to interrupt any output on the display. You can make the notification messages display immediately by using **set –b**.

† In POSIX mode, the message is slightly different: "[1]+   Done(1)   alice". The number in parentheses is the exit status of the job. POSIX mode can be selected via the **set** command or by starting *bash* in POSIX mode. For further information, see Appendix B, Table B-1, "Command-Line Options," and Table B-5, "Options."

‡ If you have an older version of UNIX, it is possible that your system does not support job control. This is particularly true for many systems derived from Xenix, System III, or early versions of System V. On such systems, *bash* does not have the **fg** and **bg** commands, job number arguments to **kill** and **wait**, typing CTRL-Z to suspend a job, or the TSTP signal.

use its job number, also preceded by %, or its process ID without a percent sign. If you don't remember which jobs are running, you can use the command **jobs** to list them.

A few examples should make this clearer. Let's say you created three background jobs as above. Then if you type **jobs**, you will see this:

```
[1]    Running                 alice &
[2]-   Running                 duchess &
[3]+   Running                 hatter &
```

jobs has a few interesting options. **jobs −l** also lists process IDs:

```
[1]       93 Running            alice &
[2]-     102 Running            duchess &
[3]+     104 Running            hatter &
```

The **−p** option tells **jobs** to list *only* process IDs:

```
93
102
104
```

(This could be useful with command substitution; see Task 8-1.) The **−n** option lists only those jobs whose status has changed since the shell last reported it—whether with a **jobs** command or otherwise. **−r** restricts the list to jobs that are running, while **−s** restricts the list to those jobs which are stopped, e.g., waiting for input from the keyboard.* Finally, you can use the **−x** option to execute a command. Any job number provided to the command will be substituted with the process ID of the job. For example, if *alice* is running in the background, then executing **jobs −x echo %1** will print the process ID of *alice*.

If you type **fg** without an argument, the shell will put **hatter** in the foreground, because it was put in the background most recently. But if you type **fg %duchess** (or **fg %2**), **duchess** will go in the foreground.

You can also refer to the job most recently put in the background by %+. Similarly, %− refers to the *next*-most-recently backgrounded job (**duchess** in this case). That explains the plus and minus signs in the above: the plus sign shows the most recent job whose status has changed; the minus sign shows the next-most-recently invoked job.†

If more than one background job has the same command, then %*command* will distinguish between them by choosing the most recently invoked job (as you'd expect). If this isn't what you want, you need to use the job number instead of the

---

* Options −r and −s are not available in *bash* prior to version 2.0.

† This is analogous to ˜+ and ˜− as references to the current and previous directory; see the footnote in Chapter 7, *Input/Output and Command-Line Processing*. Also: %% is a synonym for %+.

command name. However, if the commands have different *arguments*, you can use %?*string* instead of %*command*. %?*string* refers to the job whose command contains the string. For example, assume you started these background jobs:

```
$ hatter mad &
[1]     189
$ hatter teatime &
[2]     190
$
```

Then you can use **%?mad** and **%?teatime** to refer to each of them, although actually **%?ma** and **%?tea** are sufficient to uniquely identify them.

Table 8-1 lists all of the ways to refer to background jobs. Given how infrequently people use job control commands, job numbers or command names are sufficient, and the other ways are superfluous.

Table 8-1: Ways to Refer to Background Jobs

Reference	Background job
%*N*	Job number *N*
%*string*	Job whose command begins with *string*
%?*string*	Job whose command contains *string*
%+	Most recently invoked background job
%%	Same as above
%−	Second most recently invoked background job

Suspending a Job

Just as you can put background jobs into the foreground with **fg**, you can also put a foreground job into the background. This involves suspending a job, so that the shell regains control of your terminal.

To suspend a job, type CTRL-Z while it is running.* This is analogous to typing CTRL-C (or whatever your interrupt key is), except that you can resume the job after you have stopped it. When you type CTRL-Z, the shell responds with a message like this:

```
[1]+  Stopped                 command
```

Then it gives you your prompt back. To resume a suspended job so that it continues to run in the foreground, just type **fg**. If, for some reason, you put other jobs in the background after you typed CTRL-Z, use **fg** with a job name or number.

---

* This assumes that the CTRL-Z key is set up as your suspend key; just as with CTRL-C and interrupts, this is conventional but by no means required.

For example:

```
alice is running...
CTRL-Z
[1]+  Stopped                    alice
$ hatter &
[2] 145
$ fg %alice
alice resumes in the foreground...
```

The ability to suspend jobs and resume them in the foreground comes in very handy when you have a conventional terminal (as opposed to a windowing work-station) and you are using a text editor like *vi* on a file that needs to be processed. For example, if you are editing a file for the *troff* text processor, you can do the following:

```
$ vi myfile
edit the file... CTRL-Z
Stopped [1] vi
$ troff myfile
troff reports an error
$ fg
vi comes back up in the same place in your file
```

Programmers often use the same technique when debugging source code.

You will probably also find it useful to suspend a job and resume it in the background instead of the foreground. You may start a command in the foreground (i.e., normally) and find that it takes much longer than you expected—for example, a *grep*, *sort*, or database query. You need the command to finish, but you would also like control of your terminal back so that you can do other work. If you type CTRL-Z followed by **bg**, you will move the job to the background.*

You can also suspend a job with CTRL-Y. This is slightly different from CTRL-Z in that the process is only stopped when it attempts to read input from the terminal.

Signals

We mentioned earlier that typing CTRL-Z to suspend a job is similar to typing CTRL-C to stop a job, except that you can resume the job later. They are actually similar in a deeper way: both are particular cases of the act of sending a *signal* to a process.

A signal is a message that one process sends to another when some abnormal event takes place or when it wants the other process to do something. Most of the

---

* Be warned, however, that not all commands are "well-behaved" when you do this. Be especially careful with commands that run over a network on a remote machine; you may end up confusing the remote program.

time, a process sends a signal to a subprocess it created. You're undoubtedly already comfortable with the idea that one process can communicate with another through an I/O pipeline; think of a signal as another way for processes to communicate with each other. (In fact, any textbook on operating systems will tell you that both are examples of the general concept of *interprocess communication*, or IPC.)*

Depending on the version of UNIX, there are two or three dozen types of signals, including a few that can be used for whatever purpose a programmer wishes. Signals have numbers (from 1 to the number of signals the system supports) and names; we'll use the latter. You can get a list of all the signals on your system, by name and number, by typing **kill –l**. Bear in mind, when you write shell code involving signals, that signal names are more portable to other versions of UNIX than signal numbers.

Control-Key Signals

When you type CTRL-C, you tell the shell to send the INT (for "interrupt") signal to the current job; CTRL-Z sends TSTP (on most systems, for "terminal stop"). You can also send the current job a QUIT signal by typing CTRL-\ (control-backslash); this is sort of like a "stronger" version of CTRL-C.† You would normally use CTRL-\ when (and *only* when) CTRL-C doesn't work.

As we'll see soon, there is also a "panic" signal called KILL that you can send to a process when even CTRL-\ doesn't work. But it isn't attached to any control key, which means that you can't use it to stop the currently running process. INT, TSTP, and QUIT are the only signals you can use with control keys.‡

You can customize the control keys used to send signals with options of the *stty* command. These vary from system to system—consult your manpage for the command—but the usual syntax is **stty** *signame char. signame* is a name for the signal that, unfortunately, is often not the same as the names we use here. Table 1-7 in Chapter 1, *bash Basics*, lists *stty* names for signals found on all versions of UNIX. *char* is the control character, which you can give using the convention that ˆ (cir-

---

* Pipes and signals were the only IPC mechanisms in early versions of UNIX. More modern versions like System V and 4.x BSD have additional mechanisms, such as sockets, named pipes, and shared memory. Named pipes are accessible to shell programmers through the *mknod*(1) command, which is beyond the scope of this book.

† CTRL-\ can also cause the shell to leave a file called *core* in your current directory. This file contains an image of the process to which you sent the signal; a programmer could use it to help debug the program that was running. The file's name is a (very) old-fashioned term for a computer's memory. Other signals leave these "core dumps" as well; unless you require them, or someone else does, just delete them.

‡ Some BSD-derived systems have additional control-key signals.

cumflex) represents "control." For example, to set your INT key to CTRL-X on most systems, use:

```
stty intr ^X
```

Now that we've told you how to do this, we should add that we don't recommend it. Changing your signal keys could lead to trouble if someone else has to stop a runaway process on your machine.

Most of the other signals are used by the operating system to advise processes of error conditions, like a bad machine code instruction, bad memory address, or division by zero, or "interesting" events such as a timer ("alarm") going off. The remaining signals are used for esoteric error conditions of interest only to low-level systems programmers; newer versions of UNIX have even more signal types.

kill

You can use the built-in shell command **kill** to send a signal to any process you created—not just the currently running job. **kill** takes as an argument the process ID, job number, or command name of the process to which you want to send the signal. By default, **kill** sends the TERM ("terminate") signal, which usually has the same effect as the INT signal you send with CTRL-C. But you can specify a different signal by using the signal name (or number) as an option, preceded by a dash.

kill is so named because of the nature of the default TERM signal, but there is another reason, which has to do with the way UNIX handles signals in general. The full details are too complex to go into here, but the following explanation should suffice.

Most signals cause a process that receives them to die; therefore, if you send any one of these signals, you "kill" the process that receives it. However, programs can be set up to "trap" specific signals and take some other action. For example, a text editor would do well to save the file being edited before terminating when it receives a signal such as INT, TERM, or QUIT. Determining what to do when various signals come in is part of the fun of UNIX systems programming.

Here is an example of **kill**. Say you have an **alice** process in the background, with process ID 150 and job number 1, that needs to be stopped. You would start with this command:

```
$ kill %1
```

If you were successful, you would see a message like this:

```
[1]+  Terminated              alice
```

If you don't see this, then the TERM signal failed to terminate the job. The next step would be to try QUIT:

```
$ kill -QUIT %1
```

If that worked, you would see this message:

```
[1]+   Exit 131              alice
```

The 131 is the exit status returned by **alice**.* But if even QUIT doesn't work, the "last-ditch" method would be to use KILL:

```
$ kill -KILL %1
```

This produces the message:

```
[1]+   Killed               alice
```

It is impossible for a process to "trap" a KILL signal—the operating system should terminate the process immediately and unconditionally. If it doesn't, then either your process is in one of the "funny states" we'll see later in this chapter, or (far less likely) there's a bug in your version of UNIX.

Here's another example.

Task 8-1

Write a script called **killalljobs** that kills all background jobs.

The solution to this task is simple, relying on **jobs –p**:

```
kill "$@" $(jobs -p)
```

You may be tempted to use the KILL signal immediately, instead of trying TERM (the default) and QUIT first. Don't do this. TERM and QUIT are designed to give a process the chance to "clean up" before exiting, whereas KILL will stop the process, wherever it may be in its computation. *Use KILL only as a last resort!*

You can use the **kill** command with any process you create, not just jobs in the background of your current shell. For example, if you use a windowing system, then you may have several terminal windows, each of which runs its own shell. If one shell is running a process that you want to stop, you can **kill** it from another window—but you can't refer to it with a job number because it's running under a different shell. You must instead use its process ID.

---

* When a shell script is sent a signal, it exits with status 128+N, where N is the number of the signal it received. In this case, **alice** is a shell script, and QUIT happens to be signal number 3.

ps

This is probably the only situation in which a casual user would need to know the ID of a process. The command *ps* gives you this information; however, it can give you lots of extra information as well.

ps is a complex command. It takes several options, some of which differ from one version of UNIX to another. To add to the confusion, you may need different options on different UNIX versions to get the same information! We will use options available on the two major types of UNIX systems, those derived from System V (such as most of the versions for Intel 386/486 PCs, as well as IBM's AIX and Hewlett-Packard's HP/UX) and BSD (DEC's Ultrix, SunOS, BSD/OS). If you aren't sure which kind of UNIX version you have, try the System V options first.

You can invoke *ps* in its simplest form without any options. In this case, it will print a line of information about the current login shell and any processes running under it (i.e., background jobs). For example, if you were to invoke three background jobs, as we saw earlier in the chapter, the *ps* command on System V-derived versions of UNIX would produce output that looks something like this:

```
 PID TTY       TIME COMD
 146 pts/10    0:03 -bash
2349 pts/10    0:03 alice
2367 pts/10    0:17 hatter
2389 pts/10    0:09 duchess
2390 pts/10    0:00 ps
```

The output on BSD-derived systems looks like this:

```
 PID TT STAT   TIME COMMAND
 146 10 S      0:03 /bin/bash
2349 10 R      0:03 alice
2367 10 D      0:17 hatter teatime
2389 10 R      0:09 duchess
2390 10 R      0:00 ps
```

(You can ignore the STAT column.) This is a bit like the **jobs** command. PID is the process ID; TTY (or TT) is the terminal (or pseudo-terminal, if you are using a windowing system) the process was invoked from; TIME is the amount of processor time (not real or "wall clock" time) the process has used so far; COMD (or COMMAND) is the command. Notice that the BSD version includes the command's arguments, if any; also notice that the first line reports on the parent shell process, and in the last line, *ps* reports on itself.

ps without arguments lists all processes started from the current terminal or pseudo-terminal. But since *ps* is not a shell command, it doesn't correlate process IDs with the shell's job numbers. It also doesn't help you find the ID of the runaway process in another shell window.

To get this information, use **ps −a** (for "all"); this lists information on a different set of processes, depending on your UNIX version.

System V

Instead of listing all that were started under a specific terminal, **ps −a** on System V-derived systems lists all processes associated with any terminal that aren't group leaders. For our purposes, a "group leader" is the parent shell of a terminal or window. Therefore, if you are using a windowing system, **ps −a** lists all jobs started in all windows (by all users), but not their parent shells.

Assume that, in the previous example, you have only one terminal or window. Then **ps −a** will print the same output as plain **ps** except for the first line, since that's the parent shell. This doesn't seem to be very useful.

But consider what happens when you have multiple windows open. Let's say you have three windows, all running terminal emulators like *xterm* for the X Window System. You start background jobs **alice**, **duchess**, and **hatter** in windows with pseudo-terminal numbers 1, 2, and 3, respectively. This situation is shown in Figure 8-1.

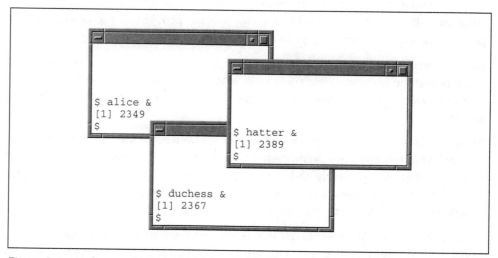

Figure 8-1: Background jobs in multiple windows

Assume you are in the uppermost window. If you type **ps**, you will see something like this:

```
 PID TTY      TIME COMD
 146 pts/1    0:03 bash
2349 pts/1    0:03 alice
2390 pts/1    0:00 ps
```

But if you type **ps −a**, you will see this:

```
PID TTY       TIME COMD
 146 pts/1    0:03 bash
2349 pts/1    0:03 alice
2367 pts/2    0:17 duchess
2389 pts/3    0:09 hatter
2390 pts/1    0:00 ps
```

Now you should see how **ps −a** can help you track down a runaway process. If it's **hatter**, you can type **kill 2389**. If that doesn't work, try **kill −QUIT 2389**, or in the worst case, **kill −KILL 2389**.

BSD

On BSD-derived systems, **ps −a** lists all jobs that were started on any terminal; in other words, it's a bit like concatenating the the results of plain **ps** for every user on the system. Given the above scenario, **ps −a** will show you all processes that the System V version shows, plus the group leaders (parent shells).

Unfortunately, **ps −a** (on any version of UNIX) will not report processes that are in certain conditions where they "forget" things like what shell invoked them and what terminal they belong to. Such processes are known as "zombies" or "orphans." If you have a serious runaway process problem, it's possible that the process has entered one of these states.

Let's not worry about why or how a process gets this way. All you need to understand is that the process doesn't show up when you type **ps −a**. You need another option to *ps* to see it: on System V, it's **ps −e** ("everything"), whereas on BSD, it's **ps −ax**.

These options tell *ps* to list processes that either weren't started from terminals or "forgot" what terminal they were started from. The former category includes lots of processes that you probably didn't even know existed: these include basic processes that run the system and so-called *daemons* (pronounced "demons") that handle system services like mail, printing, network file systems, etc.

In fact, the output of **ps −e** or **ps −ax** is an excellent source of education about UNIX system internals, if you're curious about them. Run the command on your system and, for each line of the listing that looks interesting, invoke *man* on the process name or look it up in the *UNIX Programmer's Manual* for your system.

User shells and processes are listed at the very bottom of **ps −e** or **ps −ax** output; this is where you should look for runaway processes. Notice that many processes in the listing have **?** instead of a terminal. Either these aren't supposed to have one (such as the basic daemons) or they're runaways. Therefore it's likely that if **ps −a** doesn't find a process you're trying to kill, **ps −e** (or **ps −ax**) will list it with

? in the TTY (or TT) column. You can determine which process you want by looking at the COMD (or COMMAND) column.

trap

We've been discussing how signals affect the casual user; now let's talk a bit about how shell programmers can use them. We won't go into too much depth about this, because it's really the domain of systems programmers.

We mentioned above that programs in general can be set up to "trap" specific signals and process them in their own way. The **trap** built-in command lets you do this from within a shell script. **trap** is most important for "bullet-proofing" large shell programs so that they react appropriately to abnormal events—just as programs in any language should guard against invalid input. It's also important for certain systems programming tasks, as we'll see in the next chapter.

The syntax of **trap** is:

```
trap cmd sig1 sig2 ...
```

That is, when any of *sig1*, *sig2*, etc., are received, run *cmd*, then resume execution. After *cmd* finishes, the script resumes execution just after the command that was interrupted.*

Of course, *cmd* can be a script or function. The *sig*s can be specified by name or by number. You can also invoke **trap** without arguments, in which case the shell will print a list of any traps that have been set, using symbolic names for the signals.

Here's a simple example that shows how **trap** works. Suppose we have a shell script called **loop** with this code:

```
while true; do
    sleep 60
done
```

This will just pause for 60 seconds (the *sleep* command) and repeat indefinitely. **true** is a "do-nothing" command whose exit status is always 0.† Try typing in this script. Invoke it, let it run for a little while, then type CTRL-C (assuming that is your interrupt key). It should stop, and you should get your shell prompt back.

---

* This is what *usually* happens. Sometimes the command currently running will abort (*sleep* acts like this, as we'll see soon); at other times it will finish running. Further details are beyond the scope of this book.

† This command is the same as the built-in shell no-op command ":".

Now insert this line at the beginning of the script:

```
trap "echo 'You hit control-C!'" INT
```

Invoke the script again. Now hit CTRL-C. The odds are overwhelming that you are interrupting the *sleep* command (as opposed to **true**). You should see the message "You hit control-C!", and the script will not stop running; instead, the *sleep* command will abort, and it will loop around and start another *sleep*. Hit CTRL-Z to get it to stop and then type **kill %1**.

Next, run the script in the background by typing **loop &**. Type **kill %loop** (i.e., send it the TERM signal); the script will terminate. Add TERM to the **trap** command, so that it looks like this:

```
trap "echo 'You hit control-C!'" INT TERM
```

Now repeat the process: run it in the background and type **kill %loop**. As before, you will see the message and the process will keep on running. Type **kill –KILL %loop** to stop it.

Notice that the message isn't really appropriate when you use **kill**. We'll change the script so it prints a better message in the **kill** case:

```
trap "echo 'You hit control-C!'" INT
trap "echo 'You tried to kill me!'" TERM

while true; do
    sleep 60
done
```

Now try it both ways: in the foreground with CTRL-C and in the background with **kill**. You'll see different messages.

Traps and Functions

The relationship between traps and shell functions is straightforward, but it has certain nuances that are worth discussing. The most important thing to understand is that functions are considered part of the shell that invokes them. This means that traps defined in the invoking shell will be recognized inside the function, and more importantly, any traps defined in the function will be recognized by the invoking shell once the function has been called. Consider this code:

```
settrap () {
    trap "echo 'You hit control-C!'" INT
}

settrap
while true; do
    sleep 60
done
```

If you invoke this script and hit your interrupt key, it will print "You hit control-C!" In this case the trap defined in **settrap** still exists when the function exits.

Now consider:

```
loop () {
    trap "echo 'How dare you!'" INT
    while true; do
        sleep 60
    done
}

trap "echo 'You hit control-C!'" INT
loop
```

When you run this script and hit your interrupt key, it will print "How dare you!" In this case the trap is defined in the calling script, but when the function is called the trap is redefined. The first definition is lost. A similar thing happens with:

```
loop () {
    trap "echo 'How dare you!'" INT
}

trap "echo 'You hit control-C!'" INT
loop
while true; do
    sleep 60
done
```

Once again, the trap is redefined in the function; this is the definition used once the loop is entered.

We'll now show a more practical example of traps.

Task 8-2

As part of an electronic mail system, write the shell code that lets a user compose a message.

The basic idea is to use *cat* to create the message in a temporary file and then hand the file's name off to a program that actually sends the message to its destination. The code to create the file is very simple:

```
msgfile=/tmp/msg$$
cat > $msgfile
```

Since *cat* without an argument reads from the standard input, this will just wait for the user to type a message and end it with the end-of-text character CTRL-D.

Process ID Variables and Temporary Files

The only thing new about this script is **$$** in the filename expression. This is a special shell variable whose value is the process ID of the current shell.

To see how **$$** works, type **ps** and note the process ID of your shell process (*bash*). Then type **echo "$$"**; the shell will respond with that same number. Now type **bash** to start a subshell, and when you get a prompt, repeat the process. You should see a different number, probably slightly higher than the last one.

A related built-in shell variable is ! (i.e., its value is **$!**), which contains the process ID of the most recently invoked background job. To see how this works, invoke any job in the background and note the process ID printed by the shell next to [1]. Then type **echo "$!"**; you should see the same number.

To return to our mail example: since all processes on the system must have unique process IDs, **$$** is excellent for constructing names of temporary files.

The directory */tmp* is conventionally used for temporary files. Many systems also have another directory, */usr/tmp*, for the same purpose.

Nevertheless, a program should clean up such files before it exits, to avoid taking up unnecessary disk space. We could do this in our code very easily by adding the line **rm $msgfile** after the code that actually sends the message. But what if the program receives a signal during execution? For example, what if a user changes his or her mind about sending the message and hits CTRL-C to stop the process? We would need to clean up before exiting. We'll emulate the actual UNIX *mail* system by saving the message being written in a file called *dead.letter* in the current directory. We can do this by using **trap** with a command string that includes an **exit** command:

```
trap 'mv $msgfile dead.letter; exit' INT TERM
msgfile=/tmp/msg$$
cat > $msgfile
# send the contents of $msgfile to the specified mail address...
rm $msgfile
```

When the script receives an INT or TERM signal, it will remove the temp file and then exit. Note that the command string isn't *evaluated* until it needs to be run, so **$msgfile** will contain the correct value; that's why we surround the string in single quotes.

But what if the script receives a signal before **msgfile** is created—unlikely though that may be? Then **mv** will try to rename a file that doesn't exist. To fix this, we need to test for the existence of the file **$msgfile** before trying to delete it. The code for this is a bit unwieldy to put in a single command string, so we'll use a function instead:

```
function cleanup {
    if [ -e $msgfile ]; then
        mv $msgfile dead.letter
    fi
    exit
}

trap cleanup INT TERM

msgfile=/tmp/msg$$
cat > $msgfile
# send the contents of $msgfile to the specified mail address...
rm $msgfile
```

Ignoring Signals

Sometimes a signal comes in that you don't want to do anything about. If you give the null string (`""` or `' '`) as the command argument to **trap**, then the shell will effectively ignore that signal. The classic example of a signal you may want to ignore is HUP (hangup). This can occur on some UNIX systems when a hangup (disconnection while using a modem—literally "hanging up") or some other network outage takes place.

HUP has the usual default behavior: it will kill the process that receives it. But there are bound to be times when you don't want a background job to terminate when it receives a hangup signal.

To do this, you could write a simple function that looks like this:

```
function ignorehup {
    trap "" HUP
    eval "$@"
}
```

We write this as a function instead of a script for reasons that will become clearer when we look in detail at subshells at the end of this chapter.

Actually, there is a UNIX command called *nohup* that does precisely this. The **start** script from the last chapter could include **nohup**:

```
eval nohup "$@" > logfile 2>&1 &
```

This prevents HUP from terminating your command and saves its standard and error output in a file. Actually, the following is just as good:

```
nohup "$@" > logfile 2>&1 &
```

If you understand why **eval** is essentially redundant when you use **nohup** in this case, then you have a firm grasp on the material in the previous chapter. Note that if you don't specify a redirection for any output from the command, *nohup* places it in a file called *nohup.out.*

disown

Another way to ignore the HUP signal is with the **disown** built-in.* **disown** takes as an argument a job specification, such as the process ID or job ID, and removes the process from the list of jobs. The process is effectively "disowned" by the shell from that point on, i.e., you can only refer to it by its process ID since it is no longer in the job table.

disown's -h option performs the same function as *nohup*; it specifies that the shell should stop the hangup signal from reaching the process under certain circumstances. Unlike *nohup*, it is up to you to specify where the output from the process is to go.

Resetting Traps

Another "special case" of the **trap** command occurs when you give a dash (–) as the command argument. This resets the action taken when the signal is received to the default, which usually is termination of the process.

As an example of this, let's return to Task 8-2, our mail program. After the user has finished sending the message, the temporary file is erased. At that point, since there is no longer any need to clean up, we can reset the signal trap to its default state. The code for this, apart from function definitions, is:

```
trap abortmsg INT
trap cleanup TERM

msgfile=/tmp/msg$$
cat > $msgfile
# send the contents of $msgfile to the specified mail address...
rm $msgfile

trap - INT TERM
```

The last line of this code resets the handlers for the INT and TERM signals.

At this point you may be thinking that one could get seriously carried away with signal handling in a shell script. It is true that "industrial strength" programs devote considerable amounts of code to dealing with signals. But these programs are almost always large enough so that the signal-handling code is a tiny fraction of the whole thing. For example, you can bet that the real UNIX *mail* system is pretty darn bullet-proof.

However, you will probably never write a shell script that is complex enough, and that needs to be robust enough, to merit lots of signal handling. You may write a

---

* **disown** is not available in versions of *bash* prior to 2.0.

prototype for a program as large as *mail* in shell code, but prototypes by definition do not need to be bullet-proofed.

Therefore, you shouldn't worry about putting signal-handling code in every 20-line shell script you write. Our advice is to determine if there are any situations in which a signal could cause your program to do something seriously bad and add code to deal with those contingencies. What is "seriously bad"? Well, with respect to the above examples, we'd say that the case where HUP causes your job to terminate is seriously bad, while the temporary file situation in our mail program is not.

Coroutines

We've spent the last several pages on almost microscopic details of process behavior. Rather than continue our descent into the murky depths, we'll revert to a higher-level view of processes.

Earlier in this chapter, we covered ways of controlling multiple simultaneous jobs within an interactive login session; now we'll consider multiple process control within shell programs. When two (or more) processes are explicitly programmed to run simultaneously and possibly communicate with each other, we call them *coroutines*.

This is actually nothing new: a pipeline is an example of coroutines. The shell's pipeline construct encapsulates a fairly sophisticated set of rules about how processes interact with each other. If we take a closer look at these rules, we'll be better able to understand other ways of handling coroutines—most of which turn out to be simpler than pipelines.

When you invoke a simple pipeline—say, **ls | more**—the shell invokes a series of UNIX primitive operations, or *system calls*. In effect, the shell tells UNIX to do the following things; in case you're interested, we include in parentheses the actual system call used at each step:

1. Create two subprocesses, which we'll call P1 and P2 (the *fork* system call).
2. Set up I/O between the processes so that P1's standard output feeds into P2's standard input (*pipe*).
3. Start */bin/ls* in process P1 (*exec*).
4. Start */bin/more* in process P2 (*exec*).
5. Wait for both processes to finish (*wait*).

You can probably imagine how the above steps change when the pipeline involves more than two processes.

Now let's make things simpler. We'll see how to get multiple processes to run at the same time if the processes do not need to communicate. For example, we want the processes **alice** and **hatter** to run as coroutines, without communication, in a shell script. Our initial solution would be this:

```
alice &
hatter
```

Assume for the moment that **hatter** is the last command in the script. The above will work—but only if **alice** finishes first. If **alice** is still running when the script finishes, then it becomes an *orphan*, i.e., it enters one of the "funny states" we mentioned earlier in this chapter. Never mind the details of orphanhood; just believe that you don't want this to happen, and if it does, you may need to use the "runaway process" method of stopping it, discussed earlier in this chapter.

wait

There is a way of making sure the script doesn't finish before **alice** does: the built-in command **wait**. Without arguments, **wait** simply waits until all background jobs have finished. So to make sure the above code behaves properly, we would add **wait**, like this:

```
alice &
hatter
wait
```

Here, if **hatter** finishes first, the parent shell will wait for **alice** to finish before finishing itself.

If your script has more than one background job and you need to wait for specific ones to finish, you can give **wait** the process ID of the job.

However, you will probably find that **wait** without arguments suffices for all coroutines you will ever program. Situations in which you would need to wait for specific background jobs are quite complex and beyond the scope of this book.

Advantages and Disadvantages of Coroutines

In fact, you may be wondering why you would ever need to program coroutines that don't communicate with each other. For example, why not just run **hatter** after **alice** in the usual way? What advantage is there in running the two jobs simultaneously?

Even if you are running on a computer with only one processor (CPU), then there may be a performance advantage.

Roughly speaking, you can characterize a process in terms of how it uses system resources in three ways: whether it is *CPU-intensive* (e.g., does lots of number crunching), *I/O-intensive* (does a lot of reading or writing to the disk), or *interactive* (requires user intervention).

We already know from Chapter 1 that it makes no sense to run an interactive job in the background. But apart from that, the more two or more processes differ with respect to these three criteria, the more advantage there is in running them simultaneously. For example, a number-crunching statistical calculation would do well when running at the same time as a long, I/O-intensive database query.

On the other hand, if two processes use resources in similar ways, it may even be less efficient to run them at the same time as it would be to run them sequentially. Why? Basically, because under such circumstances, the operating system often has to "time-slice" the resource(s) in contention.

For example, if both processes are "disk hogs," the operating system may enter a mode where it constantly switches control of the disk back and forth between the two competing processes; the system ends up spending at least as much time doing the switching as it does on the processes themselves. This phenomenon is known as *thrashing*; at its most severe, it can cause a system to come to a virtual standstill. Thrashing is a common problem; system administrators and operating system designers both spend lots of time trying to minimize it.

Parallelization

But if you have a computer with multiple CPUs (such as a Pyramid, Sequent, or Sun MP), you should be less concerned about thrashing. Furthermore, coroutines can provide dramatic increases in speed on this type of machine, which is often called a *parallel* computer; analogously, breaking up a process into coroutines is sometimes called *parallelizing* the job.

Normally, when you start a background job on a multiple-CPU machine, the computer will assign it to the next available processor. This means that the two jobs are actually—not just metaphorically—running at the same time.

In this case, the running time of the coroutines is essentially equal to that of the longest-running job plus a bit of overhead, instead of the sum of the run times of all processes (although if the CPUs all share a common disk drive, the possibility of I/O-related thrashing still exists). In the best case—all jobs having the same run time and no I/O contention—you get a speedup factor equal to the number of CPUs.

Parallelizing a program is often not easy; there are several subtle issues involved and there's plenty of room for error. Nevertheless, it's worthwhile to know how to parallelize a shell script whether or not you have a parallel machine, especially since such machines are becoming more and more common.

We'll show how to do this—and give you an idea of some problems involved—by means of a simple task whose solution is amenable to parallelization.

Task 8-3

Write a utility that allows you to make multiple copies of a file at the same time.

We'll call this script *mcp*. The command **mcp** *filename dest1 dest2* . . . should copy *filename* to all of the destinations given. The code for this should be fairly obvious:

```
file=$1
shift
for dest in "$@"; do
    cp $file $dest
done
```

Now let's say we have a parallel computer and we want this command to run as fast as possible. To parallelize this script, it's a simple matter of firing off the *cp* commands in the background and adding a **wait** at the end:

```
file=$1
shift
for dest in "$@"; do
    cp $file $dest &
done
wait
```

Simple, right? Well, there is one little problem: what happens if the user specifies duplicate destinations? If you're lucky, the file just gets copied to the same place twice. Otherwise, the identical *cp* commands will interfere with each other, possibly resulting in a file that contains two interspersed copies of the original file. In contrast, if you give the regular *cp* command two arguments that point to the same file, it will print an error message and do nothing.

To fix this problem, we would have to write code that checks the argument list for duplicates. Although this isn't too hard to do (see the exercises at the end of this chapter), the time it takes that code to run might offset any gain in speed from parallelization; furthermore, the code that does the checking detracts from the simple elegance of the script.

As you can see, even a seemingly trivial parallelization task has problems resulting from multiple processes having concurrent access to a given system resource (a file in this case). Such problems, known as *concurrency control* issues, become much more difficult as the complexity of the application increases. Complex concurrent programs often have much more code for handling the special cases than for the actual job the program is supposed to do!

Therefore, it shouldn't surprise you that much research has been and is being done on parallelization, the ultimate goal being to devise a tool that parallelizes code automatically. (Such tools do exist; they usually work in the confines of some narrow subset of the problem.) Even if you don't have access to a multiple-CPU machine, parallelizing a shell script is an interesting exercise that should acquaint you with some of the issues that surround coroutines.

Subshells

To conclude this chapter, we will look at a simple type of interprocess relationship: that of a subshell with its parent shell. We saw in Chapter 3, *Customizing Your Environment*, that whenever you run a shell script, you actually invoke another copy of the shell that is a subprocess of the main, or *parent*, shell process. Now let's look at subshells in more detail.

Subshell Inheritance

The most important things you need to know about subshells are what characteristics they get, or *inherit*, from their parents. These are as follows:

- The current directory
- Environment variables
- Standard input, output, and error, plus any other open file descriptors
- Signals that are ignored

Just as important are the things that a subshell does not inherit from its parent:

- Shell variables, except environment variables and those defined in the environment file (usually *.bashrc*)
- Handling of signals that are not ignored

We covered some of this in Chapter 3, but these points are common sources of confusion, so they bear repeating.

Nested Subshells

Subshells need not be in separate scripts; you can also start a subshell within the same script (or function) as the parent. You do this in a manner very similar to the command blocks we saw in the last chapter. Just surround some shell code with parentheses (instead of curly brackets), and that code will run in a subshell. We'll call this a *nested* subshell.

For example, here is the calculator program from the last chapter, with a subshell instead of a command block:

```
( while read line; do
        echo "$(alg2rpn $line)"
  done
) | dc
```

The code inside the parentheses will run as a separate process. This is usually less efficient than a command block. The differences in functionality between subshells and command blocks are very few; they primarily pertain to issues of scope, i.e., the domains in which definitions of things like shell variables and signal traps are known. First, code inside a nested subshell obeys the above rules of subshell inheritance, except that it knows about variables defined in the surrounding shell; in contrast, think of blocks as code units that inherit *everything* from the outer shell. Second, variables and traps defined inside a command block are known to the shell code after the block, whereas those defined in a subshell are not.

For example, consider this code:

```
{
    hatter=mad
    trap "echo 'You hit CTRL-C!'" INT
}
while true; do
    echo "\$hatter is $hatter"
    sleep 60
done
```

If you run this code, you will see the message **$hatter is mad** every 60 seconds, and if you hit CTRL-C, you will see the message, **You hit CTRL-C!**. You will need to hit CTRL-Z to stop it (don't forget to kill it with **kill %+**). Now let's change it to a nested subshell:

```
(
    hatter=mad
    trap "echo 'You hit CTRL-C!'" INT
)
while true; do
    echo "\$hatter is $hatter"
    sleep 60
done
```

If you run this, you will see the message **$hatter is**; the outer shell doesn't know about the subshell's definition of **hatter** and therefore thinks it's null. Furthermore, the outer shell doesn't know about the subshell's trap of the INT signal, so if you hit CTRL-C, the script will terminate.

If a language supports code nesting, then it's considered desirable that definitions inside a nested unit have a scope limited to that nested unit. In other words, nested subshells give you better control than command blocks over the scope of variables and signal traps. Therefore, we feel that you should use subshells instead of command blocks if they are to contain variable definitions or signal traps—unless efficiency is a concern.

Process Substitution

A unique but rarely used feature of *bash* is *process substitution*. Let's say that you had two versions of a program that produced large quantities of output. You want to see the differences between the output from each version. You could run the two programs, redirecting their output to files, and then use the *cmp* utility to see what the differences were.

Another way would be to use process substitution. There are two forms of this substitution. One is for input to a process: >(*list*); the other is for output from a process: <(*list*). *list* is a process that has its input or output connected to something via a *named pipe*. A named pipe is simply a temporary file that acts like a pipe with a name.

In our case, we could connect the outputs of the two programs to the input of *cmp* via named pipes:

```
cmp <(prog1) <(prog2)
```

prog1 and *prog2* are run concurrently and connect their outputs to named pipes. *cmp* reads from each of the pipes and compares the information, printing any differences as it does so.

This chapter has covered a lot of territory. Here are some exercises that should help you make sure you have a firm grasp on the material. Don't worry if you have trouble with the last one; it's especially difficult.

1. Write a shell script called *pinfo* that combines the **jobs** and *ps* commands by printing a list of jobs with their job numbers, corresponding process IDs, running times, and full commands.

2. Take a non-trivial shell script and "bullet-proof" it with signal traps.

3. Take a non-trivial shell script and parallelize it as much as possible.

4. Write the code that checks for duplicate arguments to the *mcp* script. Bear in mind that different pathnames can point to the same file. (Hint: if **$i** is "1", then **eval** ′echo \${$i}′ prints the first command-line argument. Make sure you understand why.)

9

Debugging Shell
Programs

We hope that we have convinced you that *bash* can be used as a serious UNIX programming environment. It certainly has enough features, control structures, etc. But another essential part of a programming environment is a set of powerful, integrated *support tools*. For example, there is a wide assortment of screen editors, compilers, debuggers, profilers, cross-referencers, etc., for languages like C and C++. If you program in one of these languages, you probably take such tools for granted, and you would undoubtedly cringe at the thought of having to develop code with, say, the *ed* editor and the *adb* machine-language debugger.

But what about programming support tools for *bash*? Of course, you can use any editor you like, including *vi* and *emacs*. And because the shell is an interpreted language, you don't need a compiler.* But there are no other tools available.

This chapter looks at some useful features that you can use to debug shell programs. We'll look at how you can utilize them in the first part of this chapter. We'll then look at some powerful new features of *bash*, not present in most Bourne shell workalikes, that will help in building a shell script debugging tool. At the end of the chapter, we'll show step by step how to build a debugger for *bash*. The debugger, called *bashdb*, is a basic yet functional program that will not only serve as an extended example of various shell programming techniques, but will also provide you with a useful tool for examining the workings of your own shell scripts.

---

* Actually, if you are really concerned about efficiency, there are shell code compilers on the market; they convert shell scripts to C code that often runs quite a bit faster.

Basic Debugging Aids

What sort of functionality do you need to debug a program? At the most empirical level, you need a way of determining *what* is causing your program to behave badly, and *where* the problem is in the code. You usually start with an obvious *what* (such as an error message, inappropriate output, infinite loop, etc.), try to work backwards until you find a *what* that is closer to the actual problem (e.g., a variable with a bad value, a bad option to a command), and eventually arrive at the exact *where* in your program. Then you can worry about *how* to fix it.

Notice that these steps represent a process of starting with obvious information and ending up with often obscure facts gleaned through deduction and intuition. Debugging aids make it easier to deduce and intuit by providing relevant information easily or even automatically, preferably without modifying your code.

The simplest debugging aid (for any language) is the output statement, **echo**, in the shell's case. Indeed, old-time programmers debugged their FORTRAN code by inserting **WRITE** cards into their decks. You can debug by putting lots of **echo** statements in your code (and removing them later), but you will have to spend lots of time narrowing down not only *what* exact information you want but also *where* you need to see it. You will also probably have to wade through lots and lots of output to find the information you really want.

Set Options

Luckily, the shell has a few basic features that give you debugging functionality beyond that of **echo**. The most basic of these are options to the **set −o** command (as covered in Chapter 3, *Customizing Your Environment*). These options can also be used on the command line when running a script, as Table 9-1 shows.

Table 9-1: Debugging Options

set −o Option	Command-Line Option	Action
noexec	−n	Don't run commands; check for syntax errors only
verbose	−v	Echo commands before running them
xtrace	−x	Echo commands after command-line processing

The **verbose** option simply echoes (to standard error) whatever input the shell gets. It is useful for finding the exact point at which a script is bombing. For example, assume your script looks like this:

```
alice
hatter
march
```

```
teatime
treacle
well
```

None of these commands is a standard UNIX program, and each does its work silently. Say the script crashes with a cryptic message like "segmentation violation." This tells you nothing about which command caused the error. If you type **bash −v** *scriptname*, you might see this:

```
alice
hatter
march
segmentation violation
teatime
treacle
well
```

Now you know that **march** is the probable culprit—though it is also possible that **march** bombed because of something it expected **alice** or **hatter** to do (e.g., create an input file) that they did incorrectly.

The **xtrace** option is more powerful: it echoes command lines after they have been through parameter substitution, command substitution, and the other steps of command-line processing (as listed in Chapter 7, *Input/Output and Command-Line Processing*). For example:

```
$ set -o xtrace
$ alice=girl
+ alice=girl
$ echo "$alice"
+ echo girl
girl
$ ls -l $(type -path vi)
++ type -path vi
+ ls -F -l /usr/bin/vi
lrwxrwxrwx   1 root      root       5 Jul 26 20:59 /usr/bin/vi -> elvis*
$
```

As you can see, **xtrace** starts each line it prints with **+** (each **+** representing a level of expansion). This is actually customizable: it's the value of the built-in shell variable **PS4**. So if you set **PS4** to "**xtrace—>** " (e.g., in your *.bash_profile* or *.bashrc*), then you'll get **xtrace** listings that look like this:

```
$ ls -l $(type -path vi)
xxtrace--> type -path vi
xtrace--> ls -l /usr/bin/vi
lrwxrwxrwx   1 root      root       5 Jul 26 20:59 /usr/bin/vi -> elvis*
$
```

Notice that for multiple levels of expansion, only the first character of **PS4** is printed. This makes the output more readable.

An even better way of customizing **PS4** is to use a built-in variable we haven't seen yet: **LINENO**, which holds the number of the currently running line in a shell script.* Put this line in your *.bash_profile* or environment file:

```
PS4='line $LINENO: '
```

We use the same technique as we did with **PS1** in Chapter 3: using single quotes to postpone the evaluation of the string until each time the shell prints the prompt. This will print messages of the form **line** *N:* in your trace output. You could even include the name of the shell script you're debugging in this prompt by using the positional parameter **$0**:

```
PS4='$0 line $LINENO: '
```

As another example, say you are trying to track down a bug in a script called **alice** that contains this code:

```
dbfmq=$1.fmq
...
fndrs=$(cut -f3 -d' ' $dfbmq)
```

You type **alice teatime** to run it in the normal way, and it hangs. Then you type **bash −x alice teatime**, and you see this:

```
+ dbfmq=teatime.fmq
...
+ + cut -f3 -d
```

It hangs again at this point. You notice that *cut* doesn't have a filename argument, which means that there must be something wrong with the variable **dbfmq**. But it has executed the assignment statement **dbfmq=teatime.fmq** properly... ah-*hah*! You made a typo in the variable name inside the command substitution construct.† You fix it, and the script works properly.

The last option is **noexec**, which reads in the shell script, checks for syntax errors, but doesn't execute anything. It's worth using if your script is syntactically complex (lots of loops, command blocks, string operators, etc.) and the bug has side effects (like creating a large file or hanging up the system).

You can turn on these options with **set −o** *option* in your shell scripts, and, as explained in Chapter 3, turn them off with **set +o** *option*. For example, if you're debugging a chunk of code, you can precede it with **set −o xtrace** to print out the executed commands, and end the chunk with **set +o xtrace**.

---

* In versions of *bash* prior to 2.0, **LINENO** won't give you the current line in a function. **LINENO**, instead, gives an approximation of the number of simple commands executed so far in the current function.

† We should admit that if you had turned on the **nounset** option at the top of this script, the shell would have flagged this error.

Note, however, that once you have turned **noexec** on, you won't be able to turn it off; a **set +o noexec** will never be executed.

Fake Signals

A more sophisticated set of debugging aids is the shell's "fake signals," which can be used in **trap** statements to get the shell to act under certain conditions. Recall from the previous chapter that **trap** allows you to install some code that runs when a particular signal is sent to your script.

Fake signals work in the same way, but they are generated by the shell itself, as opposed to the other signals which are generated externally. They represent run-time events that are likely to be of interest to debuggers—both human ones and software tools—and can be treated just like real signals within shell scripts. Table 9-2 lists the two fake signals available in *bash*.

Table 9-2: Fake Signals

Fake Signal	Sent When
EXIT	The shell exits from script
DEBUG	The shell has executed a statement[a]

a. The DEBUG signal is not available in *bash* versions prior to 2.0.

EXIT

The EXIT trap, when set, will run its code whenever the script within which it was set exits.[*]

Here's a simple example:

```
trap 'echo exiting from the script' EXIT
echo 'start of the script'
```

If you run this script, you will see this output:

```
start of the script
exiting from the script
```

In other words, the script starts by setting the trap for its own exit, then prints a message. The script then exits, which causes the shell to generate the signal EXIT, which in turn runs the code **echo exiting from the script**.

An EXIT trap occurs no matter how the script exits—whether normally (by finishing the last statement), by an explicit **exit** or **return** statement, or by receiving a "real" signal such as INT or TERM. Consider this inane number-guessing program:

---

[*] You can trap only the exiting of a script. Functions don't generate the EXIT signal, as they are part of the current shell invocation.

```
trap 'echo Thank you for playing!' EXIT

magicnum=$(($RANDOM%10+1))
echo 'Guess a number between 1 and 10:'
while read -p 'Guess: ' guess ; do
    sleep 4
    if [ "$guess" = $magicnum ]; then
        echo 'Right!'
        exit
    fi
    echo 'Wrong!'
done
```

This program picks a number between 1 and 10 by getting a random number (the built-in variable **RANDOM**), extracting the last digit (the remainder when divided by 10), and adding 1. Then it prompts you for a guess, and after 4 seconds, it will tell you if you guessed right.

If you did, the program will exit with the message, "Thank you for playing!", i.e., it will run the EXIT trap code. If you were wrong, it will prompt you again and repeat the process until you get it right. If you get bored with this little game and hit CTRL-C or CTRL-D while waiting for it to tell you whether you were right, you will also see the message.

The EXIT trap is especially useful when you want to print out the values of variables at the point that your script exits. For example, by printing the value of loop counter variables, you can find the most appropriate places in a complicated script, with many nested **for** loops, to enable **xtrace** or place debug output.

DEBUG

The other fake signal, DEBUG, causes the trap code to be executed after every statement in a function or script. This has two main uses. First is the use for humans, as a sort of "brute force" method of tracking a certain element of a program's state that you notice has gone awry.

For example, you notice the value of a particular variable is running amok. The naive approach is to put in a lot of **echo** statements to check the variable's value at several points. The DEBUG trap makes this easier by letting you do this:

```
function dbgtrap
{
    echo "badvar is badvar"
}

trap dbgtrap DEBUG

...section of code in which the problem occurs...

trap - DEBUG    # turn off the DEBUG trap
```

This code will print the value of the wayward variable after every statement between the two **traps**.

One important point to remember when using DEBUG is that it is not inherited by functions called from the shell in which it is set. In other words, if your shell sets a DEBUG trap and then calls a function, the statements within the function will not execute the trap. You have to set a trap for DEBUG explicitly within the function if you want to use it.

The second and far more important use of the DEBUG signal is as a primitive for implementing a *bash* debugger. In fact, it would be fair to say that DEBUG reduces the task of implementing a useful shell debugger from a large-scale software development project to a manageable exercise.

A *bash* Debugger

In this section we'll develop a basic debugger for *bash*.* Most debuggers have numerous sophisticated features that help a programmer in dissecting a program, but just about all of them include the ability to step through a running program, stop it at selected places, and examine the values of variables. These simple features are what we will concentrate on providing in our debugger. Specifically, we'll provide the ability to:

- Specify places in the program at which to stop execution. These are called *breakpoints.*

- Execute a specified number of statements in the program. This is called *stepping.*

- Examine and change the state of the program during its execution. This includes being able to print out the values of variables and change them when the program is stopped at a breakpoint or after stepping.

- Print out the source code we are debugging along with indications of where breakpoints are and what line in the program we are currently executing.

- Provide the debugging capability without having to change the original source code of the program we wish to debug in any way.

As you will see, the capability to do all of these things (and more) is easily provided by the constructs and methods we have seen in previous chapters.

---

* Unfortunately, the debugger will not work with versions of *bash* prior to 2.0, because they do not implement the DEBUG signal.

Structure of the Debugger

The *bashdb* debugger works by taking a shell script and turning it into a debugger for itself. It does this by concatenating debugger functionality and the target script, which we'll call the guinea pig script, and storing it in another file which then gets executed. The process is transparent to the user—they will be unaware that the code that is executing is actually a modified copy of their script.

The *bash* debugger has three main sections: the driver, the preamble, and the debugger functions.

The driver script

The driver script is responsible for setting everything up. It is a script called *bashdb* and looks like this:

```
# bashdb - a bash debugger
# Driver Script: concatenates the preamble and the target script
# and then executes the new script.

echo 'bash Debugger version 1.0'

_dbname=${0##*/}

if (( $# < 1 )) ; then
  echo "$_dbname: Usage: $_dbname filename" >&2
  exit 1
fi

_guineapig=$1

if [ ! -r $1 ]; then
  echo "$_dbname: Cannot read file '$_guineapig'." >&2
  exit 1
fi

shift

_tmpdir=/tmp
_libdir=.
_debugfile=$_tmpdir/bashdb.$$  # temporary file for script that is
    being debugged
cat $_libdir/bashdb.pre $_guineapig > $_debugfile
exec bash $_debugfile $_guineapig $_tmpdir $_libdir "$@"
```

bashdb takes as the first argument the name of guinea pig file. Any subsequent arguments are passed on to the guinea pig as its positional parameters.

If no arguments are given, *bashdb* prints out a usage line and exits with an error status. Otherwise, it checks to see if the file exists. If it doesn't, exist then *bashdb* prints a message and exits with an error status. If all is in order, *bashdb* constructs a temporary file in the way we saw in the last chapter. If you don't have (or don't have access to) */tmp* on your system, then you can substitute a different directory for **_tmpdir**.* The variable **_libdir** is the name of the directory that contains files needed by *bashdb* (*bashdb.pre* and *bashdb.fns*). If you are installing *bashdb* on your system for everyone to use, you might want to place them in */usr/lib*.

The **cat** statement builds the modified copy of the guinea pig file: it contains the script found in *bashdb.pre* (which we'll look at shortly) followed by a copy of the guinea pig.

exec

The last line runs the newly created script with **exec**, a statement we haven't discussed yet. We've chosen to wait until now to introduce it because—as we think you'll agree—it can be dangerous. **exec** takes its arguments as a command line and runs the command in place of the current program, in the same process. In other words, a shell that runs **exec** will *terminate immediately* and be replaced by **exec**'s arguments.†

In our script, **exec** just runs the newly constructed shell script, i.e., the guinea pig with its debugger, in another shell. It passes the new script three arguments—the name of the original guinea pig file (**$_guineapig**), the name of the temporary directory (**$_tmpdir**), and the name of the library directory (**$_libdir**)—followed by the user's positional parameters, if any.

The Preamble

Now we'll look at the code that gets prepended to the guinea pig script; we call this the preamble. It's kept in the file *bashdb.pre* and looks like this:

```
# bashdb preamble
# This file gets prepended to the shell script being debugged.
# Arguments:
# $1 = the name of the original guinea pig script
# $2 = the directory where temporary files are stored
# $3 = the directory where bashdb.pre and bashdb.fns are stored

_debugfile=$0
_guineapig=$1
```

---

* All function names and variables (except those local to functions) in *bashdb* have names beginning with an underscore (_), to minimize the possibility of clashes with names in the guinea pig script.

† **exec** can also be used with an I/O redirector only; this makes the redirector take effect for the remainder of the script or login session. For example, the line **exec 2>errlog** at the top of a script directs standard error to the file *errlog* for the rest of the script.

```
        _tmpdir=$2
        _libdir=$3

        shift 3

        source $_libdir/bashdb.fns
        _linebp=
        let _trace=0
        let _i=1

        while read; do
            _lines[$_i]=$REPLY
            let _i=$_i+1
        done < $_guineapig

        trap _cleanup EXIT
        let _steps=1
        LINENO=-2
        trap '_steptrap $LINENO' DEBUG
        :
```

The first few lines save the three fixed arguments in variables and shift them out of the way, so that the positional parameters (if any) are those that the user supplied on the command line as arguments to the guinea pig. Then, the preamble reads in another file, *bashdb.fns*, that contains all of the functions necessary for the operation of the debugger itself. We put this code in a separate file to minimize the size of the temporary file. We'll examine *bashdb.fns* shortly.

Next, *bashdb.pre* initializes a breakpoint array to empty and execution tracing to off (see the following discussion), then reads the original guinea pig script into an array of lines. We need the source lines from the original script for two reasons: to allow the debugger to print out the script showing where the breakpoints are, and to print out the lines of code as they execute if tracing is turned on. You'll notice that we assign the script lines to **_lines** from the environment variable **$REPLY** rather than reading them into the array directly. This is because **$REPLY** preserves any leading whitespace in the lines, i.e., it preserves the indentation and layout of the original script.

The last five lines of code set up the conditions necessary for the debugger to begin working. The first **trap** command sets up a clean-up routine that runs when the fake signal EXIT occurs. The clean-up routine, normally called when the debugger and guinea pig script finish, just erases the temporary file. The next line sets the variable **_steps** to 1 so that when the debugger is first entered, it will stop after the first line.

The built-in variable **LINENO**, which we saw earlier in the chapter, is used to provide line numbers in the debugger. However, if we just used **LINENO** as is, we'd get line numbers above thirty because **LINENO** would be including the lines in the preamble. To get around this, we can set **LINENO** to a new value and it will happily start counting line numbers from that value. In this case we set it to the value −2 so that the first line of the guinea pig will be line 1.*

The next line sets up the routine **_steptrap** to run when the fake signal DEBUG occurs. **_steptrap** is passed **$LINENO** as an argument when it is called.

The last line is a "do-nothing" statement (:). The shell executes this statement and enters **_steptrap** for the first time. As we have set **_steps** to 1, the debugger will stop and wait for a command from the user. We'll see how this works in the next section.

Debugger Functions

The function **_steptrap** is the entry point into the debugger; it is defined in the file *bashdb.fns*. Here is **_steptrap**:

```
# After each line of the test script is executed the shell traps to
# this function.

function _steptrap
{
    _curline=$1          # the number of the line that just ran

    (( $_trace )) && _msg "$PS4 line $_curline: ${_lines[$_curline]}"

    if (( $_steps >= 0 )); then
        let _steps="$_steps - 1"
    fi

    # First check to see if a line number breakpoint was reached.
    # If it was, then enter the debugger.
    if _at_linenumbp ; then
        _msg "Reached breakpoint at line $_curline"
        _cmdloop

    # It wasn't, so check whether a break condition exists and is true.
    # If it is, then enter the debugger.
    elif [ -n "$_brcond" ] && eval $_brcond; then
        _msg "Break condition $_brcond true at line $_curline"
        _cmdloop

    # It wasn't, so check if we are in step mode and the number of steps
    # is up. If it is then enter the debugger.
    elif (( $_steps == 0 )); then
        _msg "Stopped at line $_curline"
        _cmdloop
    fi
}
```

---

* If you are typing or scanning in the preamble code from this book, make sure that the last line in the file is the colon (:), i.e., no blank lines should appear after the colon.

_steptrap starts by setting **_curline** to the number of the guinea pig line that just ran. If execution tracing is on, it prints the PS4 execution trace prompt (like the shell's **xtrace** mode), line number, and line of code itself. It then decrements the number of steps if the number of steps still left is greater than or equal to zero.

Then it does one of two things: it enters the debugger via **_cmdloop**, or it returns so the shell can execute the next statement. It chooses the former if a breakpoint or break condition has been reached, or if the user stepped into this statement.

Commands

We'll explain shortly how **_steptrap** determines these things; now we'll look at **_cmdloop**. It's a simple combination of the case statements we saw in Chapter 5, *Flow Control*, and the calculator loop we saw in the previous chapter.

```
# The Debugger Command Loop

function _cmdloop {
    local cmd args

    while read -e -p "bashdb> " cmd args; do
        case $cmd in
            \? | h  ) _menu ;;          # print command menu
            bc ) _setbc $args ;;        # set a break condition
            bp ) _setbp $args ;;        # set a breakpoint at the given
                                        # line
            cb ) _clearbp $args ;;      # clear one or all breakpoints
            ds ) _displayscript ;;      # list the script and show the
                                        # breakpoints
            g  ) return ;;              # "go": start/resume execution of
                                        # the script
            q  ) exit ;;                # quit

            s  ) let _steps=${args:-1}  # single step N times
                                        # (default = 1)
                 return ;;
            x  ) _xtrace ;;             # toggle execution trace
            !* ) eval ${cmd#!} $args ;; # pass to the shell
            *  ) _msg "Invalid command: '$cmd'" ;;
        esac
    done
}
```

At each iteration, **_cmdloop** prints a prompt, reads a command, and processes it. We use **read −e** so that the user can take advantage of the *readline* command-line editing. The commands are all one- or two-letter abbreviations; quick for typing, but terse in the UNIX style.*

---

* There is nothing to stop you from changing the commands to something you find easier to remember. There is no "official" *bash* debugger, so feel free to change the debugger to suit your needs.

Table 9-3 summarizes the debugger commands.

Table 9-3: bashdb Commands

Command	Action
bp *N*	Set breakpoint at line *N*
bp	List breakpoints and break condition
bc *string*	Set break condition to *string*
bc	Clear break condition
cb *N*	Clear breakpoint at line *N*
cb	Clear all breakpoints
ds	Display the test script and breakpoints
g	Start/resume execution
s [*M*]	Execute *N* statements (default 1)
x	Toggle execution trace on/off
h, ?	Print the help menu
! *string*	Pass *string* to a shell
q	Quit

Before looking at the individual commands, it is important that you understand how control passes through **_steptrap**, the command loop, and the guinea pig.

_steptrap runs after every statement in the guinea pig as a result of the trap on DEBUG in the preamble. If a breakpoint has been reached or the user previously typed in a step command (s), **_steptrap** calls the command loop. In doing so, it effectively "interrupts" the shell that is running the guinea pig to hand control over to the user.

The user can invoke debugger commands as well as shell commands that run in the same shell as the guinea pig. This means that you can use shell commands to check values of variables, signal traps, and any other information local to the script being debugged. The command loop continues to run, and the user stays in control, until they type **g**, **q**, or **s**. We'll now look in detail at what happens in each of these cases.

Typing **g** has the effect of running the guinea pig uninterrupted until it finishes or hits a breakpoint. It simply exits the command loop and returns to **_steptrap**, which exits as well. The shell then regains control and runs the next statement in the guinea pig script. Another DEBUG signal occurs and the shell traps to **_steptrap** again. If there are no breakpoints then **_steptrap** will just exit. This process will repeat until a breakpoint is reached or the guinea pig finishes.

The **q** command calls the function **_cleanup**, which erases the temporary file and exits the program.

Stepping

When the user types **s**, the command loop code sets the variable _steps to the number of steps the user wants to execute, i.e., to the argument given. Assume at first that the user omits the argument, meaning that _steps is set to 1. Then the command loop exits and returns control to _steptrap, which (as above) exits and hands control back to the shell. The shell runs the next statement and returns to _steptrap, which then decrements _steps to 0. Then the second **elif** conditional becomes true because _steps is 0 and prints a "stopped" message and then calls the command loop.

Now assume that the user supplies an argument to **s**, say 3. _steps is set to 3. Then the following happens:

1. After the next statement runs, _steptrap is called again. It enters the first **if** clause, since **_steps** is greater than 0. _steptrap decrements _steps to 2 and exits, returning control to the shell.

2. This process repeats, another step in the guinea pig is run, and _steps becomes 1.

3. A third statement is run and we're back in _steptrap. _steps is decremented to 0, the second **elif** clause is run, and _steptrap breaks out to the command loop again.

The overall effect is that the three steps run and then the debugger takes over again.

All of the other debugger commands cause the shell to stay in the command loop, meaning that the user prolongs the "interruption" of the shell.

Breakpoints

Now we'll examine the breakpoint-related commands and the breakpoint mechanism in general. The **bp** command calls the function _setbp, which can do two things, depending on whether an argument is supplied or not. Here is the code for _setbp:

```
# Set a breakpoint at the given line number or list breakpoints
function _setbp
{
    local i

    if [ -z "$1" ]; then
        _listbp
    elif [ $(echo $1 | grep '^[0-9]*')  ]; then
        if [ -n "${_lines[$1]}" ]; then
            _linebp=($(echo $( (for i in ${_linebp[*]} $1; do
                echo $i; done) | sort -n) ))
            _msg "Breakpoint set at line $1"
```

```
            else
                _msg "Breakpoints can only be set on non-blank lines"
            fi
        else
            _msg "Please specify a numeric line number"
        fi
    }
```

If no argument is supplied, _setbp calls _listbp, which prints the line numbers that have breakpoints set. If anything other than a number is supplied as an argument, an error message is printed and control returns to the command loop. Providing a number as the argument allows us to set a breakpoint; however, we have to do another test before doing so.

What happens if the user decides to set a breakpoint at a nonsensical point: a blank line, or at line 1000 of a ten-line program? If the breakpoint is set well beyond the end of the program, it will never be reached and will cause no problem. If, however, a breakpoint is set at a blank line, it will cause problems. The reason is that the DEBUG trap only occurs after each executed *simple command* in a script, not each line. Blank lines never generate the DEBUG signal. The user could set a breakpoint on a blank line, in which case continuing execution with the **g** command would never break back out to the debugger.

We can fix both of these problems by making sure that breakpoints are set only on lines with text.* After making the tests, we can add the breakpoint to the breakpoint array, _linebp. This is a little more complex than it sounds. In order to make the code in other sections of the debugger simpler, we should maintain a sorted array of breakpoints. To do this, we echo all of the line numbers currently in the array, along with the new number, in a subshell and pipe them into the UNIX **sort** command. **sort −n** sorts a list into numerically ascending order. The result of this is a list of ordered numbers which we then assign back to the _linebp array with a compound assignment.

To complement the user's ability to add breakpoints, we also allow the user to delete them. The **cb** command allows the user to clear single breakpoints or all breakpoints, depending on whether a line number argument is supplied or not. For example, **cb 12** clears a breakpoint at line 12 (if a breakpoint was set at that line). **cb** on its own would clear all of the breakpoints that have been set. It is useful to look briefly at how this works; here is the code for the function that is called with the **cb** command, _clearbp:

---

* This isn't a complete solution. Certain other lines (e.g., comments) will also be ignored by the DEBUG trap. See the list of limitations and the exercises at the end of this chapter.

```
function _clearbp
{
    local i

    if [ -z "$1" ]; then
        unset _linebp[*]
        _msg "All breakpoints have been cleared"
    elif [ $(echo $1 | grep '^[0-9]*')  ]; then
        _linebp=($(echo $(for i in ${_linebp[*]}; do
                if (( $1 != $i )); then echo $i; fi; done) ))
        _msg "Breakpoint cleared at line $1"
    else
        _msg "Please specify a numeric line number"
    fi
}
```

The structure of the code is similar to that used for setting the breakpoints. If no argument was supplied to the command, the breakpoint array is unset, effectively deleting all the breakpoints. If an argument was supplied and is not a number, we print out an error message and exit.

A numeric argument to the **cb** command means the code has to search the list of breakpoints and delete the specified one. We can easily make the deletion by following a procedure similar to the one we used when we added a breakpoint in **_setbp**. We execute a loop in a subshell, printing out the line numbers in the breakpoints list and ignoring any that match the provided argument. The echoed values once again form a compound statement which can then be assigned to an array variable.*

The function **_at_linenumbp** is called by **_steptrap** after every statement; it checks whether the shell has arrived at a line number breakpoint. The code for the function is:

```
# See if this line number has a breakpoint
function _at_linenumbp
{
    local i=0

  if [ "$_linebp" ]; then
    while (( $i < ${#_linebp[@]} )); do
      if (( ${_linebp[$i]} == $_curline )); then
        return 0
      fi
      let i=$i+1
    done
  fi
```

---

* *bash* versions 2.01 and earlier have a bug in assigning arrays to themselves which prevents the code for **setbp** and **clearbp** from working. In each case, you can get around this bug by assigning **_linebp** to a local variable first, **unsetting** it, and then assigning the local variable back to it. Better yet, update to a more recent version of *bash*.

```
    return 1
}
```

The function simply loops through the breakpoint array and checks the current line number against each one. If a match is found, it returns **true** (i.e., returns 0). Otherwise, it continues looping, looking for a match until the end of the array is reached. It then returns **false**.

It is possible to find out exactly what line the debugger is up to and where the breakpoints have been set in the guinea pig by using the **ds** command. We'll see an example of the output later, when we run a sample *bashdb* debugging session. The code for this function is fairly straightforward:

```
# Print out the shell script and mark the location of breakpoints
# and the current line
function _displayscript
{
    local i=1 j=0 bp cl

    ( while (( $i < ${#_lines[@]} )); do
          if [ ${_linebp[$j]} ] && (( ${_linebp[$j]} == $i )); then
              bp='*'
              let j=$j+1
          else
              bp=' '
          fi

          if (( $_curline == $i )); then
              cl=">"
          else
              cl=" "
          fi

          echo "$i:$bp $cl  ${_lines[$i]}"
          let i=$i+1
      done
    ) | more
}
```

This function contains a subshell, the output of which is piped to the UNIX **more** command. We have done this for user-friendly reasons; a long script would scroll up the screen quickly and the users may not have displays that allows them to scroll back to previous pages of screen output. **more** displays one screenful of output at a time.

The core of the subshell code loops through the lines of the guinea pig script. It first tests to see if the line it is about to display is in the array of breakpoints. If it is, a breakpoint character (*) is set and the local variable j is incremented. j was initialized to 0 at the beginning of the function; it contains the current breakpoint that we are up to. It should now be apparent why we went to the trouble of sorting the breakpoints in _setbp: both the line numbers and the breakpoint numbers increment sequentially, and once we pass a line number that has a breakpoint and find it in the breakpoint array, we know that future breakpoints in the script must be further on in the array. If the breakpoint array contained line numbers in a random order, we'd have to search the entire array to find out if a line number was in the array or not.

The core of the subshell code then checks to see if the current line and the line it is about to display are the same. If they are, a "current line" character (>) is set. The current displayed line number (stored in i), breakpoint character, current line character, and script line are then printed out.

We think you'll agree that the added complexity in the handling of breakpoints is well worth it. Being able to display the script and the location of breakpoints is an important feature in any debugger.

Break conditions

bashdb provides another method of breaking out of the guinea pig script: the *break condition*. This is a string that the user can specify that is evaluated as a command; if it is true (i.e., returns exit status 0), the debugger enters the command loop.

Since the break condition can be any line of shell code, there's a lot of flexibility in what can be tested. For example, you can break when a variable reaches a certain value—e.g., (($x < 0))—or when a particular piece of text has been written to a file (**grep** *string file*). You will probably think of all kinds of uses for this feature.* To set a break condition, type **bc** *string*. To remove it, type **bc** without arguments—this installs the null string, which is ignored.

_steptrap evaluates the break condition **$_brcond** only if it's not null. If the break condition evaluates to 0, then the **if** clause is true and, once again, **_steptrap** calls the command loop.

Execution tracing

The final feature of the debugger is execution tracing, available with the **x** command.

The function **_xtrace** "toggles" execution tracing simply by assigning to the variable **_trace** the logical "not" of its current value, so that it alternates between 0 (off) and 1 (on). The preamble initializes it to 0.

---

* Bear in mind that if your break condition sends anything to standard output or standard error, you will see it after every statement executed. Also, make sure your break condition doesn't take a long time to run; otherwise your script will run very, very slowly.

Debugger limitations

We have kept *bashdb* reasonably simple so that you can see the fundamentals of building a shell script debugger. Although it contains some useful features and is designed to be a real tool, not just a scripting example, it has some important limitations. The ones that we know of are described in the list that follows.

1. Debuggers tend to run programs slower than if they were executed on their own. *bashdb* is no exception. Depending upon the script you use it on, you'll find the debugger runs everything anywhere from eight to thirty times more slowly. This isn't so much of a problem if you are stepping through a script in small increments, but bear it in mind if you have, say, initialization code with large looping constructs.

2. One problem with setting breakpoints is that when they are set on lines with no simple commands (actual UNIX commands, shell built-ins, function calls, and aliases), the DEBUG signal is never generated and the trap code never executes. This includes reserved words like **while**, **if**, **for**, and so on, unless a simple command is on the same line.

3. The debugger will not "step down" into shell scripts that are called from the guinea pig. To do this, you'd have to edit your guinea pig script and change a call to *scriptname* to **bashdb** *scriptname*.

4. Similarly, nested subshells are treated as one gigantic statement; you cannot step down into them at all.

5. The guinea pig should not trap on the fake signals DEBUG and EXIT; otherwise the debugger won't work.

6. Command error handling could be significantly improved.

7. The shell should really have the ability to trap *before* each statement, not after. This is the way most commercial source code debuggers work. At the very least, the shell should provide a variable that contains the number of the line about to run instead of (or in addition to) the number of the line that just ran.

Many of these are not insurmountable; see the exercises at the end of this chapter.

A Sample bashdb Session

Now we'll show a transcript of an actual session with *bashdb*, in which the guinea pig is the solution to Task 6-1, the script *ndu*. Here is the transcript of the debugging session:

```
[bash]$ bashdb ndu
bash Debugger version 1.0
Stopped at line 0
bashdb> ds
```

```
1:      for dir in ${*:-.}; do
2:         if [ -e $dir ]; then
3:            result=$(du -s $dir | cut -f 1)
4:            let total=$result*1024
5:
6:            echo -n "Total for $dir = $total bytes"
7:
8:            if [ $total -ge 1048576 ]; then
9:              echo " ($((total/1048576)) Mb)"
10:            elif [ $total -ge 1024 ]; then
11:              echo " ($((total/1024)) Kb)"
12:            fi
13:         fi
14:      done
bashdb> s
Stopped at line 2
bashdb> bp 4
Breakpoint set at line 4
bashdb> bp 8
Breakpoint set at line 8
bashdb> bp 11
Breakpoint set at line 11
bashdb> ds
1:      for dir in ${*:-.}; do
2:  >       if [ -e $dir ]; then
3:            result=$(du -s $dir | cut -f 1)
4:*           let total=$result*1024
5:
6:            echo -n "Total for $dir = $total bytes"
7:
8:*           if [ $total -ge 1048576 ]; then
9:              echo " ($((total/1048576)) Mb)"
10:            elif [ $total -ge 1024 ]; then
11:*             echo " ($((total/1024)) Kb)"
12:            fi
13:         fi
14:      done
bashdb> g
Reached breakpoint at line 4
bashdb> !echo $total
6840032
bashdb> cb 8
Breakpoint cleared at line 8
bashdb> ds
1:      for dir in ${*:-.}; do
2:         if [ -e $dir ]; then
3:            result=$(du -s $dir | cut -f 1)
4:* >        let total=$result*1024
5:
6:            echo -n "Total for $dir = $total bytes"
7:
8:            if [ $total -ge 1048576 ]; then
9:              echo " ($((total/1048576)) Mb)"
10:            elif [ $total -ge 1024 ]; then
```

```
11:*            echo " ($((total/1024)) Kb)"
12:         fi
13:      fi
14:   done
bashdb> bp
Breakpoints at lines: 4 11
Break on condition:

bashdb> !total=5600
bashdb> g
Total for . = 5600 bytes (5 Kb)
Reached breakpoint at line 11
bashdb> cb
All breakpoints have been cleared
bashdb> ds
1:     for dir in ${*:-.}; do
2:       if [ -e $dir ]; then
3:         result=$(du -s $dir | cut -f 1)
4:         let total=$result*1024
5:
6:         echo -n "Total for $dir = $total bytes"
7:
8:         if [ $total -ge 1048576 ]; then
9:           echo " ($((total/1048576)) Mb)"
10:        elif [ $total -ge 1024 ]; then
11:   >       echo " ($((total/1024)) Kb)"
12:        fi
13:      fi
14:   done
bashdb> g
[bash]$
```

First, we display the script with **ds** and then perform a step, taking execution to line 2 of *ndu*. We then set breakpoints at lines 4, 8, and 11 and display the script again. This time the breakpoints are clearly marked by asterisks (*). The right angle bracket (>) indicates that line 2 was the most recent line executed.

Next, we continue execution of the script that breaks at line 4. We print out the value of **total** now and decide to clear the breakpoint at line 8. Displaying the script confirms that the breakpoint at line 8 is indeed gone. We can also use the **bp** command, and it too shows that the only breakpoints set are at lines 4 and 11.

At this stage we might decide that we want to check the logic of the **if** branch at line 11. This requires that **$total** be greater than or equal to 1024, but less than 1048576. As we saw previously, **$total** is very large, so we set its value to 5600 so that it will execute the second part of the **if** and continue execution. The script enters that section of the **if** correctly, prints out the value, and stops at the breakpoint.

To finish off, we clear the breakpoints, display the script again, and then continue execution, which exits the script.

Exercises

The *bashdb* debugger is available via anonymous FTP, as discussed in Appendix E, *Obtaining Sample Programs*; if you don't have access to the Internet, you can type or scan the code in. Either way, you can use *bashdb* to debug your own shell scripts, and you should feel free to enhance it. We'll conclude this chapter with some suggested enhancements and a complete listing of the debugger command source code.

1. Improve command error handling in these ways:

    a. Check that the arguments to **s** are valid numbers and print an appropriate error message if they aren't.

    b. Check that a breakpoint actually exists before clearing it and warn the user if the line doesn't have a breakpoint.

    c. Any other error handling that you can think of.

2. Add code to remove duplicate breakpoints (more than one breakpoint on one line).

3. Enhance the **cb** command so that the user can specify more than one breakpoint to be cleared at a time.

4. Implement an option that causes a break into the debugger whenever a command exits with non-zero status:

    a. Implement it as the command-line option **−e**.

    b. Implement it as the debugger command **e** to toggle it on and off. (Hint: when you enter **_steptrap**, **$?** is still the exit status of the last command that ran.)

5. Implement a command that prints out the status of the debugger: whether execution trace is on/off, error exit is on/off, and the number of the last line to be executed. In addition, move the functionality for displaying the breakpoints from **bp** to the new option.

6. Add support for multiple break conditions, so that *bashdb* stops execution whenever one of them becomes true and prints a message indicating which one became true. Do this by storing the break conditions in an array. Try to make this as efficient as possible, since the checking will take place after every statement.

7. Add the ability to watch variables.

    a. Add a command **aw** that takes a variable name as an argument and adds it to a list of variables to watch. Any watched variables are printed out when execution trace is toggled on.

b. Add another command **cw** that, without an argument, removes all of the variables from the watch list. With an argument, it removes the specified variable.

8. As we saw earlier, unless breakpoints are set on lines with simple commands, they are ignored and never cause the program to break out into the debugger. Add code that solves this problem. (Hint: if the user sets a breakpoint on such a line, move it forward on to a line that contains a simple command. Alternatively, you might consider ways to insert the "do-nothing" command (:) when creating the temporary file from the guinea pig and preamble scripts.)

9. Although placing an underscore at the start of the debugger identifiers will avoid name clashes in most cases, think of ways to automatically detect name clashes with the guinea pig script and how to get around this problem. (Hint: you could rename the clashing names in the guinea pig script at the point where it gets combined with the preamble and placed in the temporary file.)

10. Add any other features you can think of.

Finally, here is a complete source listing of the debugger function file *bashdb.fns*:

```
# After each line of the test script is executed the shell traps to
# this function.

function _steptrap
{
    _curline=$1          # the number of the line that just ran

    (( $_trace )) && _msg "$PS4 line $_curline: ${_lines[$_curline]}"

    if (( $_steps >= 0 )); then
        let _steps="$_steps - 1"
    fi

    # First check to see if a line number breakpoint was reached.
    # If it was, then enter the debugger.
    if _at_linenumbp ; then
        _msg "Reached breakpoint at line $_curline"
        _cmdloop

    # It wasn't, so check whether a break condition exists and is true.
    # If it is, then enter the debugger
    elif [ -n "$_brcond" ] && eval $_brcond; then
        _msg "Break condition $_brcond true at line $_curline"
        _cmdloop

    # It wasn't, so check if we are in step mode and the number of
    # steps is up. If it is, then enter the debugger.
    elif (( $_steps == 0 )); then
        _msg "Stopped at line $_curline"
        _cmdloop
```

```
        fi
}

# The Debugger Command Loop

function _cmdloop {
  local cmd args

    while read -e -p "bashdb> " cmd args; do
      case $cmd in
        \? | h  ) _menu ;;              # print command menu
        bc ) _setbc $args ;;           # set a break condition
        bp ) _setbp $args ;;           # set a breakpoint at the given line
        cb ) _clearbp $args ;;         # clear one or all breakpoints
        ds ) _displayscript ;;         # list the script and show the
                                       # breakpoints
        g  ) return ;;                 # "go": start/resume execution of
                                       # the script
        q  ) exit ;;                   # quit
        s  ) let _steps=${args:-1}     # single step N times (default = 1)
             return ;;
        x  ) _xtrace ;;                # toggle execution trace
       * ) eval ${cmd#!} $args ;; # pass to the shell
        *  ) _msg "Invalid command: '$cmd'" ;;
      esac
  done
}



# See if this line number has a breakpoint
function _at_linenumbp
{
    local i=0

    # Loop through the breakpoints array and check to see if any of
    # them match the current line number. If they do return true (0)
    # otherwise return false.

    if [ "$_linebp" ]; then
        while (( $i < ${#_linebp[@]} )); do
            if (( ${_linebp[$i]} == $_curline )); then
                return 0
            fi
            let i=$i+1
        done
    fi
    return 1
}



# Set a breakpoint at the given line number or list breakpoints
function _setbp
{
    local i
```

```
    # If there are no arguments call the breakpoint list function.
    # Otherwise check to see if the argument was a positive number.
    # If it wasn't then print an error message. If it was then check
    # to see if the line number contains text. If it doesn't then
    # print an error message. If it does then echo the current
    # breakpoints and the new addition and pipe them to "sort" and
    # assign the result back to the list of breakpoints. This results
    # in keeping the breakpoints in numerical sorted order.

    # Note that we can remove duplicate breakpoints here by using
    # the -u option to sort which uniquifies the list.

    if [ -z "$1" ]; then
        _listbp
    elif [ $(echo $1 | grep '^[0-9]*')  ]; then
        if [ -n "${_lines[$1]}" ]; then
            _linebp=($(echo $( (for i in ${_linebp[*]} $1; do
                    echo $i; done) | sort -n) ))
            _msg "Breakpoint set at line $1"
        else
            _msg "Breakpoints can only be set on non-blank lines"
        fi
    else
        _msg "Please specify a numeric line number"
    fi
}


# List breakpoints and break conditions
function _listbp
{
    if [ -n "$_linebp" ]; then
        _msg "Breakpoints at lines: ${_linebp[*]}"
    else
        _msg "No breakpoints have been set"
    fi

    _msg "Break on condition:"
    _msg "$_brcond"
}


# Clear individual or all breakpoints
function _clearbp
{
    local i bps

    # If there are no arguments, then delete all the breakpoints.
    # Otherwise, check to see if the argument was a positive number.
    # If it wasn't, then print an error message. If it was, then
    # echo all of the current breakpoints except the passed one
    # and assign them to a local variable. (We need to do this because
    # assigning them back to _linebp would keep the array at the same
    # size and just move the values "back" one place, resulting in a
```

```
    # duplicate value). Then destroy the old array and assign the
    # elements of the local array, so we effectively recreate it,
    # minus the passed breakpoint.

    if [ -z "$1" ]; then
        unset _linebp[*]
        _msg "All breakpoints have been cleared"
    elif [ $(echo $1 | grep '^[0-9]*') ]; then
            bps=($(echo $(for i in ${_linebp[*]}; do
                    if (( $1 != $i )); then echo $i; fi; done) ))
            unset _linebp[*]
            _linebp=(${bps[*]})
            _msg "Breakpoint cleared at line $1"
    else
        _msg "Please specify a numeric line number"
    fi
}


# Set or clear a break condition
function _setbc
{
    if [ -n "$*" ]; then
        _brcond=$args
        _msg "Break when true: $_brcond"
    else
        _brcond=
        _msg "Break condition cleared"
    fi
}


# Print out the shell script and mark the location of breakpoints
# and the current line

function _displayscript
{
    local i=1 j=0 bp cl

    ( while (( $i < ${#_lines[@]} )); do
        if [ ${_linebp[$j]} ] && (( ${_linebp[$j]} == $i )); then
            bp='*'
            let j=$j+1
        else
            bp=' '
        fi
        if (( $_curline == $i )); then
            cl=">"
        else
            cl=" "
        fi
        echo "$i:$bp $cl  ${_lines[$i]}"
        let i=$i+1
    done
```

```
    ) | more
}


# Toggle execution trace on/off
function _xtrace
{
    let _trace="! $_trace"
    _msg "Execution trace    if (( $_trace )); then
        _msg "on"
    else
        _msg "off"
    fi
}


# Print the passed arguments to Standard Error
function _msg
{
    echo -e "$@" >&2
}


# Print command menu
function _menu {
    _msg 'bashdb commands:
        bp N                    set breakpoint at line N
        bp                      list breakpoints and break condition
        bc string               set break condition to string
        bc                      clear break condition
        cb N                    clear breakpoint at line N
        cb                      clear all breakpoints
        ds                      displays the test script and breakpoints
        g                       start/resume execution
        s [N]                   execute N statements (default 1)
        x                       toggle execution trace on/off
        h, ?                    print this menu
        ! string                passes string to a shell
        q                       quit'
}


# Erase the temporary file before exiting
function _cleanup
{
    rm $_debugfile 2>/dev/null
}
```

In this chapter:
- *Installing bash as the Standard Shell*
- *Environment Customization*
- *System Security Features*

10

bash Administration

There are two areas in which system administrators use the shell as part of their job: setting up a generic environment for users and system security. In this chapter, we'll discuss *bash*'s features that relate to these tasks. We assume that you already know the basics of UNIX system administration.*

Installing bash as the Standard Shell

As a prelude to system-wide customization, we want to emphasize that *bash* can be installed as if it were the standard Bourne shell, */bin/sh*. Indeed, some systems, such as Linux, come with *bash* installed instead of the Bourne shell.

If you want to do this with your system, you can just save the original Bourne shell to another filename (in case someone needs to use it) and either install *bash* as *sh* in the */bin* directory, or better yet install *bash* in the */bin* directory and create a symbolic link from */bin/sh* to */bin/bash* using the command **ln −s /bin/bash /bin/sh**. The reason we think that the second option is better is because *bash* changes its behavior slightly if started as *sh*, as we will see shortly.

As detailed in Appendix A, *Related Shells*, *bash* is backward-compatible with the Bourne shell, except that it doesn't support ˆ as a synonym for the pipe character |. Unless you have an ancient UNIX system, or you have some very, very old shell scripts, you needn't worry about this.

But if you want to be absolutely sure, simply search through all shell scripts in all directories in your **PATH**. An easy way to perform the search is to use the *file* command, which we saw in Chapter 5, *Flow Control*, and Chapter 9, *Debugging Shell*

---

* A good source of information on system administration is *Essential System Administration* by Æleen Frisch (O'Reilly & Associates).

Programs. file prints "executable shell script" when given the name of one.* Here is a script that looks for ^ in shell scripts in every directory in your **PATH**:

```
IFS=:
for d in $PATH; do
    echo checking $d:
    cd $d
    scripts=$(file * | grep 'shell script' | cut -d: -f1)
    for f in $scripts; do
        grep '\^' $f /dev/null
    done
done
```

The first line of this script makes it possible to use **$PATH** as an item list in the **for** loop. For each directory, it **cd**s there and finds all shell scripts by piping the *file* command into *grep* and then, to extract the filename only, into *cut*. Then for each shell script, it searches for the ^ character.[†]

If you run this script, you will probably find several occurrences of ^—but these carets should be used within regular expressions in *grep*, *sed*, or *awk* commands, not as pipe characters. As long as carets are never used as pipes, it is safe for you to install *bash* as */bin/sh*.

As we mentioned earlier, if *bash* is started as *sh* (because the executable file has been renamed *sh* or there is a link from *sh* to *bash*) its startup behavior will change slightly to mimic the Bourne shell as closely as possible. For login shells it only attempts to read */etc/profile* and ~/*.profile*, ignoring any other startup files like ~/*.bash_profile*. For interactive shells it won't read the initialization file ~/*.bashrc*.[‡]

POSIX Mode

Besides its native operating mode, *bash* can also be switched into POSIX mode. The POSIX (Portable Operating System Interface) standard, described in detail in Appendix A, defines guidelines for standardizing UNIX. One part of the POSIX standard covers shells.

bash is nearly 100% POSIX-compliant in its native mode. If you want strict POSIX adherence, you can either start *bash* with the **–posix** option, or set it from within the shell with **set –o posix**.

---

* The exact message varies from system to system; make sure that yours prints this message when given the name of a shell script. If not, just substitute the message your *file* command prints for "shell script" in the following code.

† The inclusion of */dev/null* in the *grep* command is a kludge that forces *grep* to print the names of files that contain a match, even if there is only one such file in a given directory.

‡ *bash* also enters POSIX mode when started as *sh*. Versions of *bash* prior to 2.0 don't—POSIX mode has to be explicitly set with the **––posix** command-line option.

Only in very rare circumstances would you ever have to use POSIX mode. The differences, outlined in Appendix A, are small and are mostly concerned with the command lookup order and how functions are handled. Most *bash* users should be able to get through life without ever having to use this option.

Command-Line Options

bash has several command-line options that change the behavior and pass information to the shell. The options fall into two sets; single character options, like we've seen in previous chapters of this book, and *multicharacter* options, which are a relatively recent improvement to UNIX utilities.* Table 10-1 lists all of the options.†

Table 10-1: bash Command-Line Options

Option	Meaning
−c *string*	Commands are read from *string*, if present. Any arguments after *string* are interpreted as positional parameters, starting with $0.
−D	A list of all double-quoted strings preceded by $ is printed on the standard ouput. These are the strings that are subject to language translation when the current locale is not C or POSIX. This also turns on the −n option.
−i	Interactive shell. Ignore signals TERM, INT, and QUIT. With job control in effect, TTIN, TTOU, and TSTP are also ignored.
−o *option*	Takes the same arguments as set −o.
−s	Read commands from the standard input. If an argument is given to *bash*, this flag takes precedence (i.e., the argument won't be treated as a script name and standard input will be read).
−r	Restricted shell. Described later in this chapter.
−	Signals the end of options and disables further option processing. Any options after this are treated as filenames and arguments. −− is synonymous with −.
−−dump-strings	Does the same as −D.
−−help	Displays a usage message and exits.
−−login	Makes *bash* act as if invoked as a login shell.
−−noediting	Does not use the GNU *readline* library to read command lines if interactive.
−−noprofile	Does not read the startup file */etc/profile* or any of the personal initialization files.

---

* Multicharacter options are far more readable and easier to remember than the old, and usually cryptic, single character options. All of the GNU utilities have multicharacter options, but many applications and utilities (certainly those on old UNIX systems) allow only single-character options.

† See Appendix A for a list of options for versions of *bash* prior to 2.0.

Table 10-1: bash Command-Line Options (continued)

Option	Meaning
−−norc	Does not read the initialization file ˜/.bashrc if the shell is interactive. This is on by default if the shell is invoked as *sh*.
−−posix	Changes the behavior of *bash* to follow the POSIX guidelines more closely where the default operation of *bash* is different.
−−quiet	Shows no information on shell startup. This is the default.
−−rcfile *file*	Executes commands read from *file* instead of the initialization file ˜/.bashrc, if the shell is interactive.
−−version	Shows the version number of this instance of *bash* and then exits.

The multicharacter options have to appear on the command line before the single-character options. In addition to these, any **set** option can be used on the command line. Like shell built-ins, using a + instead of − turns an option off.

Of these options, the most useful are −i (interactive), −r (restricted), −s (read from standard input), −p (privileged), and −m (enable job control). Login shells are usually run with the −i, −s, and −m flags. We'll look at restricted and privileged modes later in this chapter.

Environment Customization

Like the Bourne shell, *bash* uses the file */etc/profile* for system-wide customization. When a user logs in, the shell reads and runs */etc/profile* before running the user's *.bash_profile*.

We won't cover all the possible commands you might want to put in */etc/profile*. But *bash* has a few unique features that are particularly relevant to system-wide customization; we'll discuss them here.

We'll start with two built-in commands that you can use in */etc/profile* to tailor your users' environments and constrain their use of system resources. Users can also use these commands in their *.bash_profile*, or at any other time, to override the default settings.

umask

umask, like the same command in most other shells, lets you specify the default permissions that files have when users create them. It takes the same types of arguments that the *chmod* command does, i.e., absolute (octal numbers) or symbolic permission values.

The **umask** contains the permissions that are turned off by default whenever a process creates a file, regardless of what permission the process specifies.*

We'll use octal notation to show how this works. As you probably know, the digits in a permission number stand (left to right) for the permissions of the owner, owner's group, and all other users, respectively. Each digit, in turn, consists of three bits, which specify read, write, and execute permissions from left to right. (If a file is a directory, the "execute" permission becomes "search" permission, i.e., permission to **cd** to it, list its files, etc.)

For example, the octal number 640 equals the binary number 110 100 000. If a file has this permission, then its owner can read and write it; users in the owner's group can only read it; everyone else has no permission on it. A file with permission 755 gives its owner the right to read, write, and execute it and everyone else the right to read and execute (but not write).

022 is a common **umask** value. This implies that when a file is created, the "most" permission it could possibly have is 755—which is the usual permission of an executable that a compiler might create. A text editor, on the other hand, might create a file with 666 permission (read and write for everyone), but the **umask** forces it to be 644 instead.

ulimit

The **ulimit** command was originally used to specify the limit on file creation size. But *bash*'s version has options that let you put limits on several different system resources. Table 10-2 lists the options.

Table 10-2: ulimit Resource Options

Option	Resource Limited
−a	All limits (for printing values only)
−c	Core file size (1 Kb blocks)
−d	Process data segment (Kb)
−f	File size (1 Kb blocks)
−l	Maximum size of a process that can be locked in memory (Kb)[a]
−m	Maximum resident set size
−n	File descriptors
−p	Pipe size (512 byte blocks)
−s	Process stack segment (Kb)
−t	Process CPU time (seconds)

---

* If you are comfortable with Boolean logic, think of the **umask** as a number that the operating system logically ANDs with the permission given by the creating process.

Table 10-2: ulimit Resource Options (continued)

Option	Resource Limited
−u	Maximum number of processes available to a user
−v	Virtual memory (Kb)

a. Not available in versions of *bash* prior to 2.0.

Each takes a numerical argument that specifies the limit in units shown in the table. You can also give the argument "unlimited" (which may actually mean some physical limit), or you can omit the argument, in which case it will print the current limit. **ulimit −a** prints limits (or "unlimited") of all types. You can specify only one type of resource at a time. If you don't specify any option, −f is assumed.

Some of these options depend on operating system capabilities that don't exist in older UNIX versions. In particular, some older versions have a fixed limit of 20 file descriptors per process (making −n irrelevant), and some don't support virtual memory (making −v irrelevant).

The −d and −s options have to do with *dynamic memory allocation*, i.e., memory for which a process asks the operating system at runtime. It's not necessary for casual users to limit these, though software developers may want to do so to prevent buggy programs from trying to allocate endless amounts of memory due to infinite loops.

The −v and −m options are similar; −v puts a limit on all uses of memory, and −m limits the amount of physical memory that a process is allowed to use. You don't need these unless your system has severe memory constraints or you want to limit process size to avoid thrashing.

The −u option is another option which is useful if you have system memory constraints or you wish just wish to stop individual users from hogging the system resources.

You may want to specify limits on file size (−f and −c) if you have constraints on disk space. Sometimes users actually mean to create huge files, but more often than not, a huge file is the result of a buggy program that goes into an infinite loop. Software developers who use debuggers like *sdb*, *dbx*, and *gdb* should not limit core file size, because core dumps are necessary for debugging.

The −t option is another possible guard against infinite loops. However, a program that is in an infinite loop but isn't allocating memory or writing files is not particularly dangerous; it's better to leave this unlimited and just let the user kill the offending program.

In addition to the types of resources you can limit, **ulimit** lets you specify hard or soft limits. Hard limits can be lowered by any user but only raised by the superuser (**root**); users can lower soft limits and raise them—but only as high as the hard limit for that resource.

If you give **−H** along with one (or more) of the options above, **ulimit** will set hard limits; **−S** sets soft limits. Without either of these, **ulimit** sets the hard and soft limit. For example, the following commands set the soft limit on file descriptors to 64 and the hard limit to unlimited:

```
ulimit -Sn 64
ulimit -Hn unlimited
```

When **ulimit** prints current limits, it prints soft limits unless you specify **−H**.

Types of Global Customization

The best possible approach to globally available customization would be a system-wide environment file that is separate from each user's environment file—just like */etc/profile* is separate from each user's *.bash_profile*. Unfortunately, *bash* doesn't have this feature.

Nevertheless, the shell gives you a few ways to set up customizations that are available to all users at all times. Environment variables are the most obvious; your */etc/profile* file will undoubtedly contain definitions for several of them, including **PATH** and **TERM**.

The variable **TMOUT** is useful when your system supports dialup lines. Set it to a number *N*, and if a user doesn't enter a command within *N* seconds after the shell last issued a prompt, the shell will terminate. This feature is helpful in preventing people from "hogging" the dialup lines.

You may want to include some more complex customizations involving environment variables, such as the prompt string **PS1** containing the current directory (as seen in Chapter 4, *Basic Shell Programming*).

You can also turn on options, such as *emacs* or *vi* editing modes, or **noclobber** to protect against inadvertent file overwriting. Any shell scripts you have written for general use also contribute to customization.

Unfortunately, it's not possible to create a global alias. You can define aliases in */etc/profile*, but there is no way to make them part of the environment so that their definitions will propagate to subshells. (In contrast, users can define global aliases by putting their definitions in ˜*.bashrc*.)

However, you can set up global functions. These are an excellent way to customize your system's environment, because functions are part of the shell, not separate processes.

System Security Features

UNIX security is a problem of legendary notoriety. Just about every aspect of a UNIX system has some security issue associated with it, and it's usually the system administrator's job to worry about this issue.

bash has two features that help solve this problem: the *restricted shell*, which is intentionally "brain damaged," and *privileged mode*, which is used with shell scripts that run as if the user were **root**.

Restricted Shell

The restricted shell is designed to put the user into an environment where his or her ability to move around and write files is severely limited. It's usually used for "guest" accounts.* You can make a user's login shell restricted by putting **rbash** in the user's */etc/passwd* entry.†

The specific constraints imposed by the restricted shell disallow the user from doing the following:

- Changing working directories: **cd** is inoperative. If you try to use it, you will get the error message **bash: cd: restricted**.
- Redirecting output to a file: the redirectors **>**, **>|**, **<>**, and **>>** are not allowed.
- Assigning a new value to the environment variables **SHELL** or **PATH**.
- Specifying any pathnames with slashes (/) in them. The shell will treat files outside of the current directory as "not found."
- Using the **exec** built-in.
- Specifying a filename containing a / as an argument to the . built-in command.
- Importing function definitions from the shell environment at startup.
- Adding or deleting built-in commands with the **−f** and **−d** options to the **enable** built-in command.
- Specifying the **−p** option to the **builtin** command.
- Turning off restricted mode with **set +r**.

These restrictions go into effect after the user's *.bash_profile* and environment files are run. In addition, it is wise to change the owner of the users' *.bash_profile* and *.bashrc* to root, and make these files read-only. The users' home directory should also be made read-only.

---

* This feature is not documented in the manual pages for old versions of *bash*.

† If this option has been included when the shell was compiled. See Chapter 11, *bash for Your System*, for details on configuring *bash*.

This means that the restricted shell user's entire environment is set up in */etc/profile* and *.bash_profile*. Since the user can't access */etc/profile* and can't overwrite *.bash_profile*, this lets the system administrator configure the environment as he or she sees fit.

Two common ways of setting up such environments are to set up a directory of "safe" commands and have that directory be the only one in **PATH**, and to set up a command menu from which the user can't escape without exiting the shell.

A System Break-In Scenario

Before we explain the other security features, here is some background information on system security that should help you understand why they are necessary.

Many problems with UNIX security hinge on a UNIX file attribute called the *suid* (set user ID) bit. This is like a permission bit (see **umask** earlier in this chapter): when an executable file has it turned on, the file runs with an effective user ID equal to the owner of the file, which is usually **root**. The effective user ID is distinct from the real user ID of the process.

This feature lets administrators write scripts that do certain things that require **root** privilege (e.g., configure printers) in a controlled way. To set a file's *suid* bit, the superuser can type **chmod 4755** *filename*; the 4 is the *suid* bit.

Modern system administration wisdom says that creating *suid* shell scripts is a very, very bad idea.* This has been especially true under the C shell, because its *.cshrc* environment file introduces numerous opportunities for break-ins. *bash*'s environment file feature creates similar security holes, although the security feature we'll see shortly make this problem less severe.

We'll show why it's dangerous to set a script's *suid* bit. Recall that in Chapter 3, *Customizing Your Environment*, we mentioned that it's not a good idea to put your personal *bin* directory at the front of your **PATH**. Here is a scenario that shows how this placement combines with *suid* shell scripts to form a security hole: a variation of the infamous "Trojan horse" scheme. First, the computer cracker has to find a user on the system with an *suid* shell script. In addition, the user must have a **PATH** with his or her personal *bin* directory listed before the public *bin* directories, and the cracker must have write permission on the user's personal *bin* directory.

Once the cracker finds a user with these requirements, he or she does the following steps.

---

* In fact, some versions of UNIX intentionally disable the *suid* feature for shell scripts.

- Looks at the *suid* script and finds a common utility that it calls. Let's say it's *grep*.

- Creates the Trojan horse, which is this case is a shell script called *grep* in the user's personal *bin* directory. The script looks like this:

```
cp /bin/bash filename
chown root filename
chmod 4755 filename
/bin/grep "$@"
rm ~/bin/grep
```

  filename should be some unremarkable filename in a directory with public read and execute permission, such as */bin* or */usr/bin*. The file, when created, will be that most heinous of security holes: an *suid* interactive shell.

- Sits back and waits for the user to run the *suid* shell script—which calls the Trojan horse, which in turn creates the *suid* shell and then self-destructs.

- Runs the *suid* shell and creates havoc.

Privileged Mode

The one way to protect against Trojan horses is *privileged mode*. This is a **set −o** option (**set −o privileged** or **set −p**), but the shell enters it automatically whenever it executes a script whose *suid* bit is set.

In privileged mode, when an *suid bash* shell script is invoked, the shell does not run the user's environment file—i.e., it doesn't expand the user's **BASH_ENV** environment variable.

Since privileged mode is an option, it is possible to turn it off with the command **set +o privileged** (or **set +p**). But this doesn't help the potential system cracker: the shell automatically changes its effective user ID to be the same as the real user ID—i.e., if you turn off privileged mode, you also turn off *suid*.

Privileged mode is an excellent security feature; it solves a problem that originated when the environment file idea first appeared in the C shell.

Nevertheless, we still strongly recommend against creating *suid* shell scripts. We have shown how *bash* protects against break-ins in one particular situation, but that certainly does not imply that *bash* is "safe" in any absolute sense. If you really must have *suid* scripts, you should carefully consider all relevant security issues.

Finally, if you would like to learn more about UNIX security, we recommend *Practical UNIX and Internet Security*, by Gene Spafford and Simson Garfinkel (O'Reilly & Associates).

11

bash for Your System

The first ten chapters of this book have looked at nearly all aspects of *bash*, from navigating the file system and command-line editing to writing shell scripts and functions using lesser-known features of the shell. This is all very well and good, but what if you have an old version of *bash* and want the new features shown in this book (or worse yet, you don't have *bash* at all)?

In this chapter we'll show you how to get the latest version of *bash* and how to install it on your system, and we'll discuss potential problems you might encounter along the way. We'll also look briefly at the examples that come with *bash* and how you can report bugs to the *bash* maintainer.

Obtaining bash

If you have a direct connection to the Internet, you should have no trouble obtaining *bash*; otherwise, you'll have to do a little more work.

bash is available from a number of anonymous FTP sites. The following list (giving host name, IP address, and directory name) is a good starting point:

prep.ai.mit.edu	(18.159.0.42)	*/pub/gnu*
sunsite.unc.edu	(152.2.254.81)	*/pub/gnu*
plaza.aarnet.edu.au	(139.130.23.2)	*/gnu*
ftp.isy.liu.se	(130.236.20.12)	*/pub/gnu*
unix.bensa.ac.uk	(129.12.200.129)	*/mirrors/gnu*

prep.ai.mit.edu is the official GNU site and will always have the most up-to-date copy of *bash*. The other sites listed mirror the official site, so barring any major changes, they should also have the most recent version. To reduce load on the GNU site, it's best to get *bash* from one of the other sources.

If you've never used anonymous *ftp* we'll provide a quick example. The following sample session shows what you type in boldface and comments in italics:

```
$ ftp unix.hensa.ac.uk
Connected to sesame.hensa.ac.uk.
220 sesame FTP server (Version wu-2.4(20) Fri Jul 28 15:46 GMT 1995) ready.
Name (unix.hensa.ac.uk:cam): anonymous
331 Guest login ok, send your complete e-mail address as password.
Password: alice@wonderland.oreilly.com (use your login name and host here)
230- ************************************************************************
230-
230-                     Welcome to HENSA
230-
230-        the Higher Education National Software Archive
230-            at the University of Kent at Canterbury
230-                    funded by JISC
230-
230-     HENSA Unix maintains copies of electronic archives from all
230-     over the world. Over 40 archives are currently available,
230-     providing access to a wide range of material, including
230-     software, documentation, bibliographic and multimedia collections.
230-     To access the mirrors, change directory to mirrors.
 .

 .

 .
230-Please read the file README
230-  it was last modified on Mon Apr  7 14:25:03 1997 - 121 days ago
230 Guest login ok, access restrictions apply.
Remote system type is UNIX.
Using binary mode to transfer files.
ftp> cd /mirrors/gnu
250-Please read the file README
250-  it was last modified on Mon Jul  8 23:00:00 1996 - 393 days ago
250-Please read the file README-about-.diff-files
250-  it was last modified on Thu Mar 20 14:08:00 1997 - 139 days ago
250-Please read the file README-about-.gz-files
250-  it was last modified on Tue Jul  9 16:18:00 1996 - 392 days ago
250 CWD command successful.
ftp> binary (you must specify binary transfer for compressed files)
200 Type set to I.
ftp> get bash-2.01.tar.gz
local: bash-2.01.tar.gz remote: bash-2.01.tar.gz
200 PORT command successful.
150 Opening BINARY mode data connection for bash-2.01.tar.gz (1342563 bytes).
226 Transfer complete.
1342563 bytes received in 556 secs (2.4 Kbytes/sec)
 .

 . (repeat this step for each file that you want)
 .
ftp> quit
221 Goodbye.
$
```

You can also retrieve the files by FTPMAIL, BITFTP, and UUCP. To find out how to use these methods, please refer to Appendix E, *Obtaining Sample Programs*.

Failing these methods, you can always get *bash* on tape or CD-ROM by ordering it directly from the Free Software Foundation:

> The Free Software Foundation (FSF)
> 675 Massachusetts Avenue
> Cambridge MA, 02139
> email: *gnu@prep.ai.mit.edu*
> phone: (617) 876-3296

Unpacking the Archive

Having obtained the archive file by one of the above methods, you need to unpack it and install it on your system. Unpacking can be done anywhere—we'll assume you're unpacking it in your home directory. Installing it on the system requires you to have root privileges. If you aren't a system administrator with root access, you can still compile and use *bash*; you just can't install it as a system-wide utility. The first thing to do is uncompress the archive file by typing **gunzip bash-2.01.tar.gz**.* Then you need to "untar" the archive by typing **tar -xf bash-2.01.tar**. The **-xf** means "extract the archived material from the specified file." This will create a directory called *bash-2.01* in your home directory.

The archive contains all of the source code needed to compile *bash* and a large amount of documentation and examples. We'll look at these things and how you go about making a *bash* executable in the rest of this chapter.

What's in the Archive

The *bash* archive contains a main directory (*bash-2.01* for the current version) and a set of files and subdirectories. Among the first files you should examine are:

- *MANIFEST*, a list of all the files and directories in the archive

- *COPYING*, the GNU Copyleft for *bash*

- *NEWS*, a list of bug fixes and new features since the last *version*

- *README*, a short introduction and instructions for compiling *bash*

---

* *gunzip* is the GNU decompression utility. *gunzip* is popular but relatively new and some systems don't have it. If your system doesn't, you can obtain it by the same methods as you obtained *bash*. *gunzip* is available from the FSF. **gzip -d** does the same thing as *gunzip*.

You should also be aware of two directories:

- *doc*, information related to *bash* in various formats

- *examples*, examples of startup files, scripts, and functions

The other files and directories in the archive are mostly things that are needed during the build. Unless you are going to go hacking into the internal workings of the shell, they shouldn't concern you.

Documentation

The *doc* directory contains a few articles that are worth reading. Indeed, it would be well worth printing out the manual entry for *bash* so you can use it in conjunction with this book. The *README* file gives a short summary of what the files are.

The document you'll most often use is the manual page entry (*bash.1*). The file is in *troff* format—that used by the manual pages. You can read it by processing it with the text-formatter *nroff* and piping the output to a pager utility: **nroff –man bash.1 | more** should do the trick. You can also print it off by piping it to the lineprinter (*lp*). This summarizes all of the facilities your version of *bash* has and is the most up-to-date reference you can get. This document is also available through the *man* facility once you've installed the package, but sometimes it's nice to have a hard copy so you can write notes all over it.

Of the other documents, *FAQ* is a *Frequently Asked Questions* document with answers, *readline.3* is the manual entry for the *readline* facility, and *article.ms* is an article about the shell that appeared in *Linux Journal*, by the current *bash* maintainer, Chet Ramey.

Configuring and Building bash

To compile *bash* "straight out of the box" is easy;* you just type **configure** and then **make**! The *bash configure* script attempts to work out if you have various utilities and C library functions, and where abouts they reside on your system. It then stores the relevant information in the file *config.h*. It also creates a file called *config.status* that is a script you can run to recreate the current configuration information. While the *configure* is running, it prints out information on what it is searching for and where it finds it.

The *configure* script also sets the location that *bash* will be installed, the default being the */usr/local* area (*/usr/local/bin* for the executable, */usr/local/man* for the

---

* This configuration information pertains to *bash* version 2.0 and later. The configuration and installation for earlier versions is fairly easy, although it differs in certain details. For further information, refer to the *INSTALL* instructions that came with your version of *bash*.

manual entries etc.). If you don't have root privilages and want it in your own home directory, or you wish to install *bash* in some other location, you'll need to specify a path to configure. You can do this with the −−**exec-prefix** option. For example:

```
$ configure --exec-prefix /usr
```

specifies that the *bash* files will be placed under the */usr* directory.

After the configuration finishes and you type **make**, the *bash* executable is built. A script called *bashbug* is also generated which allows you to report bugs in the format the *bash* maintainers want. We'll look at how you use it later in this chapter.

Once the build finishes, you can see if the *bash* executable works by typing ./**bash**. If it doesn't, turn to the section "Potential Problems," later in this chapter.

To install *bash*, type **make install**. This will create all of the necessary directories (*bin, info, man* and its subdirectories) and copy the files to them.

If you've installed *bash* in your home directory, be sure to add your own *bin* path to your **PATH** and your own *man* path to **MANPATH**.

bash comes preconfigured with nearly all of its features enabled, but it is possible to customize your version by specifying what you want with the −−**enable**-*feature* and −−**disable**-*feature* command-line options to *configure*.

Table 11-1 is a list of the configurable features and a short description of what those features do.

Table 11-1: Configurable Features

Feature	Description
alias	Support for aliases
array-variables	Support for one dimensional arrays
bang-history	C-shell-like history expansion and editing
brace-expansion	Brace expansion
command-timing	Support for the **time** command
directory-stack	Support for the **pushd**, **popd**, and **dirs** directory manipulation commands
disabled-builtins	Whether a built-in can be run with the **builtin** command, even if it has been disabled with **enable −n**
dparen-arithmetic	Support for ((...))
help-builtin	Support for the **help** built-in
history	History via the **fc** and **history** commands
job-control	Job control via **fg**, **bg**, and **jobs** if supported by the operating system

Table 11-1: Configurable Features (continued)

Feature	Description
process-substitution	Whether process substitution occurs, if supported by the operating system
prompt-string-decoding	Whether backslash escaped characters in PS1, PS2, PS3, and PS4 are allowed
readline	*readline* editing and history capabilities
restricted	Support for the restricted shell, the **−r** option to the shell, and **rbash**
select	The **select** construct
usg-echo-default	Whether **echo −e** is the default for **echo**

The options **disabled-builtins** and **usg-echo-default** are disabled by default. The others are enabled.

Many other shell features can be turned on or off by modifying the file *config.h.top*. For further details on this file and configuring *bash* in general, see *INSTALL*.

Finally, to clean up the source directory and remove all of the object files and executables, type **make clean**. Make sure you run **make install** first, otherwise you'll have to rerun the installation from scratch.

Testing bash

There are a series of tests that can be run on your newly built version of *bash* to see if it is running correctly. The tests are scripts that are derived from problems reported in earlier versions of the shell. Running these tests on the latest version of *bash* shouldn't cause any errors.

To run the tests just type **make tests** in the main *bash* directory. The name of each test is displayed, along with some warning messages, and then it is run. Successful tests produce no output (unless otherwise noted in the warning messages).

If any of the tests fail, you'll see a list of things that represent differences between what is expected and what happened. If this occurs you should file a bug report with the *bash* maintainer. See the "Reporting Bugs" section of this chapter for information on how to do this.

Potential Problems

Although *bash* has been installed on a large number of different machines and operating systems, there are occasional problems. Usually the problems aren't serious and a bit of investigation can result in a quick solution.

If *bash* didn't compile, the first thing to do is check that *configure* guessed your machine and operating system correctly. Then check the file *NOTES*, which contains some information on specific UNIX systems. Also look in *INSTALL* for additional information on how to give *configure* specific compilation instructions.

Installing bash as a Login Shell

Having installed *bash* and made sure it is working correctly, the next thing to do is to make it your login shell. This can be accomplished in two ways.

Individual users can use the *chsh* (change shell) command after they log in to their accounts. *chsh* asks for their password and displays a list of shells to choose from. Once a shell is chosen, *chsh* changes the appropriate entry in */etc/passwd*. For security reasons, *chsh* will only allow you to change to a shell if it exists in the file */etc/shells* (if */etc/shells* doesn't exist, *chsh* asks for the pathname of the shell).

Another way to change the login shell is to edit the password file directly. On most systems, */etc/passwd* will have lines of the form:

```
cam:pK1Z9BCJbzCrBNrkjRUdUiTtFOh/:501:100:Cameron Newham:/home/cam:/bin/bash
cc:kfDKDjfkeDJKJySFgJFWErrElpe:502:100:Cheshire Cat:/home/cc:/bin/bash
```

As **root** you can just edit the last field of the lines in the password file to the pathname of whatever shell you choose.

If you don't have root access and *chsh* doesn't work, you can still make *bash* your login shell. The trick is to replace your current shell with *bash* by using **exec** from within one of the startup files for your current shell.

If your current shell is similar to *sh* (e.g., *ksh*), you have to add the line:

```
[ -f /pathname/bash ] && exec /pathname/bash --login
```

to your *.profile*, where *pathname* is the path to your *bash* executable.

You will also have to create an empty file called *.bash_profile*. The existence of this file prevents *bash* from reading your *.profile* and re-executing the **exec**—thus entering an infinite loop. Any initialization code that you need for *bash* can just be placed in *.bash_profile*.

If your current shell is similar to *csh* (e.g., *tcsh*) things are slightly easier. You just have to add the line:

```
if ( -f /pathname/bash ) exec /pathname/bash --login
```

to your *.login*, where *pathname* is the path to your *bash* executable.

Examples

The *bash* archive also includes an examples directory. This directory contains some subdirectories for scripts, functions, and examples of startup files.

The startup files in the *startup-files* directory provide many examples of what you can put in your own startup files. In particular, *bash_aliases* gives many useful aliases. Bear in mind that if you copy these files wholesale, you'll have to edit them for your system because many of the paths will be different. Refer to Chapter 3, *Customizing Your Environment*, for further information on changing these files to suit your needs.

The *functions* directory contains about twenty files with function definitions that you might find useful. Among them are:

- *basename*, the *basename* utility, missing from some systems
- *dirfuncs*, directory manipulation facilities
- *dirname*, the *dirname* utility, missing from some systems
- *whatis*, an implementation of the 10th Edition Bourne shell **whatis** builtin
- *whence*, an almost exact clone of the Korn shell **whence** builtin

Especially helpful, if you come from a Korn shell background, is *kshenv*. This contains function definitions for some common Korn facilities such as **whence**, **print**, and the two-parameter **cd** builtins.

The *scripts* directory contains four examples of *bash* scripts. The two largest scripts are examples of the complex things you can do with shell scripts. The first is a (rather amusing) adventure game interpreter and the second is a C shell interpreter. The other scripts include examples of precedence rules, a scrolling text display, a "spinning wheel" progress display, and how to prompt the user for a particular type of answer.

Not only are the script and function examples useful for including in your environment, they also provide many alternative examples that you can learn from when reading this book. We encourage you to experiment with them.

Who Do I Turn to?

No matter how good something is or how much documentation comes with it, you'll eventually come across something that you don't understand or that doesn't work. In such cases it can't be stressed enough to *carefully read the documenta-*

tion (in computer parlance: RTFM).* In many cases this will answer your question or point out what you're doing wrong.

Sometimes you'll find this only adds to your confusion or confirms that there is something wrong with the software. The next thing to do is to talk to a local *bash* guru to sort out the problem. If that fails, or there is no guru, you'll have to turn to other means (currently only via the Internet).

Asking Questions

If you have any questions about *bash*, there are currently two ways to go about getting them answered. You can email questions to *bug-bash@prep.ai.mit.edu* or you can post your question to the USENET newsgroup *gnu.bash.bug*.

In both cases either the *bash* maintainer or some knowledgeable person on USENET will give you advice. When asking a question, try to give a meaningful summary of your question in the subject line.

Reporting Bugs

Bug reports should be sent to *bash-maintainers@prep.ai.mit.edu* and should include the version of *bash* and the operating system it is running on, the compiler used to compile *bash*, a description of the problem, a description of how the problem was produced and, if possible, a fix for the problem. The best way to do this is by using the *bashbug* script which is installed when you install *bash*.

Before you run *bashbug*, make sure you've set your **EDITOR** environment variable to your favorite editor and have exported it (*bashbug* defaults to *emacs*, which may not be installed on your system). When you execute *bashbug* it will enter the editor with a partially blank report form. Some of the information (*bash* version, operating system version, etc.) will have been filled in automatically. We'll take a brief look at the form, but most of it is self-explanatory.

The **From:** field should be filled out with your email address. For example:

```
From: confused@wonderland.oreilly.com
```

Next comes the **Subject:** field; make an effort to fill it out, as this makes it easier for the maintainers when they need to look up your submission. Just replace the line surrounded by square brackets with a meaningful summary of the problem.

The next few lines are a description of the system and should not be touched. Next comes the **Description:** field. You should provide a detailed description of

---

* RTFM stands for "Read The F(laming) Manual."

the problem and how it differs from what is expected. Try to be as specific and concise as possible when describing the problem.

The **Repeat-By**: field is where you describe how you generated the problem; if necessary, list the exact keystrokes you used. Sometimes you won't be able to reproduce the problem yourself, but you should still fill out this field with the events leading up to the problem. Attempt to reduce the problem to the smallest possible form. For example, if it was a large shell script, try to isolate the section that produced the problem and include only that in your report.

Lastly, the **Fix**: field is where you can provide the necessary patch to fix the problem if you've investigated it and found out what was going wrong. If you have no idea what caused the problem, just leave the field blank.

Once you've finished filling in the form, save it and exit your editor. The form will automatically be sent to the maintainers.

Related Shells

The fragmentation of the UNIX marketplace has had its advantages and disadvantages. The advantages came mostly in the early days: lack of standardization and proliferation among technically knowledgeable academics and professionals contributed to a healthy "free market" for UNIX software, in which several programs of the same type (e.g., shells, text editors, system administration tools) would often compete for popularity. The best programs would usually become the most widespread, while inferior software tended to fade away.

But often there was no single "best" program in a given category, so several would prevail. This led to the current situation, where multiplicity of similar software has led to confusion, lack of compatibility, and—most unfortunate of all—the inability of UNIX to capture as big a share of the market as other operating platforms (MS-DOS, Microsoft Windows, Novell NetWare, etc.).

The "shell" category has probably suffered in this way more than any other type of software. As we said in the Preface and in Chapter 1, *bash Basics*, several shells are currently available; the differences between them are often not all that great.

Therefore we felt it necessary to include information on shells similar to *bash*. This appendix summarizes the differences between the latter and the following:

- The standard Version 7 Bourne shell, as a kind of "baseline"

- The IEEE POSIX 1003.2 shell Standard, to which *bash* and other shells will adhere in the future

- The Korn shell (*ksh*), a popular commercial shell provided with many UNIX systems

- *pdksh*, a widely used public domain Korn shell
- Shell workalikes on desktop PC platforms, including the MKS Toolkit shell

The Bourne Shell

bash is almost completely backward-compatible with the Bourne shell. The only significant feature of the latter that *bash* doesn't support is ˆ (caret) as a synonym for the pipe (|) character. This is an archaic feature that the Bourne shell includes for its own backward compatibility with earlier shells. No modern UNIX version has any shell code that uses ˆ as a pipe.

To describe the differences between the Bourne shell and *bash*, we'll go through each chapter of this book and enumerate the features discussed in the chapter that the Bourne shell does *not* support. Although some versions of the Bourne shell exist that include a few *bash* features,* we refer to the standard, Version 7 Bourne shell that has been around for many years.

Chapter 1, *bash Basics*
> The **cd** – form of the **cd** command; tilde (˜) expansion; the **jobs** command; the **help** built-in.

Chapter 2, *Command-Line Editing*
> All. (That is, the Bourne shell doesn't support any of the *readline*, history, and editing features discussed in this chapter.)

Chapter 3, *Customizing Your Environment*
> Aliases; prompt string customization; **set** options. The Bourne shell supports only the following: –e, –k, –n, –t, –u, –v, –x, and –. It doesn't support option names (–o). The **shopt** built-in. Environment files aren't supported.
>
> The following built-in variables aren't supported:
>
> | | |
> |---|---|
> | BASH | BASH_VERSION |
> | BASH_ENV | BASH_VERSINFO |
> | CDPATH | DIRSTACK |
> | FCEDIT | GROUPS |
> | HISTCMD | HISTCONTROL |
> | HISTFILE | HISTIGNORE |
> | HISTSIZE | HISTFILESIZE |
> | HOSTFILE | HOSTNAME |
> | HOSTTYPE | IGNOREEOF |

---

* For example, the Bourne shell distributed with System V supports functions and a few other shell features common to *bash* and the Korn shell.

INPUTRC	LANG
LC_ALL	LC_COLLATE
LC_MESSAGES	LINENO
MAILCHECK	OLDPWD
OPTARG	OPTERR
OPTIND	OSTYPE
PROMPT_COMMAND	PIPESTATUS
PS3	PS4
PWD	RANDOM
REPLY	SECONDS
SHELLOPTS	SHLVL
TIMEFORMAT	TMOUT
auto_resume	histchars

Chapter 4, *Basic Shell Programming*

Functions; the **type** command; the **local** command; the **${#parameter}** operator; pattern-matching variable operators (%, %%, #, ##). Command-substitution syntax is different: use the older `command` instead of $(command). The built-in **pushd** and **popd** commands.

Chapter 5, *Flow Control*

The **!** keyword; the **select** construct isn't supported. The Bourne shell **return** doesn't exit a script when it is sourced with . (dot).

Chapter 6, *Command-Line Options and Typed Variables*

Use the external command *getopt* instead of **getopts**, but note that it doesn't really do the same thing. Integer arithmetic isn't supported: use the external command *expr* instead of the $((*arithmetic-exp*)) syntax. The arithmetic conditional ((*arithmetic-exp*)) isn't supported; use the old condition test syntax and the relational operators **–lt**, **–eq**, etc. Array variables are not supported. **declare** and **let** aren't supported.

Chapter 7, *Input/Output and Command-Line Processing*

The **command, builtin,** and **enable** built-ins. The **–e** and **–E** options to **echo** are not supported. The I/O redirectors **>|** and **<>** are not supported. None of the options to **read** is supported.

Chapter 8, *Process Handling*

Job control—specifically, the **jobs, fg,** and **bg** commands. Job number notation with **%**, i.e., the **kill** and **wait** commands only accept process IDs. The **–** option to **trap** (reset trap to the default for that signal). **trap** only accepts signal numbers, not logical names. The **disown** built-in.

Chapter 9, *Debugging Shell Programs*

> The DEBUG fake signal is not supported. The EXIT fake signal is supported as
> signal 0.

Chapter 10, *bash Administration*

> The **ulimit** command and privileged mode aren't supported. The **–S** option to
> **umask** is not supported. The Bourne shell's restrictive counterpart, *rsh*, only
> inhibits assignment to **PATH**.

The IEEE 1003.2 POSIX Shell Standard

There have been many attempts to standardize UNIX. Hardware companies'
monolithic attempts at market domination, fragile industry coalitions, marketing
failures, and other such efforts are the stuff of history—and the stuff of frustration.

Only one standardization effort has not been tied to commercial interests: the
Portable Operating System Interface, known as POSIX. This effort started in 1981
with the */usr/group* (now UniForum) Standards Committee, which produced the
/usr/group Standard three years later. The list of contributors grew to include the
Institute of Electrical and Electronic Engineers (IEEE) and the International Organi-
zation for Standardization (ISO).

The first POSIX standard was published in 1988. This one, called IEEE P1003.1,
covers low-level issues at the system-call level. IEEE P1003.2, covering the shell,
utility programs, and user interface issues, was ratified in September 1992 after a
six-year effort.

The POSIX standards were never meant to be rigid and absolute. The committee
members certainly weren't about to put guns to the heads of operating system
implementors and force them to adhere. Instead, the standards are designed to be
flexible enough to allow for both coexistence of similar available software, so that
existing code isn't in danger of obsolescence, and the addition of new features, so
that vendors have the incentive to innovate. In other words, they are supposed to
be the kind of third-party standards that vendors might actually be interested in
following.

As a result, most UNIX vendors currently comply with POSIX 1003.1. Now that
POSIX 1003.2 is available, the most important shells will undoubtedly adhere to it
in the future. *bash* is no exception; it is nearly 100% POSIX-compliant already and
will continue to move towards full compliance in future releases.

POSIX 1003.2 itself consists of two parts. The first, 1003.2, addresses shell script
portability; it defines the shell and the standard utilities. The second, 1003.2a,
called the User Portability Extensions (UPE), defines standards of interactive shell
use and interactive utilities like the *vi* editor. The combined document—on the

order of 2000 pages—is available through the IEEE; for information, call (800) 678-IEEE.

The committee members had two motivating factors to weigh when they designed the 1003.2 shell standard. On the one hand, the design had to accommodate, as much as possible, existing shell code written under various Bourne-derived shells (the Version 7, System V, BSD, and Korn shells). These shells are different in several extremely subtle ways, most of which have to do with the ways certain syntactic elements interact with each other.

It must have been quite difficult and tedious to spell out these differences, let alone to reach compromises among them. Throw in biases of some committee members towards particular shells, and you might understand why it took six years to ratify 1003.2.

On the other hand, the shell design had to serve as a standard on which to base future shell implementations. This implied goals of simplicity, clarity, and precision—objectives that seem especially elusive in the context of the above problems.

The designers found one way of ameliorating this dilemma: they decided that the standard should include not only the features included in the shell, but also those explicitly omitted and those included but with unspecified functionality. The latter category allows some of the existing shells' innovations to "sneak through" without becoming part of the standard, while listing omitted features helps programmers determine which features in existing shell scripts won't be portable to future shells.

The POSIX standard is primarily based on the System V Bourne shell, which is a superset of the Version 7 shell discussed earlier in this appendix. Therefore you should assume that *bash* features that aren't present in the Bourne shell also aren't included in the POSIX standard.

The following *bash* features are left "unspecified" in the standard, meaning that their syntax is acceptable but their functionality is not standardized:

- The other syntax for functions shown in Chapter 4 is supported; see the following discussion.

- The **select** control structure.

- Code blocks ({ ... }) are supported, but for maximum portability, the curly brackets should be quoted (for reasons too complicated to go into here).

- Signal numbers are only allowed if the numbers for certain key signals (INT, TERM, and a few others) are the same as on the most important historical versions of UNIX. In general, shell scripts should use symbolic names for signals.

The POSIX standard supports functions, but the semantics are weaker: it is not possible to define local variables, and functions can't be exported.

The command lookup order has been changed to allow certain built-in commands to be overridden by functions—since aliases aren't included in the standard. Built-in commands are divided into two sets by their positions in the command lookup order: some are processed before functions, some after. Specifically, the built-in commands **break**, **:** (do nothing), **continue**, **.** (source), **eval**, **exec**, **exit**, **export**, **readonly**, **return**, **set**, **shift**, **trap**, and **unset** take priority over functions.

Finally, because the POSIX standard is meant to promote shell script portability, it explicitly avoids mention of features that only apply to interactive shell use—including aliases, editing modes, control keys, and so on. The UPE covers these. It also avoids mentioning certain fundamental implementation issues: in particular, there is no requirement that multitasking be used for background jobs, subshells, etc. This was done to allow portability to non-multitasking systems like MS-DOS, so that, for example, the MKS Toolkit (see the following discussion) can be POSIX-compliant.

The Korn Shell

One of the first major alternatives to the "traditional" shells, Bourne and C, was the Korn shell, publicly released in 1986 as part of AT&T's "Experimental Toolchest." The Korn shell was written by David Korn at AT&T. The first version was unsupported, but eventually UNIX System Laboratories (USL) decided to give it support when they released it with their version of UNIX (System V Release 4) in 1989. The November 1988 Korn shell is the most widely used version of this shell.

The 1988 release is not fully POSIX-compliant—less so than *bash*. The latest release (1993) has brought the Korn shell into better compliance as well as providing more features and streamlining existing features.

Unlike *bash*, the Korn shell is a commercial product; the source code is not available and you have to purchase the executable (which is usually bundled with the other utilities on most commercial versions of UNIX).

The 1988 Korn shell and *bash* share many features, but there are some important differences in the Korn shell:

*   Functions are more like separate entities than part of the invoking shell (traps and options are not shared with the invoking shell).

*   Coroutines are supported. Two processes can communicate with one another by using the **print** and **read** commands.

- The command **print** replaces **echo**. **print** can have a file descriptor specified and can be used to communicate with coroutines.

- Function autoloading is supported. Functions are read into memory only when they are called.

- String conditional tests have a new syntax of the form [[. . .]].

- There is an additional "fake" signal, ERR. This signal is sent when a script or function exits with a non-zero status.

- One-dimensional arrays are supported, although they are limited to a maximum size of 1024 elements.

- Filename generation capabilities are substantially increased by expanding on pattern matching and including *regular expression* operators.

- The history list is kept in a file rather than in memory. This allows concurrent instantiations of the shell to access the same history list, a possible advantage in certain circumstances.

- There is no default startup file. If the environment variable **ENV** is not defined, nothing is read.

- The **type** command is replaced with the more restrictive **whence**.

- The primary prompt string (**PS1**) doesn't allow escaped commands.

- There are no built-in equivalents to **builtin**, **command**, and **enable**.

- There is no provision for key bindings and no direct equivalent to *readline*.

- There are no built-in equivalents to **pushd**, **popd**, and **dirs**. They have to be defined as functions if you want them.

- The history substitution mechanism is not supported.

- Brace expansion is not supported in the default configuration, but is a compile-time option.

- ! is not a keyword.

- Prompt strings don't allow backslash-escaped special characters.

- There is no provision for online help.

- Many of the *bash* environment variables don't exist, notably:

BASH	BASH_VERSION
BASH_VERSINFO	DIRSTACK
EUID	FIGNORE
GLOBIGNORE	HISTCMD
HISTFILESIZE	HISTIGNORE
HISTCONTROL	HOSTFILE

HOSTNAME	HOSTTYPE
IGNOREEOF	INPUTRC
MACHTYPE	OPTERR
OSTYPE	PROMPT_COMMAND
PIPESTATUS	SHELLOPTS
SHLVL	TIMEFORMAT
UID	auto_resume
histchars	

In addition, the startup and environment files for Korn are different, consisting of *.profile* and the file specified by the **ENV** variable. The default environment file can be overridden by using the variable **ENV**. There is no logout file.

For a more detailed list of the differences between *bash* and the 1988 Korn shell, plus differences with the 1993 Korn shell, see the *FAQ* file in the *doc* directory of the *bash* archive.

The Korn shell is a good alternative to *bash*. Its only major drawbacks are that it isn't freely available and is upgraded only every few years.

pdksh

A free alternative to *bash* is a version of the Korn shell known as *pdksh* (standing for Public Domain Korn shell). *pdksh* is available as source code in various places on the Internet, including the USENET newsgroup *comp.sources.unix*, and the *pdksh* World Wide Web home page (*http://www.cs.mun.ca/˜michael/pdksh/*) of the current maintainer, Michael Rendell.

pdksh was originally written by Eric Gisin, who based it on Charles Forsyth's public domain Version 7 Bourne shell. It has all Bourne shell features plus some of the POSIX extensions and a few features of its own.

pdksh's additional features include user-definable tilde notation, in which you can set up ˜ as an abbreviation for anything, not just usernames.

Otherwise, *pdksh* lacks a few features of the official Korn version and *bash*. In particular, it lacks the following *bash* features:

- The built-in variable **PS4**
- The advanced I/O redirectors **>|** and **<>**
- The options **errexit**, **noclobber**, and **privileged**

One important advantage that *pdksh* has over *bash* is that the executable is only about a third the size and it runs considerably faster. Weighed against this is that it is less POSIX-compliant, has had numerous people add code to it (so it hasn't been as strongly controlled as *bash*), and isn't as polished a product as *bash* (for example, the documentation isn't anywhere near as detailed or complete).

However, *pdksh* is a worthwhile alternative for those who want something other than *bash* and can't obtain the Korn shell.

Workalikes on PC Platforms

The proliferation of shells has not stopped at the boundaries of UNIX-dom. Many programmers who got their initial experience on UNIX systems and subsequently crossed over into the PC world wished for a nice UNIX-like environment (especially when faced with the horrors of the MS-DOS command line!), so it's not surprising that several UNIX shell-style interfaces to small-computer operating systems have appeared, Bourne shell emulations among them.

A Korn shell workalike is provided in the MKS Toolkit, available from Mortice Kern Systems, Inc. The Toolkit is actually a complete UNIX-like environment for MS-DOS (version 2.0 and later) and OS/2 (version 1.2 and later). In addition to its shell, it comes with a *vi* editor and many UNIX-style utilities, including major ones like *awk*, *uucp*, and *make*.

The MKS shell itself is very much compatible with the 1988 UNIX Korn shell, and it has a well-written manual.

Most of the differences between the MKS shell and the Korn shell and *bash* are due to limitations in the underlying operating systems rather than the shell itself. Most importantly, MS-DOS does not support multitasking or file permissions, so the MS-DOS version supports none of the relevant features. The OS/2 version doesn't support file permissions either.

If you want to know more details about the differences between the 1988 Korn shell and the MKS shell, see Appendix A, *Related Shells*, of the O'Reilly & Associates Nutshell Handbook, *Learning the Korn Shell*, by Bill Rosenblatt.

Many UNIX users who have moved to DOS PCs swear by the MKS Toolkit; it's inexpensive, and it makes MS-DOS into a reasonable environment for advanced users and software developers.

The Toolkit is available through most dealers that sell software tools, or through MKS itself. For more information, contact:

MKS
185 Columbia Street West
Waterloo, Ontario, Canada N2L 5Z5

Or electronically as follows:

Telephone	(800) 265-2797 (US & Canada)
Fax	(519) 884 8861
Internet	*info@mks.com*
CompuServe	73260,1043
BIX	mks
WWW	*http://www.mks.com/*

B

Reference Lists

Invocation

Tables B–1 and B–2 list the options you can use when invoking *bash* 2.*x* and 1.*x*, respectively.* The multicharacter options must appear on the command line before the single-character options. In addition to these, any **set** option can be used on the command line; see Table B-6. Login shells are usually invoked with the options **−i** (interactive), **−s** (read from standard input), and **−m** (enable job control).

Table B-1: Command-Line Options

Option	Meaning
−c *string*	Commands are read from *string*, if present. Any arguments after *string* are interpreted as positional parameters, starting with **$0**.
−D	A list of all double-quoted strings preceded by **$** is printed on the standard ouput. These are the strings that are subject to language translation when the current locale is not C or POSIX. This also turns on the **−n** option.
−i	Interactive shell. Ignore signals TERM, INT, and QUIT. With job control in effect, TTIN, TTOU, and TSTP are also ignored.
−o *option*	Takes the same arguments as **set −o**.
−s	Read commands from the standard input. If an argument is given to *bash*, this flag takes precedence (i.e., the argument won't be treated as a script name and standard input will be read).
−r	Restricted shell. See Chapter 10, *bash Administration*.

---

* At the time of writing, the old 1.*x* versions of *bash* are still widely used. We strongly recommend that you upgrade to the latest version. We have included a table of old options (Table B–2) just in case you encounter an old version of the shell.

Table B-1: Command-Line Options (continued)

Option	Meaning
–	Signals the end of options and disables further option processing. Any options after this are treated as filenames and arguments. – – is synonymous with –.
– –dump-strings	Does the same as **–D**.
– –help	Displays a usage message and exits.
– –login	Makes *bash* act as if invoked as a login shell.
– –noediting	Does not use the GNU *readline* library to read command lines if interactive.
– –noprofile	Does not read the startup file */etc/profile* or any of the personal initialization files.
– –norc	Does not read the initialization file *˜/.bashrc* if the shell is interactive. This is on by default if the shell is invoked as *sh*.
– –posix	Changes the behavior of *bash* to follow the POSIX guidelines more closely where the default operation of *bash* is different.
– –quiet	Shows no information on shell startup. This is the default.
– –rcfile *file*	Executes commands read from *file* instead of the initialization file *˜/.bashrc*, if the shell is interactive.
– –version	Shows the version number of this instance of *bash* and then exits.

Table B-2: Old Command-Line Options

Option	Meaning
–c *string*	Commands are read from *string*, if present. Any arguments after *string* are interpreted as positional parameters, starting with **$0**.
–i	Interactive shell. Ignore signals TERM, INT, and QUIT. With job control in effect, TTIN, TTOU, and TSTP are also ignored.
–s	Read commands from the standard input. If an argument is given to *bash*, this flag takes precedence (i.e., the argument won't be treated as a script name and standard input will be read).
–r	Restricted shell. See Chapter 10, *bash Administration*.
–	Signals the end of options and disables further option processing. Any options after this are treated as filenames and arguments. – – is synonymous with –.
–norc	Does not read the initialization file *˜/.bashrc* if the shell is interactive. This is on by default if the shell is invoked as *sh*.
–noprofile	Does not read the startup file */etc/profile* or any of the personal initialization files.
–rcfile *file*	Executes commands read from *file* instead of the initialization file *˜/.bashrc*, if the shell is interactive.
–version	Shows the version number of this instance of *bash* when starting.

Table B-2: Old Command-Line Options (continued)

Option	Meaning
−quiet	Shows no information on shell startup. This is the default.
−login	Makes *bash* act as if invoked as a login shell.
−nobraceexpansion	Does not perform curly brace expansion.
−nolineediting	Does not use the GNU *readline* library to read command lines if interactive.
−posix	Changes the behavior of *bash* to follow the POSIX guidelines more closely where the default operation of *bash* is different.

Built-In Commands and Reserved Words

Table B-3 shows a summary of all built-in commands and reserved words.

Table B-3: Commands and Reserved Words

Command	Chapter	Summary
!	5	Reserved word. Logical NOT of a command exit status.
:	7	Do nothing (just do expansions of any arguments).
.	4	Read file and execute its contents in current shell.
alias	3	Set up shorthand for command or command line.
bg	8	Put job in background.
bind	2	Bind a key sequence to a *readline* function or macro.
break	5	Exit from surrounding **for**, **select**, **while**, or **until** loop.
builtin	5	Execute the specified shell built-in.
case	5	Reserved word. Multi-way conditional construct.
cd	1	Change working directory.
command	7	Run a command bypassing shell function lookup.
continue		Skip to next iteration of **for**, **select**, **while**, or **until** loop.
declare	6	Declare variables and give them attributes.
dirs	6	Display the list of currently remembered directories.
disown	8	Remove a job from the job table.
do	5	Reserved word. Part of a **for**, **select**, **while**, or **until** looping construct.
done	5	Reserved word. Part of a **for**, **select**, **while**, or **until** looping construct.
echo	4	Expand and print any arguments.
elif	5	Reserved word. Part of an **if** construct.
else	5	Reserved word. Part of an **if** construct.
enable	7	Enable and disable built-in shell commands.
esac	5	Reserved word. Part of a **case** construct.
eval	7	Run the given arguments through command-line processing.

Table B-3: Commands and Reserved Words (continued)

Command	Chapter	Summary
exec	9	Replace the shell with the given program.
exit	5	Exit from the shell.
export	3	Create environment variables.
fc	2	Fix command (edit history file).
fg	8	Put background job in foreground.
fi	5	Reserved word. Part of an **if** construct.
for	5	Reserved word. Looping construct.
function	4	Define a function.
getopts	6	Process command-line options.
hash	3	Full pathnames are determined and remembered.
help	1	Display helpful information on built-in commands.
history	1	Display command history.
if	5	Reserved word. Conditional construct.
in	5	Reserved word. Part of a **case** construct.
jobs	1	List any background jobs.
kill	8	Send a signal to a process.
let	6	Arithmetic variable assignment.
local	4	Create a local variable.
logout	1	Exits a login shell.
popd	4	Removes a directory from the directory stack.
pushd	4	Adds a directory to the directory stack.
pwd	1	Print the working directory.
read	7	Read a line from standard input.
readonly	6	Make variables read-only (unassignable).
return	5	Return from the surrounding function or script.
select	5	Reserved word. Menu-generation construct.
set	3	Set options.
shift	6	Shift command-line arguments.
suspend		Suspend execution of a shell.
test	5	Evaluates a conditional expression.
then	5	Reserved word. Part of an **if** construct.
time		Reserved word. Run command pipeline and print execution times. The format of the output can be controlled with **TIMEFORMAT**.
times		Print the accumulated user and system times for processes run from the shell.
trap	8	Set up a signal-catching routine.
type	3	Identify the source of a command.
typeset	6	Declare variables and give them attributes. Same as **declare**.
ulimit	10	Set/show process resource limits.
umask	10	Set/show file permission mask.
unalias	3	Remove alias definitions.

Table B-3: Commands and Reserved Words (continued)

Command	Chapter	Summary
unset	3	Remove definitions of variables or functions.
until	5	Reserved word. Looping construct.
wait	8	Wait for background job(s) to finish.
while	5	Reserved word. Looping construct.

Environment Variables

Table B-4 shows a complete list of environment variables available in *bash* 2.0. The letters in the **Type** column of the table have the following meanings: A = Array, L = colon separated list, R = read-only, U = unsetting it causes it to lose its special meaning.

Note that the variables **BASH_VERSINFO**, **DIRSTACK**, **GLOBIGNORE**, **GROUPS**, **HISTIGNORE**, **HOSTNAME**, **LANG**, **LC_ALL**, **LC_COLLATE**, **LC_MESSAGE**, **MACHTYPE**, **PIPESTATUS**, **SHELLOPTS**, and **TIMEFORMAT** are not available in versions prior to 2.0. **BASH_ENV** replaces **ENV** found in earlier versions.

Table B-4: Environment Variables

Variable	Chapter	Type	Description
*	4	R	The positional parameters given to the current script or function.
@	4	R	The positional parameters given to the current script or function.
#	4	R	The number of arguments given to the current script or function.
-		R	Options given to the shell on invocation.
?	5	R	Exit status of the previous command.
_		R	Last argument to the previous command.
$	8	R	Process ID of the shell process.
!	8	R	Process ID of the last background command.
0	4	R	Name of the shell or shell script.
BASH	3		The full pathname used to invoke this instance of *bash*.
BASH_ENV	3		The name of a file to run as the environment file when the shell is invoked.
BASH_VERSION	3		The version number of this instance of *bash*.
BASH_VERSINFO	3,6	AR	Version information for this instance of *bash*. Each element of the array holds parts of the version number.

Table B-4: Environment Variables (continued)

Variable	Chapter	Type	Description
CDPATH	3	L	A list of directories for the *cd* command to search.
DIRSTACK	4,6	ARU	The current contents of the directory stack.
EUID		R	The effective user ID of the current user.
FCEDIT	2		The default editor for *fc* command.
FIGNORE		L	A list of names to ignore when doing filename completion.
GLOBIGNORE		L	A list of patterns defining filenames to ignore during pathname expansion.
GROUPS		AR	An array containing a list of groups of which the current user is a member.
IFS	7		The Internal Field Separator: a list of characters that act as word separators. Normally set to SPACE, TAB, and NEWLINE.
HISTCMD	3	U	The history number of the current command.
HISTCONTROL	3		Controls what is entered in the command history.
HISTFILE	2		The name of the command history file.
HISTIGNORE	3		A list of patterns to decide what should be retained in the history list.
HISTSIZE	2		The number of lines kept in the command history.
HISTFILESIZE	3		The maximum number of lines kept in the history file.
HOME	3		The home (login) directory.
HOSTFILE	3		The file to be used for hostname completion.
HOSTNAME			The name of the current host.
HOSTTYPE	3		The type of machine *bash* is running on.
IGNOREEOF	3		The number of EOF characters received before exiting an interactive shell.
INPUTRC	2		The *readline* startup file.
LANG			Used to determine the locale category for any category not specifically selected with a variable starting with LC_.
LC_ALL			Overrides the value of LANG and any other LC_ variable specifying a locale category.
LC_COLLATE			Determines the collation order used when sorting the results of pathname expansion.
LC_MESSAGES			This variable determines the locale used to translate double-quoted strings preceded by a $.

Table B-4: Environment Variables (continued)

Variable	Chapter	Type	Description
LINENO	9	U	The number of the line that just ran in a script or function.
MACHTYPE			A string describing the system on which *bash* is executing.
MAIL	3		The name of the file to check for new mail.
MAILCHECK	3		How often (in seconds) to check for new mail.
MAILPATH	3	L	A list of file names to check for new mail, if MAIL is not set.
OLDPWD	3		The previous working directory.
OPTARG	6		The value of the last option argument processed by **getopts**.
OPTERR	6		If set to 1, display error messages from **getopts**.
OPTIND	6		The number of the first argument after options.
OSTYPE			The operating system on which *bash* is executing.
PATH	3	L	The search path for commands.
PIPESTATUS	6	A	An array variable containing a list of exit status values from the processes in the most recently executed foreground pipeline.
PROMPT_COMMAND			The value is executed as a command before the primary prompt is issued.
PS1	3		The primary command prompt string.
PS2	3		The prompt string for line continuations.
PS3	5		The prompt string for the **select** command.
PS4	9		The prompt string for the **xtrace** option.
PPID	8	R	The process ID of the parent process.
PWD	3		The current working directory.
RANDOM	9	U	A random number between 0 and 32767 $(2^{15}-1)$.
REPLY	5, 7		The user's response to the **select** command; result of the **read** command if no variable names are given.
SECONDS	3	U	The number of seconds since the shell was invoked.
SHELL	3		The full pathname of the shell.
SHELLOPTS		LR	A list of enabled shell options.
SHLVL			Incremented by one each time an instance of *bash* is invoked.

Table B-4: Environment Variables (continued)

Variable	Chapter	Type	Description
TIMEFORMAT			Specifies the format for the output from using the **time** reserved word on a command pipeline.
TMOUT	10		If set to a positive integer, the number of seconds after which the shell automatically terminates if no input is received.
UID		R	The user ID of the current user.
auto_resume			Controls how job control works.
histchars			Specifies what to use as the history control characters. Normally set to the string '!#'.

Test Operators

Table B-5 lists the operators that are used with **test** and the [. . .] construct. They can be logically combined with -a ("and") and -o ("or") and grouped with escaped parenthesis (\(. . . \)). The string comparisons < and > are not available in versions of *bash* prior to 2.0.

Table B-5: Test Operators

Operator	True If . . .
–b *file*	*file* exists and is a block device file
–c *file*	*file* exists and is a character device file
–d *file*	*file* exists and is a directory
–e *file*	*file* exists
–f *file*	*file* exists and is a regular file
–g *file*	*file* exists and has its setgid bit set
–G *file*	*file* exists and is owned by the effective group ID
–k *file*	*file* exists and has its sticky bit set
–L *file*	*file* exists and is a symbolic link
–n *string*	*string* is non-null
–O *file*	*file* exists and is owned by the effective user ID
–p *file*	*file* exists and is a pipe or named pipe (FIFO file)
–r *file*	*file* exists and is readable
–s *file*	*file* exists and is not empty
–S *file*	*file* exists and is a socket
–t *N*	File descriptor *N* points to a terminal
–u *file*	*file* exists and has its setuid bit set
–w *file*	*file* exists and is writeable
–x *file*	*file* exists and is executable, or *file* is a directory that can be searched

Table B-5: Test Operators (continued)

Operator	True If . . .
−z *string*	*string* has a length of zero
fileA −nt *fileB*	*fileA* is newer than *fileB*
fileA −ot *fileB*	*fileA* is older than *fileB*
fileA −ef *fileB*	*fileA* and *fileB* point to the same file
stringA = *stringB*	*stringA* equals *stringB*
stringA != *stringB*	*stringA* does not match *stringB*
stringA < *stringB*	*stringA* sorts before *stringB* lexicographically
stringA > *stringB*	*stringA* sorts after *stringB* lexicographically
exprA −eq *exprB*	Arithmetic expressions *exprA* and *exprB* are equal
exprA −ne *exprB*	Arithmetic expressions *exprA* and *exprB* are not equal
exprA −lt *exprB*	*exprA* is less than *exprB*
exprA −gt *exprB*	*exprA* is greater than *exprB*
exprA −le *exprB*	*exprA* is less than or equal to *exprB*
exprA −ge *exprB*	*exprA* is greater than or equal to *exprB*
exprA −a *exprB*	*exprA* is true and *exprB* is true
exprA −o *exprB*	*exprA* is true or *exprB* is true

set Options

Table B-6 lists the options that can be turned on with the **set** −*arg* command. All are initially off except where noted. **Full Names**, where listed, are arguments to **set** that can be used with **set** −o. The **Full Names braceexpand, histexpand, history, keyword,** and **onecmd** are not available in versions of *bash* prior to 2.0. Also, in those versions, hashing is switched with −**d**.

Table B-6: Options to set

Option	Full Name	Meaning
−a	allexport	Export all subsequently defined or modified variables.
−B	braceexpand	The shell performs brace expansion. This is on by default.
−b	notify	Report the status of terminating background jobs immediately.
−C	noclobber	Don't allow redirection to overwrite existing files.
−e	errexit	Exit the shell when a simple command exits with non-zero status. A simple command is a command not part of a **while**, **until**, or **if**; or part of a **&&** or **||** list; or a command whose return value is inverted by **!**.
	emacs	Use *emacs*-style command-line editing.
−f	noglob	Disable pathname expansion.
−H	histexpand	Enable ! style history substitution. On by default in an interactive shell.

Table B-6: Options to set (continued)

Option	Full Name	Meaning
	history	Enable command history. On by default in interactive shells.
–h	hashall	Disable the hashing of commands.
	ignoreeof	Disallow CTRL-D to exit the shell.
–k	keyword	Place keyword arguments in the environment for a command.
–m	monitor	Enable job control (on by default in interactive shells).
–n	noexec	Read commands and check syntax but do not execute them. Ignored for interactive shells.
–P	physical	Do not follow symbolic links on commands that change the current directory. Use the physical directory.
–p	privileged	Script is running in *suid* mode.
	posix	Change the default behavior to that of POSIX 1003.2 where it differs from the standard.
–t	onecmd	Exit after reading and executing one command.
–u	nounset	Treat undefined variables as errors, not as null.
–v	verbose	Print shell input lines before running them.
	vi	Use *vi*-style command-line editing.
–x	xtrace	Print commands (after expansions) before running them.
–		Signals the end of options. All remaining arguments are assigned to the positional parameters. –x and –v are turned off. If there are no remaining arguments to set, the positional arguments remain unchanged.
––		With no arguments following, unset the positional parameters. Otherwise, the positional parameters are set to the following arguments (even if they begin with –).

shopt Options

The *shopt* options are set with **shopt –s***arg* and unset with **shopt –u***arg*. See Table B-7 for options to *shopt*. Versions of *bash* prior to 2.0 had environment variables to perform some of these settings. Setting them equated to **shopt –s**.

The variables (and corresponding **shopt** options) were: **allow_null_glob_expansion** (**nullglob**), **cdable_vars** (**cdable_vars**), **command_oriented_history** (**cmdhist**), **glob_dot_filenames** (**dotglob**), **no_exit_on_failed_exec** (**execfail**). These variables no longer exist.

Table B-7: Options to shopt

Option	Meaning if Set
cdable_vars	An argument to **cd** that is not a directory is assumed to be the name of a variable whose value is the directory to change to.
cdspell	Minor errors in the spelling of a directory supplied to the **cd** command will be corrected if there is a suitable match. This correction includes missing letters, incorrect letters, and letter transposition. It works for interactive shells only.
checkhash	Commands found in the hash table are checked for existence before being executed and non-existence forces a **PATH** search.
checkwinsize	Checks the window size after each command and, if it has changed, updates the variables **LINES** and **COLUMNS** accordingly.
cmdhist	Attempt to save all lines of a multiline command in a single history entry.
dotglob	Filenames beginning with a . are included in pathname expansion.
execfail	A non-interactive shell will not exit if it cannot execute the argument to an **exec**. Interactive shells do not exit if **exec** fails.
expand_aliases	Aliases are expanded.
histappend	The history list is appended to the file named by the value of the variable **HISTFILE** when the shell exits, rather than overwriting the file.
histreedit	If *readline* is being used, the opportunity is given for re-editing a failed history substitution.
histverify	If *readline* is being used, the results of history substitution are not immediately passed to the shell parser. Instead, the resulting line is loaded into the *readline* editing buffer, allowing further modification.
hostcomplete	If *readline* is being used, an attempt will be made to perform hostname completion when a word beginning with @ is being completed.
interactive_comments	Allows a word beginning with # and all subsequent characters on the line to be ignored in an interactive shell.
lithist	If the **cmdhist** option is enabled, multiline commands are saved to the history with embedded newlines rather than using semicolon separators where possible.
mailwarn	If the file being checked for mail has been accessed since the last time it was checked, the message "The mail in *mailfile* has been read" is displayed.
nullglob	Allows patterns which match no files to expand to null strings rather than themselves.

Table B-7: Options to shopt (continued)

Option	Meaning if Set
promptvars	Prompt strings undergo variable and parameter expansion after being expanded.
shift_verbose	The **shift** built-in prints an error if it has shifted past the last positional parameter.
sourcepath	The **source** built-in uses the value of **PATH** to find the directory containing the file supplied as an argument.

I/O Redirection

Table B-8 shows a complete list of I/O redirectors. (This table is also included earlier as Table 7-1.) Note that there are two formats for specifying standard output and error redirection: **&>file** and **>&file**. The second of these, and the one used throughout this book, is the preferred way.

Table B-8: I/O Redirectors

Redirector	Function
cmd1 | *cmd2*	Pipe; take standard output of *cmd1* as standard input to *cmd2*
> *file*	Direct standard output to *file*
< *file*	Take standard input from *file*
>> *file*	Direct standard output to *file*; append to *file* if it already exists
>| *file*	Force standard output to *file* even if **noclobber** is set
n>| *file*	Force output to *file* from file descriptor
n	even if **noclobber** set
<> *file*	Use *file* as both standard input and standard output
n<> *file*	Use *file* as both input and output for file descriptor *n*
<< *label*	Here-document
n> *file*	Direct file descriptor *n* to *file*
n< *file*	Take file descriptor *n* from *file*
>> *file*	Direct file descriptor *n* to *file*; append to *file* if it already exists
n>&	Duplicate standard output to file descriptor *n*
n<&	Duplicate standard input from file descriptor *n*
n>&*m*	File descriptor *n* is made to be a copy of the output file descriptor
n<&*m*	File descriptor *n* is made to be a copy of the input file descriptor
&>*file*	Directs standard output and standard error to *file*
<&–	Close the standard input
>&–	Close the standard output
n>&–	Close the output from file descriptor *n*
n<&–	Close the input from file descriptor *n*

emacs Mode Commands

Table B-9 shows a complete list of *emacs* editing mode commands.

Table B-9: emacs Mode Commands

Command	Meaning
CTRL-A	Move to beginning of line
CTRL-B	Move backward one character
CTRL-D	Delete one character forward
CTRL-E	Move to end of line
CTRL-F	Move forward one character
CTRL-G	Abort the current editing command and ring the terminal bell
CTRL-J	Same as RETURN
CTRL-K	Delete (kill) forward to end of line
CTRL-L	Clear screen and redisplay the line
CTRL-M	Same as RETURN
CTRL-N	Next line in command history
CTRL-O	Same as RETURN, then display next line in history file
CTRL-P	Previous line in command history
CTRL-R	Search backward
CTRL-S	Search forward
CTRL-T	Transpose two characters
CTRL-U	Kill backward from point to the beginning of line
CTRL-V	Make the next character typed verbatim
CTRL-V TAB	Insert a TAB
CTRL-W	Kill the word behind the cursor, using whitespace as the boundary
CTRL-X /	List the possible filename completions of the current word
CTRL-X ˜	List the possible username completions of the current word
CTRL-X $	List the possible shell variable completions of the current word
CTRL-X @	List the possible hostname completions of the current word
CTRL-X !	List the possible command name completions of the current word
CTRL-X (	Begin saving characters into the current keyboard macro
CTRL-X)	Stop saving characters into the current keyboard macro
CTRL-X e	Re-execute the last keyboard macro defined
CTRL-X CTRL-R	Read in the contents of the *readline* initialization file
CTRL-X CTRL-V	Display version information on this instance of *bash*
CTRL-Y	Retrieve (yank) last item killed
DEL	Delete one character backward
CTRL-[	Same as ESC (most keyboards)
ESC-B	Move one word backward
ESC-C	Change word after point to all capital letters
ESC-D	Delete one word forward
ESC-F	Move one word forward

Table B-9: emacs Mode Commands (continued)

Command	Meaning
ESC-L	Change word after point to all lowercase letters
ESC-N	Non-incremental forward search
ESC-P	Non-incremental reverse search
ESC-R	Undo all the changes made to this line
ESC-T	Transpose two words
ESC-U	Change word after point to all uppercase letters
ESC-CTRL-E	Perform shell alias, history, and word expansion on the line
ESC-CTRL-H	Delete one word backward
ESC-CTRL-Y	Insert the first argument to the previous command (usually the second word) at point
ESC-DEL	Delete one word backward
ESC-^	Perform history expansion on the line
ESC-<	Move to first line of history file
ESC->	Move to last line of history file
ESC-.	Insert last word in previous command line after point
ESC-_	Same as above
TAB	Attempt filename completion on current word
ESC-?	List the possible completions of the text before point
ESC-/	Attempt filename completion on current word
ESC-~	Attempt username completion on current word
ESC-$	Attempt variable completion on current word
ESC-@	Attempt hostname completion on current word
ESC-!	Attempt command name completion on current word
ESC-TAB	Attempt completion from text in the command history
ESC-~	Attempt tilde expansion on the current word
ESC-\	Delete all the spaces and TABs around point
ESC-*	Insert all of the completions that would be generated by ESC-= before point
ESC-=	List the possible completions before point
ESC-{	Attempt filename completion and return the list to the shell enclosed within braces

vi Control Mode Commands

Table B-10 shows a complete list of all *vi* control mode commands.

Table B-10: vi Control Mode Commands

Command	Meaning
h	Move left one character
l	Move right one character
w	Move right one word
b	Move left one word
W	Move to beginning of next non-blank word
B	Move to beginning of preceding non-blank word
e	Move to end of current word
E	Move to end of current non-blank word
0	Move to beginning of line
^	Move to first non-blank character in line
$	Move to end of line
i	Insert text before current character
a	Insert text after current character
I	Insert text at beginning of line
A	Insert text at end of line
R	Overwrite existing text
dh	Delete one character backward
dl	Delete one character forward
db	Delete one word backward
dw	Delete one word forward
dB	Delete one non-blank word backward
dW	Delete one non-blank word forward
d$	Delete to end of line
d0	Delete to beginning of line
D	Equivalent to **d$** (delete to end of line)
dd	Equivalent to **0d$** (delete entire line)
C	Equivalent to **c$** (delete to end of line, enter input mode)
cc	Equivalent to **0c$** (delete entire line, enter input mode)
x	Equivalent to **dl** (delete character forwards)
X	Equivalent to **dh** (delete character backwards)
k or −	Move backward one line
j or +	Move forward one line
G	Move to line given by repeat count
/*string*	Search forward for *string*
?*string*	Search backward for *string*
n	Repeat search forward
N	Repeat search backward
f*x*	Move right to next occurrence of *x*
F*x*	Move left to previous occurrence of *x*
t*x*	Move right to next occurrence of *x*, then back one space
T*x*	Move left to previous occurrence of *x*, then forward one space

Table B-10: vi Control Mode Commands (continued)

Command	Meaning
;	Redo last character finding command
,	Redo last character finding command in opposite direction
\	Do filename completion
*	Do wildcard expansion (onto command line)
\=	Do wildcard expansion (as printed list)
~	Invert (twiddle) case of current character(s)
_	Append last word of previous command, enter input mode
CTRL-L	Start a new line and redraw the current line on it
#	Prepend # (comment character) to the line and send it to history

C

Loadable Built-Ins

bash 2.0 introduces a new feature that increases the flexibility of the shell: dynamically loadable built-ins. On systems that support dynamic loading, you can write your own built-ins in C, compile them into shared objects, and load them at any time from within the shell with the **enable** built-in (see Chapter 7, *Input/Output and Command-Line Processing*, for details on all of the **enable** options).

This appendix will discuss briefly how to go about writing a built-in and loading it in *bash*. The discussion assumes that you have experience with writing C programs, compiling, and linking them.

The *bash* archive contains a number of pre-written built-ins in the directory *examples/loadables/*. You can build them by uncommenting the lines in the file *Makefile* that are relevent to your system, and typing **make**. We'll take one of these built-ins, **tty**, and use it as a "case study" for built-ins in general.

tty will mimic the standard UNIX command *tty*. It will print the name of the terminal that is connected to standard input. The built-in will, like the command, return true if the device is a TTY and false if it isn't. In addition, it will take an option, **–s**, which specifies that it should work silently, i.e., print nothing and just return a result.

The C code for a built-in can be divided into three distinct sections: the code that implements the functionality of the built-in, a help text message definition, and a structure describing the built-in so that *bash* can access it.

The description structure is quite straightforward and takes the form:

```
struct builtin structname = {
    "builtin_name",
    function_name,
    BUILTIN_ENABLED,
```

```
        help_array,
        "usage",
        0
};
```

builtin_name is the name of the built-in as it appears in *bash*. The next field, *function-name*, is the name of the C function that implements the built-in. We'll look at this in a moment. BUILTIN_ENABLED is the initial state of the built-in; whether it is enabled or not. This field should always be set to BUILTIN_ENABLED. *help_array* is an array of strings which are printed when **help** is used on the built-in. *usage* is the shorter form of help; the command and its options. The last field in the structure should be set to 0.

In our example we'll call the built-in **tty**, the C function **tty_builtin**, and the help array **tty_doc**. The usage string will be **tty [-s]**. The resulting structure looks like this:

```
struct builtin tty_struct = {
    "tty",
    tty_builtin,
    BUILTIN_ENABLED,
    tty_doc,
    "tty [-s]",
    0
};
```

The next section is the code that does the work. It looks like this:

```
tty_builtin (list)
    WORD_LIST *list;
{
    int opt, sflag;
    char *t;

    reset_internal_getopt ();
    sflag = 0;
    while ((opt = internal_getopt (list, "s")) != -1)
    {
      switch (opt)
      {
          case 's':
              sflag = 1;
              break;
          default:
              builtin_usage ();
              return (EX_USAGE);
      }
    }
    list = loptend;

    t = ttyname (0);
    if (sflag == 0)
```

```
        puts (t ? t : "not a tty");
      return (t ? EXECUTION_SUCCESS : EXECUTION_FAILURE);
 }
```

Built-in functions are always given a pointer to a list of type WORD_LIST. If the built-in doesn't actually take any options, you must call *no_options(list)* and check its return value before any further processing. If the return value is non-zero, your function should immediately return with the value EX_USAGE.

You must always use *internal_getopt* rather than the standard C library *getopt* to process the built-in options. Also, you must reset the option processing first by calling *reset_internal_getopt*.

Option processing is performed in the standard way, except if the options are incorrect, in which case you should return EX_USAGE. Any arguments left after option processing are pointed to by *loptend*. Once the function is finished, it should return the value EXECUTION_SUCCESS or EXECUTION_FAILURE.

In the case of our **tty** built-in, we then just call the standard C library routine *ttyname*, and if the −s option wasn't given, print out the name of the tty (or "not a tty" if the device wasn't). The function then returns success or failure, depending upon the result from the call to *ttyname*.

The last major section is the help definition. This is simply an array of strings, the last element of the array being NULL. Each string is printed to standard output when **help** is run on the built-in. You should, therefore, keep the strings to 76 characters or less (An 80-character standard display minus a 4-character margin). In the case of **tty**, our help text looks like this:

```
char *tty_doc[] = {
  "tty writes the name of the terminal that is opened for standard",
  "input to standard output.  If the '-s' option is supplied, nothing",
  "is written; the exit status determines whether or not the standard",
  "input is connected to a tty.",
  (char *)NULL
};
```

The last things to add to our code are the necessary C header files. These are *stdio.h* and the *bash* header files *config.h*, *builtins.h*, *shell.h*, and *bashgetopt.h*.

Here is the C program in its entirety:

```
#include "config.h"
#include <stdio.h>
#include "builtins.h"
#include "shell.h"
#include "bashgetopt.h"
```

```c
extern char *ttyname ();

tty_builtin (list)
    WORD_LIST *list;
{
    int opt, sflag;
    char *t;

    reset_internal_getopt ();
    sflag = 0;
    while ((opt = internal_getopt (list, "s")) != -1)
    {
        switch (opt)
        {
            case 's':
                sflag = 1;
                break;
            default:
                builtin_usage ();
                return (EX_USAGE);
        }
    }
    list = loptend;

    t = ttyname (0);
    if (sflag == 0)
        puts (t ? t : "not a tty");
    return (t ? EXECUTION_SUCCESS : EXECUTION_FAILURE);
}

char *tty_doc[] = {
    "tty writes the name of the terminal that is opened for standard",
    "input to standard output.  If the '-s' option is supplied, nothing",
    "is written; the exit status determines whether or not the standard",
    "input is connected to a tty.",
    (char *)NULL
};

struct builtin tty_struct = {
    "tty",
    tty_builtin,
    BUILTIN_ENABLED,
    tty_doc,
    "tty [-s]",
    0
};
```

We now need to compile and link this as a dynamic shared object. Unfortunately, different systems have different ways to specify how to compile dynamic shared objects. Table C-1 lists some common systems and the commands needed to compile and link *tty.c*. Replace *archive* with the path of the top level of the *bash* archive.

Table C-1: Shared Object Compilation

System	Commands
SunOS 4	cc –pic –I*archive* –I*archive*/builtins –I*archive*/lib –c tty.c
	ld –assert pure-text –o tty tty.o
SunOS 5	cc –K pic –I*archive* –I*archive*/builtins –I*archive*/lib –c tty.c
	cc –dy –z text –G –i –h tty –o tty tty.o
SVR4, SVR4.2, Irix	cc –K PIC –I*archive* –I*archive*/builtins –I*archive*/lib –c tty.c
	ld –dy –z text –G –h tty –o tty tty.o
AIX	cc –K –I*archive* –I*archive*/builtins –I*archive*/lib –c tty.c
	ld –bdynamic –bnoentry –bexpall –G –o tty tty.o
Linux	cc –fPIC –I*archive* –I*archive*/builtins –I*archive*/lib –c tty.c
	ld –shared –o tty tty.o
NetBSD, FreeBSD	cc –fpic –I*archive* –I*archive*/builtins –I*archive*/lib –c tty.c
	ld –x –Bshareable –o tty tty.o

Further examples are given in the file *examples/loadables/Makefile* in the archive.

After you have compiled and linked the program, you should have a shared object called **tty**. To load this into *bash*, just type **enable –f** *path*/**tty tty**, where *path* is the full pathname of the shared object. You can remove a loaded built-in at any time with the **–d** option, e.g., **enable –d tty**.

You can put as many built-ins as you like into one shared object; all you need are the three main sections that we saw above for each built-in in the same C file. It is best, however, to keep the number of built-ins per shared object small. You will also probably find it best to keep similar built-ins, or built-ins that work together (e.g., **pushd**, **popd**, **dirs**), in the same shared object.

bash loads a shared object as a whole, so if you ask it to load one built-in from a shared object that has twenty built-ins, it will load all twenty (but only one will be enabled). For this reason, keep the number of built-ins small to save loading memory with unnecessary things, and group similar built-ins so that if the user enables one of them, all of them will be loaded and ready in memory for enabling.

D

Syntax

Reserved Words

The following words are *reserved words* and have a special meaning to the shell when they are unquoted:

if	then	else	elif	fi	case
esac	for	while	until	do	done
function	in	select	!	{	}
time					

BNF for bash

The following is the syntax of *bash* 2.0 in Backus-Naur Form (BNF):

```
<letter> ::= a|b|c|d|e|f|g|h|i|j|k|l|m|n|o|p|q|r|s|t|u|v|w|x|y|z|
             A|B|C|D|E|F|G|H|I|J|K|L|M|N|O|P|Q|R|S|T|U|V|W|X|Y|Z

<digit> ::= 0|1|2|3|4|5|6|7|8|9

<number> ::= <digit>
           | <number> <digit>

<word> ::= <letter>
         | <word> <letter>
         | <word> '_'

<word_list> ::= <word>
              | <word_list> <word>

<assignment_word> ::= <word> '=' <word>
```

```
<redirection> ::=   '>' <word>
                |   '<' <word>
                |   <number> '>' <word>
                |   <number> '<' <word>
                |   '>>' <word>
                |   <number> '>>' <word>
                |   '<<' <word>
                |   <number> '<<' <word>
                |   '<&' <number>
                |   <number> '<&' <number>
                |   '>&' <number>
                |   <number> '>&' <number>
                |   '<&' <word>
                |   <number> '<&' <word>
                |   '>&' <word>
                |   <number> '>&' <word>
                |   '<<-' <word>
                |   <number> '<<-' <word>
                |   '>&' '-'
                |   <number> '>&' '-'
                |   '<&' '-'
                |   <number> '<&' '-'
                |   '&>' <word>
                |   <number> '<>' <word>
                |   '<>' <word>
                |   '>|' <word>
                |   <number> '>|' <word>

<simple_command_element> ::= <word>
                         |   <assignment_word>
                         |   <redirection>

<redirection_list> ::= <redirection>
                   |   <redirection_list> <redirection>

<simple_command> ::=  <simple_command_element>
                  |   <simple_command> <simple_command_element>

<command> ::=  <simple_command>
           |   <shell_command>
           |   <shell_command> <redirection_list>

<shell_command> ::=   <for_command>
                  |   <case_command>
                  |   while <compound_list> do <compound_list> done
                  |   until <compound_list> do <compound_list> done
                  |   <select_command>
                  |   <if_command>
                  |   <subshell>
                  |   <group_command>
                  |   <function_def>

<for_command> ::=  for <word> <newline_list> do <compound_list> done
              |   for <word> <newline_list> '{' <compound_list> '}'
```

```
            |  for <word> ';' <newline_list> do <compound_list> done
            |  for <word> ';' <newline_list> '{' <compound_list> '}'
            |  for <word> <newline_list> in <word_list> <list_terminator>
                  <newline_list> do <compound_list> done
            |  for <word> <newline_list> in <word_list> <list_terminator>
                  <newline_list> '{' <compound_list> '}'

<select_command> ::=  select <word> <newline_list> do <list> done
                   |  select <word> <newline_list> '{' <list> '}'
                   |  select <word> ';' <newline_list> do <list> done
                   |  select <word> ';' <newline_list> '{' list '}'
                   |  select <word> <newline_list> in <word_list>
                          <list_terminator> <newline_list> do <list> done
                   |  select <word> <newline_list> in <word_list>
                          <list_terminator> <newline_list> '{' <list> '}'

<case_command> ::=  case <word> <newline_list> in <newline_list> esac
                 |  case <word> <newline_list> in <case_clause_sequence>
                        <newline_list> esac
                 |  case <word> <newline_list> in <case_clause> esac

<function_def> ::=  <word> '(' ')' <newline_list> <group_command>
                 |  function <word> '(' ')' <newline_list> <group_command>
                 |  function <word> <newline_list> <group_command>

<subshell> ::=  '(' <compound_list> ')'

<if_command> ::= if <compound_list> then <compound_list> fi
             | if <compound_list> then <compound_list> else <compound_list> fi
             | if <compound_list> then <compound_list> <elif_clause> fi

<group_command> ::=  '{' <list> '}'

<elif_clause> ::= elif <compound_list> then <compound_list>
              | elif <compound_list> then <compound_list> else <compound_list>
              | elif <compound_list> then <compound_list> <elif_clause>

<case_clause> ::=  <pattern_list>
                |  <case_clause_sequence> <pattern_list>

<pattern_list> ::=  <newline_list> <pattern> ')' <compound_list>
                 |  <newline_list> <pattern> ')' <newline_list>
                 |  <newline_list> '(' <pattern> ')' <compound_list>
                 |  <newline_list> '(' <pattern> ')' <newline_list>

<case_clause_sequence> ::=  <pattern_list> ';;'
                         |  <case_clause_sequence> <pattern_list> ';;'

<pattern> ::=  <word>
           |  <pattern> '|' <word>


<list> ::=   <newline_list> <list0>
```

```
<compound_list> ::=  <list>
                  |  <newline_list> <list1>

<list0> ::=  <list1> '\n' <newline_list>
          |  <list1> '&' <newline_list>
          |  <list1> ';' <newline_list>

<list1> ::=  <list1> '&&' <newline_list> <list1>
          |  <list1> '||' <newline_list> <list1>
          |  <list1> '&' <newline_list> <list1>
          |  <list1> ';' <newline_list> <list1>
          |  <list1> '\n' <newline_list> <list1>
          |  <pipeline_command>

<list_terminator> ::= '\n'
                   |  ';'

<newline_list> ::=
                  |  <newline_list> '\n'

<simple_list> ::=  <simple_list1>
                |  <simple_list1> '&'
                |  <simple_list1> ';'

<simple_list1> ::=  <simple_list1> '&&' <newline_list> <simple_list1>
                 |  <simple_list1> '||' <newline_list> <simple_list1>
                 |  <simple_list1> '&' <simple_list1>
                 |  <simple_list1> ';' <simple_list1>
                 |  <pipeline_command>

<pipeline_command> ::= <pipeline>
                    |  '!' <pipeline>
                    |  <timespec> <pipeline>
                    |  <timespec> '!' <pipeline>
                    |  '!' <timespec> <pipeline>

<pipeline> ::=
          <pipeline> '|' <newline_list> <pipeline>
       |  <command>

<time_opt> ::= '-p'

<timespec> ::=  time
             |  time <time_opt>
```

E

Obtaining Sample Programs

Some of the examples in this book are available electronically by both FTP and FTPMAIL. Use FTP if you are directly on the Internet. Use FTPMAIL if you are not on the Internet but can send and receive electronic mail to Internet sites.

FTP

If you have an Internet connection (permanent or dialup), the easiest way to use FTP is via your web browser or an FTP client. To get the examples, point your browser to *ftp://ftp.oreilly.com/published/oreilly/nutshell/bash/examples.tar.gz*. If you don't have a web browser, you can use the command-line FTP client included with Windows NT or Windows 95.

A sample session is shown below, with what you should type in boldface.

```
% ftp ftp.oreilly.com
Connected to ftp.oreilly.com.
220 FTP server (Version 6.21 Tue Mar 10 22:09:55 EST 1992) ready.
Name (ftp.oreilly.com:username): anonymous
331 Guest login OK, send email address as password.
Password: username@hostname  (Use your username and host here)
230 Guest login OK, access restrictions apply.
ftp> cd /published/oreilly/nutshell/bash
250 CWD command successful.
ftp> binary  (Very important! You must specify binary transfer for compressed files.)
200 Type set to I.
ftp> get examples.tar.gz
200 PORT command successful.
150 Opening BINARY mode data connection for examples.tar.gz (xxxx bytes).
226 Transfer complete. local: exercise remote: exercises
xxxx bytes received in xxx seconds (xxx Kbytes/s)
ftp> quit
221 Goodbye.
%
```

FTPMAIL

FTPMAIL is a mail server available to anyone who can send electronic mail to, and receive electronic mail from, Internet sites. Any company or service provider that allows email connections to the Internet can access FTPMAIL.

You send mail to *ftpmail@online.oreilly.com*. In the message body, give the name of the anonymous FTP host and the FTP commands you want to run. The server will run anonymous FTP for you, and mail the files back to you. To get a complete help file, send a message with no subject and the single word "help" in the body. The following is an example mail session that gets you the examples. This command sends you a listing of the files in the selected directory, and the requested examples file. The listing is useful if you are interested in a later version of the examples.

```
Subject:
reply-to username@hostname          (Where you want files mailed)
open
cd /published/oreilly/nutshell/bash
dir
mode binary
uuencode
get examples.tar.gz
quit
.
```

A signature at the end of the message is acceptable as long as it appears after "quit."

Index

Symbols

& (ampersand)
   bitwise and operator, 152
   running commands in background, 18,
      197
   && (logical and) operator, 116, 122, 152
   &> I/O redirector, 163
* (asterisk)
   multiplication operator, 152
   pattern-matching operator, 100
   positional parameter variable, 89, 92
   special array index, 161
   vi command, 46
   wildcard, 11–12, 179
@ (at sign)
   for hostname expansion, 35
   positional parameter variable, 89, 92
   special array index, 161
\ (backslash)
   command completion (vi), 46
   escaping, 23
   line continuation character, 24, 177
! (bang)
   bitwise not operator, 152
   conditional not operator, 117, 122
   history command, 50, 261
   negation wildcard, 12
   process ID shell variable, 210
   !! history command, 50
   != (not equal to) operator, 152
   != (string comparison) operator, 118

[ ] (brackets)
   for condition tests, 117–125
   range wildcards, 12–13
^ (caret)
   in Bourne shell, 268
   exclusive or operator, 152
   representing CTRL key, 201
: (colon)
   := string operator, 98
   :– string operator, 96
   :+ string operator, 98
   :? string operator, 109
   in string operators, 94
{ } (curly brackets)
   brace expansion wildcards, 14, 179
   for command blocks, 174–175, 271
   with shell variable names, 93
   for string operators, 94–103
$ (dollar sign)
   in arithmetic expressions, 151
   move to end of line (vi), 39
   for variable substitution, 35, 65–66, 179
   $* string, 89, 92
   $@ string, 89, 92
   $$ shell variable, 210–211
   $# string, 89
   (see also string operators)
. (dot)
   current directory shortcut, 10
   repeat last modification command (vi),
      42